SOAR

A Spiritual Journey through Divorce, Transformation, and Self-Actualization

Dear David -
I am delighted that our
paths have crossed, and am
so looking forward to being a guest
on Office Hours in a few weeks:
You are doing amazing work in this
world, my friend. Keep shining that bright
light of yours and... Happy Soaring!
Love and light -
Pam

PAMELA SAVINO

First edition February 2020

Book design, front cover and illustrations by Pamela Savino

ISBN 978-1-7344252-6-0 (paperback)
ISBN 978-1-7344252-0-8 (ebook)
ISBN 978-1-7344252-1-5 (audiobook)

Live Authentically, LLC
440 W. Colfax
Palatine, IL 60078-552
www.liveauthentically.today

DISCLAIMER

This book is designed to provide information, motivation and entertainment to our readers. It is based on the author's personal opinions and experiences with the subject matter and is made available to the public with the understanding that neither the author nor the publisher are engaged to render any type of psychological, legal, accounting, medical, nutritional, or any other kind of professional advice. Any statements made about food, supplements and mental health represent the author's views only, and are not intended to diagnose, treat, cure, or prevent any condition or disease. Please consult with your physician or healthcare specialist regarding any health, wellness and/or nutritional information contained in this book.

The author and publisher are providing this book and its contents on an "as is" basis and make no representations, warranties or guarantees of any kind, expressed or implied, with respect to this book or its contents. The author and publisher disclaim all such representations and warranties, including but not limited to merchantability, healthcare, or fitness for a particular purpose. In addition, while every effort was made to ensure that the information in this book was correct at press time, the author and publisher do not represent or warrant that the information accessible via this book is accurate, complete or current.

Neither the publisher nor any authors, contributors or other representatives shall be held liable or responsible to any person or entity with respect to any loss, injury, disruption or damage, including but not limited to any physical, psychological, emotional, financial, commercial, or any other damages caused, or alleged to have been caused, directly or indirectly, by the use of this book or the information contained herein. This is a comprehensive limitation of liability that applies to all damages of any kind, including (without limitation) compensatory, direct, indirect, special, incidental or consequential damages; loss of income or profit; loss of or damage to property, and claims of third parties. No warranty may be created or extended by sales representatives or by any written or electronic sales materials used in the sale and distribution of this book.

Every person and every life situation is different, and the information contained in this book may not be suitable for all readers. Reading this book does not guarantee that all readers' experience will be comparable to that of the author or of other readers. It is advised that all readers seek the services of a competent professional before beginning any legal course of action, lifestyle change, health practice, or other improvement program. Your use of this book signifies your acceptance of this disclaimer.

CONTENTS

PART IV: TAKING FLIGHT

PART V: SOARING

FOREWORD

To many people, a divorce attorney may not seem like the most fitting individual to draft the foreword to a book as inspirational as this one. While I understand that sentiment, I am both honored and grateful to write this message on behalf of my former client and current dear friend. Furthermore, I believe that as I share just a small piece of my journey and how it intersects with Pam's, you will begin to see how powerful the book you're holding really is.

I have practiced family law for over 25 years. Ten years ago, I had an epiphany. I realized that I could use my empathy to help people. While I knew it could help, I didn't yet know how, and figuring that out became a mission for me. This idea led me to Collaborative Law, a team-based approach that balances the needs and interests of both parties. This way of practicing family law resonated with me because it supported my desire to help everyone involved to find the best possible resolution out of what is often an extremely challenging and emotional situation.

What does this have to do with Pam? As an attorney, I often need to guide my clients through the process of divorce, but in Pam's case, she guided the course of action. No doubt, this approach would unnerve any number of attorneys, but her calm demeanor, poise, confidence and trust in the Universe as she navigated this situation made one thing clear: Pam is unique. I had never worked with another client like her before, and I knew I needed to let her strength shine through.

I believe people are placed on this Earth for a reason. As I walked alongside Pam during this part of her journey, I knew that she would need to share her story. There simply had to be a bigger reason behind what led her to where she was. As you read her story, you will get a sense of exactly what I mean.

Pam could have followed the path so many people in her situation do — a path of anger, hatred and pain. But, Pam had the capacity to see that she had also received a tremendous gift. She could peer through the mist and discern what really deserved her energy. She thoughtfully contemplated which path she needed to take to move forward and bring herself to a higher place. It's very easy to cast blame, but Pam chose compassion and a steadfast commitment to growth and transformation.

While Pam acknowledged her marriage was irreparable, she knew her life, and her family, could take a whole new path. In fact, she knew they could be better than ever, even if she didn't have a concrete plan. As you read and come to understand her story, you will see just how instrumental her mindset was in this time of transition.

The Universe always strategically places people exactly where they need to be at every moment in time. It knew exactly what it was doing when it ensured that our paths would intersect. I was the right attorney to help her strength shine through during her divorce, and she, in turn, helped me to become open to a level of consciousness that I wouldn't have achieved without her in my life. The lessons I learned from Pam have, and will continue to impact me in my personal life, my professional life and the way I interact with everyone I encounter.

A relationship quickly blossomed between us, extending far beyond what one might expect between an attorney and a client. While she no longer needs my services, we have a lasting friendship that nothing can diminish. For that reason, I'm honored to write this foreword, but I also understand that my role is larger than our friendship. Just as the Universe meticulously arranged the pieces so that Pam and I would work together on legal formalities, it knew Pam wanted my energy signature to be a part of this book, and in true Universe fashion, it knew just how to make that happen.

How do I know this? Because on one cold February day when Pam and I were catching up over coffee and she was telling me about her book, I enthusiastically asked if I could write the foreword. Little did I know, she had intended to ask me to write it before I made the request. The Universe never misses an opportunity to put the people and things that you need right where you need them. Just as the Universe put us together, it put this book in your hands for a reason. Whatever is going on in your life, I wholeheartedly believe as you read this, you will find exactly what you need to embrace your own authenticity.

Early in our journey together, during one of our meetings, I unwaveringly declared to Pam, "You are going to change the world." I knew it then, and I know it now. Remember, no matter where you are on your journey, this book has all the elements you need to transform your life. With a healthy sense of open-mindedness and a willingness to approach life in a new way, you will be well on your way to creating your new reality.

It was both humbling and inspiring to work with Pam during this process, and I have been honored to walk alongside her during this part of her journey. Now, through this book, she wants to walk beside you during yours.

I can tell you from experience, reading this book will be one of the most worthwhile and impactful investments you make in yourself.

- Beth McCormack
Family Law Partner, Beermann LLP

PREFACE

I wrote this book with the hope that it would prompt a stirring in your soul at whatever magnitude your current state of evolution is ready for and to encourage you to begin the process of shifting your paradigm so that you may step more fully into your authentic reality, whatever that may look like.

The floodgates have just opened in my world and I'm delighted and grateful that you have consciously chiseled out a piece of your reality to experience the tsunami of transformative ideas that are about to be released into this world. The Universe and I have been crafting our strategy for helping you claim your personal power, and I'm honored to walk this journey with you.

The one thing life guarantees is that there will always be challenges to navigate. Nobody is exempt from that, as challenges don't discriminate based on gender, race, religion, sexual orientation, financial standing, social status or any other delineation. While we can't undo or re-create events in our lives, what we can do is reframe them and choose to see them through spiritual lenses. When we do that, an entirely new world opens up to us. Much of what we see in our physical world are only illusions. Life can feel complicated and frenzied and stressful, and what might appear to be chaos on the surface is in actuality a divinely orchestrated plan with perfect order as the underlying element. Life becomes so sweet when we learn to surrender, relax and trust the Universe and its magical process. We learn to stop forcing things that aren't meant for us and become observers and co-creators in a reality that unfolds organically.

In the spiritual world, there is no such thing as a mistake. There are no accidents. There is no such thing as a waste of time. Everything always unfolds in a divinely orchestrated manner, and the people and experiences that are meant for us are placed in our path with pristine timing. The Universe never ceases to amaze me, as it always knows the magnitude of the catalyst that is necessary to shake up our own current realities and launch us into our own authentic realities. I have arrived at a place where I can say I look at the way in which my story unfolded with extreme gratitude, as it gradually and gracefully escorted all of us to a place where were are all perfectly poised to become the best version of ourselves, as we now exist in an environment with freedom and authenticity at its core. I can say with certainty that would not have been a possibility in our prior realities.

The Universe always has grander plans and our highest good in mind, and if we surrender and trust the process, we are catapulted to unprecedented levels of personal spiritual growth.

My wish for everyone in this world, regardless of any delineation that creates the illusion of separatism, is that we all live deeply fulfilling and authentic lives. My hope is that everyone will get to a place where they have the determination to find their own voices and the willingness to speak their own truths. Achieving this goal often requires radical change, and I am vowing to embody, embrace and model this change to inspire others to find their own voice and leave this world a better place than we found it.

We live in an extremely exciting time because we are on the cusp of our collective consciousness starting to make a huge shift. We are seeing people start to wake up and examine their lives in ways they have never looked at them before. They're looking for more fulfillment; people aren't satisfied with the standard norms, customs, traditions and beliefs that have been handed down to them that had worked well for prior generations. We are beginning to see these antiquated paradigms start to break down across the entire spectrum of our lives, from significant primary relationships to day-to-day lifestyle choices. People are looking for deeper meaning and are starting to make more conscious choices. When we make a commitment and a practice to turn our unconscious patterns into conscious choices on a daily basis, we open ourselves up to an entirely new dimension. It is through this expansion of our awareness and the commitment to choosing love that we are able to access Universal Energy on a continual basis and claim our personal power.

We all have a story, and this book is mine. In it, I share my life experiences in an authentic way and demonstrate how I use spiritual universal truths to navigate my Earthly journey. It is only through vulnerability and transparency that we unlock the doors to personal growth and transformation and through that process we discover our Higher Selves and step into our authentic realities. Implicit in one's willingness to enter vulnerable territory is the statement "I trust you." As I open my heart wide enough to share my story with you, it is my hope that it creates fertile ground for you to take a deep, introspective dive into who you are today as you simultaneously explore your own truth. Setting the precedent for openness and transparency allows us to connect with each other on a much deeper level and has a synergistic effect as we all achieve unprecedented levels of consciousness together.

Spirituality and writing are two of my passions, so it only made sense to blend these together in an experiential account of how I partner with the Universe to create my reality. I love how words can be used to prompt a stirring in the soul. I love how words, when sequenced in a purpose-driven way, can prompt people to make huge shifts in their own lives. I am grateful that you have chosen to chisel out a few hours of your reality to step into mine. You made a conscious choice with a very clear intention; you want to grow. It is my sincere hope that you will take these truths and sprinkle them throughout your own life, as well as the lives of others. We are all in this together.

By making the resolution to transform your own life, you are effectively changing the world. If you're wondering if what you do on an individual level matters, it does. If you're wondering if your actions can actually have a broadscale impact, they can. Everything we do has a ripple effect and even the smallest, seemingly insignificant actions work their way through collective consciousness and eventually reverberate back to you. Together we can prompt huge shifts in collective consciousness. We have to start somewhere, and that somewhere is right where you are, right now. Your paradigm shift is underway.

Nothing sets my soul on fire more than demystifying esoteric, metaphysical concepts by showing people how to apply them in their daily lives so they are empowered and in a position to create a life they love. For this plan to work, though, I need you to be willing to learn a new language, the language of the Universe. You need to be willing to "unlearn" certain things that you have learned and be willing to replace your old, antiquated programming with programming that launches you into higher realms of consciousness to unleash your true potential. In exchange for your promise to do that, I will make these promises:

I WILL

I WILL challenge conventional programming
I WILL overturn antiquated modes of operation
I WILL shift stagnant paradigms
I WILL defy odds
I WILL transform lives
I WILL have unlimited potential by helping others achieve theirs
I WILL fuel this mission via multiple pathways
I WILL dazzle the naysayers
I WILL awaken slumbering souls
I WILL open hearts
I WILL radiate light
I WILL scatter the energy of creation
I WILL impart infinite wisdom
I WILL share my divine essence
I WILL ignite this world and all the while
I WILL LOVE what I do

The journey from your head to your heart is the best trip you'll ever take. Let's take this trip together.

The journey from your head to your heart is the best trip you'll ever take.

WITH GRATITUDE

To Mom and Dad: Your unwavering support over the years is absolutely unparalleled. Among an endless list of other values, you've modeled and taught me tenacity, positivity and that triumph in the face of insurmountable odds is the only option. The foundation of faith that you have worked so relentlessly to bestow upon me will forever be the cornerstone of who I am, as that has enabled me to surrender and trust the process, knowing that no matter what chaos may be ensuing in front of us, behind the scenes everything is always in perfect divine order.

To my children: Of all the moms you could have chosen, it is truly humbling to know that you chose me. You have added more depth and richness to my life than I could ever articulate, and I am so proud of all of you. I can hardly wait to watch as you imprint your unique energy signature on this world.

To my tribe: None of you were placed in my path by accident. You were strategically positioned to propel me on my journey and assist me in my own personal transformation. Thank you for helping me to commit to a lifestyle that is anchored to growth and has catapulted me into fulfilling my soul's purpose. You have always known what I needed, from challenging me when I needed to be challenged, to helping me celebrate small victories along the way. You have each played an essential role in helping me craft the version of who I am today.

To my motivators: For everyone who helped me turn my dream of writing this book into a reality, to my trainers at the gym who don't allow me to stop until I finish all my reps, to all those who inspired me to follow a plant-based diet and kept challenging the way I ate until I finally got it and everyone in between. I find inspiration in every interaction with each of you.

To my lessons of life, love and loss: These experiences have stripped me to my core, caused me to dig deep and prompted me to contemplate every belief I've ever known. It is these experiences that have shaped who I am and have encouraged me to not only step into my truth but to also impart my message to a broader audience.

To my audience: I am grateful that you are open-minded enough to purposefully carve out a slice of your reality to step into my human experience for a brief moment in time. It is my hope that you use your own life experiences to align yourself more closely with the essence of who you are. Each of you possesses a unique gift that the world is waiting for you to share, and it is my hope that this book prompts a stirring in your soul.

To the Universe: You have my back every moment of every day. Your timing is divine. Your execution is flawless. Your wisdom is infinite. Because of you, this journey gets sweeter every single day.

INTRODUCTION

I've long believed that the Universe provides me with opportunities to work with clients who I'm meant to serve, and I've equally experienced great growth, often as much as my clients, from the work we do in therapy. My connection with Pam, and the transformative development that occurred for us both is a wonderful example of the benevolence of the Universe, and the healing and forward movement that can happen when open hearts, searching psyches and spirits craving evolution come together.

I've witnessed firsthand the intelligence, courage and grace Pam has brought to her journey to make sense of the challenges in her life. She is relentless in her self-examination and embraces the truths she uncovers with bravery matched only by the size of her heart and the resilience of her spirit. This book is the result of her willingness to face, speak and live her truth, and her commitment to the evolution of the planet by choosing to share her journey with all of us. In these pages, Pam will challenge readers with questions that encourage them to find, own and choose from their own innate, perhaps buried, wisdom. As a human being, she has done the work. She is willing to walk the walk, alongside her readers. She is willing to be vulnerable in as public a place as the written page, and she doesn't shy away from sharing herself completely, from her most devastating, fear-based queries into the future of her and her children's lives as she began her path toward divorce, to the pinnacle of her moments of achievement and transformation, as she grew a business, attended to her children's healing, and created a life of authenticity and empowerment. Pam's story is one of courage, perseverance, humility and the willingness to jump into the deep end of what was a whirlpool time in her life and to rise above the waves more connected than ever to herself and the riches the Universe offered her.

Pam's story makes for inspiring reading on its own. But she knows the purpose of her challenges reach far beyond her own experience. Pam was aware, through her own spiritual work and the corresponding efforts she's made with clients as a spiritual coach, that the lessons were applicable to everyone, and that the transformation she's experienced could be replicated by anyone willing to have an open heart and mind and be open to a new way of thinking. Pam's philosophy flies in the face of conventional thinking, engendering new ways to consider and develop your definition and makeup of family, spirituality and the divorce process. She guides the reader to moments of blossoming through the use of thoughtful suggestions and concrete tools to maximize growth and spiritual development. Hers is a positive process, but one that is far from saccharine. Her humility, hopefulness and unflinching honesty will inspire readers to believe in their own possibilities, even to unearth a life of abundance, peace and joy beyond their previous imaginings.

I wholeheartedly encourage you to join Pam in jumping into the pool of limitless possibilities. She will buoy you, inspire you and celebrate with you as the Universe's waves carry you to your authentic self and purpose.

- Susan De Luca, LCSW
June, 2019

PART I

LEARNING TO FLY

Before you can embark on a new trajectory, you must open your mind to different perspectives.

1

WHAT WOULD LOVE DO?

Don't worry about what they do. Ask yourself "What would love do?" and do that. Love is the answer, every single time.

We don't always get to choose what happens to us in life, but we always get to choose how we respond. Challenging situations in life have the potential to be highly transformative, as long as we are willing to abandon the conditioning that has been imprinted on us. You have a choice in how your life unfolds. There is a way to partner with the Universe in co-creating your new reality to take your life from mediocre to mind-blowing. Join me as I usher you out of fear mode into a space that embraces change and uncertainty and step into a new beginning where anything is possible, by making conscious choices coming from a place of love every moment of every day.

This book is an experiential account of stepping out of **fear** and into **love** in the context of a personal, experiential account with the divorce process as the underlying storyline, but the tenets and beliefs can be applied to **any** situation in life by learning to access the most abundant and freely-available source of energy

... Universal Energy. It's unlimited, **and** it's free. My divorce process is simply the life experience that unleashed me into my new reality and inspired me to impart the knowledge and wisdom the Universe has bestowed upon me, and I have used this as the underlying storyline to illustrate how I have interwoven spiritual truths into my life. When I first started writing this book, it was initially intended to be a guide for helping people navigate the divorce process consciously and holistically. As my writing progressed and evolved, I realized that many of the underlying elements of divorce, like fear, regret, resentment, grief and dealing with change are found in many other life experiences. The ideologies presented in this book are universal in their application and can be used to navigate any life experience.

Many of us are living realities that are not authentic to who we are. You may be in a relationship that has run its course and no longer works. You may be working at a job that is mundane and unfulfilling. You may be living in a geographic location that stifles creativity and adventure. Whatever your current situation is, there is a way through it. The issue is that many people don't realize that they are infinitely powerful and embody the fortitude to totally transform their world. Our thoughts create our reality and we must first accept the truth that we are where we are because of our prior thoughts. The same thought patterns that delivered us to our current situations will not be the same thought patterns that usher us out. Old ways of thinking must be abandoned and you must be willing to rewire your mind and establish new patterns.

This book is not about helping you decide whether or not you should make a life-changing decision, whether it surrounds relationships, career or any other significant area of your life. Your heart already knows the answer. It's about introducing you to spiritual concepts and showing you how to apply these concepts in a natural and organic way until it becomes your new way of living. It's about expanding your awareness to include alternative ways of thinking and empowering you so you have the confidence to make the right choices for yourself. By incorporating new holistic lifestyle practices, you will gain the courage to stand unabashedly in your truth and in doing so your magnetism and zest for life will encourage others to do the same.

My wish for you is that by the end of this book you have reached a place where you feel empowered to navigate any life experience with unprecedented levels of open-mindedness and a willingness to use your life experiences as tools of transformation and self-actualization.

In some respects, staying within the boundaries of old paradigms, whether they pertain to relationships or any other life situation, may be easier in the moment. You may feel inclined to cling on to comfort and familiarity. You may be fearful of making a change. You may be unwilling to step into the unknown. We all have that fight or flight instinct where our bodies naturally want to choose anger or other self-protecting mechanisms. Our natural inclinations may be to put on the boxing gloves, dig our heels in, and defend our positions. When another person starts a mud-slinging contest, you may feel the pull to join in and show them that you can sling mud farther. You may feel the thrill of a small victory in the moment, but I can assure you that this is not the path that will deliver long-term fulfillment and certainly will not foster an environment where everyone can coexist harmoniously.

It's hard to walk uphill. It's hard to go against the grain. It's hard to take the high-road. Growth does not come easy. Like anything else worth having, it takes commitment and consistency.

Heart-centered living is a choice and a commitment. It doesn't happen overnight and it doesn't come easily. There's no "on" switch. No easy button. No magic bullet. It takes work. It takes open-mindedness. It takes a willingness to own your stuff. It takes courage. It takes uncomfortableness. It takes vulnerability. It takes transparency. It takes silencing the chatter in your mind. It takes learning to trust your intuition. It takes finding your voice. It takes stepping into your truth. But, it also takes you to places your fear-based, conscious mind can't even comprehend. Are you ready to take this journey into your soul?

This is your life, and it is completely your right and your responsibility to craft a reality that represents who you are at your core, the deepest level of your being. Regardless of what has happened to you, through opening up your mind to a new approach, you will start to view the world through new lenses and unleash your full potential.

Navigating any life experience the spiritual way takes authenticity. Positivity is important, but that's only part of the picture. Showing up authentically requires a level of honesty with oneself that may be unprecedented for you depending on where you are on your journey. Rest assured that wherever you are is where you are meant to be, and the only thing that is required is that you show up as you are, with an open and curious mind, willing and ready to deprogram yourself from what you have previously been taught so that you can reprogram your mind with more progressive, avant-garde ways of thinking in accordance with the language of the Universe.

I firmly believe that the best outcomes are achieved when we become active, conscious co-creators with the Universe as our partner. Each situation comes with a unique set of circumstances, terms and conditions, and as a result, there is no one blueprint that can be used ubiquitously for each situation without a healthy dose of conscious thought and conscious creativity behind it. Allow your unique situation to run through the filter of this experiential account as you experience what it feels like for words to prompt a stirring in your soul.

At this point, I invite you to check your ego at the door. The ideas in this book require a healthy dose of open-mindedness and a willingness to view the world and your human experience through new lenses. The limitations of our conscious minds, fear-based egos, other self-limiting factors and societal conditioning can all work together to create barriers against embracing a new way of thinking, but these hurdles can be overcome. The extent to which you allow your mind to stretch into an open-minded territory and remain there will directly influence the degree to which you will experience growth, expansion and transformation. In this book, I'm going to show you how thriving under any set of circumstances is only one mindset away. The Universe always has our highest good at the forefront of its agenda, and when we learn how to shift over from the driver's seat to the passenger seat and become the observer of our own lives rather than the controller, each of our lives transforms from mediocre to magical.

While this book provides a general framework and presents various modalities for navigating the divorce process mindfully and holistically, the spiritual truths that we will explore together are universal in their application. My hope is that you will use them as a guiding light not only during this time of transition and your period of healing but also throughout the rest of your journey through this Earthly Classroom.

This book doesn't attempt to give you "10 easy steps to navigate divorce with a smile" or anything like that. It doesn't work that way. No two situations are exactly alike, and therefore there is no one recipe that works for everyone.

It takes challenging yourself every moment of every day. The first powerful question I will ask and encourage you to ask at every decision point, from the most minute to the grandest, is "What would love do?"

The real question, though, is **how**? How do you do this? How exactly do you go from a place of feeling stuck or lost or fearful or hopeless or overwhelmed or all of the above and step into an authentic life where your new state of being is love and peace and joy and bliss and freedom? Through asking yourself some powerful questions coupled with a willingness to take a deep dive, you will begin to discover the truths that reside deep within your soul. Nothing sets my soul on fire quite like the process of igniting the spark in others, and I am grateful that you've given me this opportunity to show you.

Discovering Your Authenticity

- What are the three most significant experiences in your life that shook you to your core?
- Did these experiences prompt you to make any changes? Did you choose to help transform the lives of others as a result of your experience?
- What is an experience in your life where the outcome could have been drastically different if you had chosen to come from love?
- Is there a challenging relationship in your life for which you haven't been coming from love?
- What is one small action you could do to be the first to come from love in this relationship?
- How do you prioritize loving yourself?

2

YOU

The best thing you can do for yourself and for humanity is to commit to your authentic reality and pour all of your energy into it.

I'm going to start this chapter off with this universal truth: We are all on this Earth for a limited time. Sobering as it may be, it's reality. You have this one life and you deserve to be happy and are entitled to do your life **your** way.

I'm a firm believer that we all already have our answers deep within us. They're like tiny jewels just waiting to be discovered and dusted off so that they glisten and allow you to shine your light into the world.

The issue is that through a combination of self-imposed limitations like doubt, fear, procrastination or guilt, and external factors like societal conditioning or feeling the need to follow other people's paths or reactions, we allow ourselves to remain stuck. Those are all examples of the ego getting in the way and trying to limit us. The ego tries to keep us tethered to physical world considerations and constraints, but our souls will always usher us to the truth. It's a dance between the ego and the soul, and the more in touch we become with our souls the easier it will become to step into our own truths with intentionality and assuredness.

You have this one life and it's up to you to take personal responsibility for the way you want to live it. The only way to do it the "right way" is to go deep within and do the work that allows you to discover your deeper truths and live them out. As much as I would love to give you a roadmap, I can't. It's not because I don't want to; it's because there isn't one. Even if there were, that wouldn't be the preferred approach because there's no growth in that. No conscious thought. No digging deep and sitting quietly with your thoughts and learning to listen to what your intuition is telling you at each juncture. We are not going for the unconscious route through this; we are going for conscious, active, co-creation with the Universe.

You have to be willing to look in the mirror and say to yourself, "I am the one who is responsible for getting myself through this," and that may sound and feel like a daunting task. The good news is that you already have everything you need within you. You always have. You are limitless beyond measure and powerful beyond your wildest dreams. You've just been directing your time and energy toward things that are stifling your personal power rather than unleashing it. A lifestyle rooted in superficial pursuits may fill you up today, or it may fill you up through next week, but it won't provide the type of long-lasting fulfillment or happiness that will sustain you for the long haul. I know. I've been there. I pulled out all the stops trying to find it. I finally have, and I couldn't be more thrilled to share my experiential journey with you so that you may become empowered to take your life by the reigns and get to a place where you feel the flow of Universal Energy coursing through your veins every moment of every day.

You have to look in the mirror and say, "I am the one who is responsible for getting myself through this."

Spiritual growth and transformation is such an exciting process because it can withstand mega-doses of creativity. We live in a world where anything is possible and nothing is ever totally off the table. It calls for you to think outside the box and apply your unique energy signature to the process. We are conditioned in this society of instant gratification to look for the magic bullet or the quick fix. Anything worth having takes a serious amount of work and dedication and the desire to change needs to come from within you. You have to be willing to take your life by the reigns and own your spiritual development. Nobody wants to be told what to do, and the fun part is navigating your own way through your journey. I don't love the idea of "10 steps to a happier you"-type lists because everyone's journey is highly individual and there is an implicit expectation that you will achieve a particular outcome after following the steps. What happens if the outcome isn't achieved? What does that do to your self-confidence? The reward is the journey and everything you discover about yourself throughout it.

You have to want it, and you have to want it bad. It's up to you. You have to believe that there is a better way to navigate life than your old way of operating and be willing to roll up your sleeves and try a new approach. You have to embody the desire to run your life or else it will run you. Nobody's coming to rescue you.

You're the one who needs to do the heavy lifting. It's up to you to climb out of whatever deep dark hole you may be in and follow the light so you can be the light.

You have to be willing to stop following the masses and set out on your own path. We often hold ourselves back and resist the direction in which our soul is pulled to satisfy others or live a life that is conventional, compromising our own happiness and growth in the process. Do not let the fear of other people's reactions hold you back. You only have this one life and every day that goes by that you are not living your truth is another day that you have deprived yourself and the world of your true potential and the gifts you can bring forward.

The best gift we can give is the gift of aligning with our true selves. Not only do we benefit, but everyone else in our lives benefits. Humanity benefits. Living a life that is authentic to who we are allows us to access Universal Energy which is unequivocally the most powerful resource available to each and every one of us.

My heart breaks for the people who are living split realities, whose day to day lives look one way, but their hearts and minds are wishing they were somewhere else. The best thing you can do for yourself and for humanity is to commit to your authentic reality and pour all of your energy into it. If you're not passionate about it, don't do it. If your heart's not in it, don't do it. If it doesn't set your soul on fire, don't do it. Arrange the pieces so that your life on the outside reflects what you hold in your heart and mind. If you've spent your life wishing you lived in a warmer climate with a mountainous backdrop, pick up and move. If you've spent your life as a homosexual but are scared to live your life out loud, move in the direction of stepping into it. If you're stuck in a job that depletes you rather than fuels you, consider a career change. If you're struggling with an addiction that you've kept hidden from your friends and family, share your story with them.

You have to be willing to bust through the chains that have been binding you. **You** need to be the one to make the first move. Don't wait for someone to come and push you off the edge of the diving board. Just jump and trust the Universe and its process. Whatever reality you are stepping into, the people who are meant to be in your life will meet you where you are and as you are with compassion, acceptance, kindness and love, and the ones who don't weren't your people to begin with. As you step into your authentic reality, the Universe will naturally exploit these misalignments and will align you with people who are at your vibrational level. Goodbyes are never easy and it can be difficult to weather these disconnections, but if we don't make conscious choices to create space for new relationships, we will never connect with the people who are meant to be in our lives.

This world has no shortage of people, 7.6 billion to be exact, and regardless of whatever your truth is, I can assure you that you will be able to find a community of like-minded people who speak your language, share your beliefs and are ready and excited to greet you on the other side and rally around you.

Everyone is dealing with something. None of us is exempt from that. Whether it's divorce, grief, loss, anxiety, depression or any other condition that plagues us, they are all similar in that they all embody elements of some type of fear. Whatever you are dealing with, the situation as it is today is temporary. You are not stuck in this place forever and the good news is that your situation and the way in which you allow it to affect you is highly responsive to the choices you make.

Any situation that challenges us has the potential to be highly transformative if we let our soul lead the way. There will always be a cloud of emptiness, dissatisfaction, and a sense of incompleteness hovering over us everywhere we go unless we learn to approach life from the soul. It takes a level of honesty with oneself and highly potent doses of transparency and vulnerability that may be unprecedented for you depending on where you are on your journey. That's okay. You are here, and you are exactly where you're meant to be. Showing up as you are is the first step, and is precisely the genesis of your personal growth and transformation.

You have already begun your paradigm shift. Simply picking up this book symbolizes the desire to take a deeper dive and explore your life at unprecedented depths. It's a vulnerable and bold statement that says "I'm seeking more. I want to approach life in a new way." Your transformation is already underway.

Whatever decisions you make in your life, people may feel the need to weigh in and express their opinion. Don't worry about what people may think. That's irrelevant. What you decide to do with your life is **your business** and **your business only**. You don't owe anyone any explanations for what you're doing or why you're doing it, and you don't need to solicit input or validation or approval from anyone. Your life is not a democratic entity; you're the decision-maker. What it comes down to is if it resonates with **your** soul, then it's the right thing to do. Everything in your physical reality will fall into place the way it's supposed to when you learn how to co-create your reality with the Universe.

Don't despair when your ideas or new way of living is considered to be bold; bold is precisely what you want to be. You want to be on the progressive end of the spectrum. You want to be a thought leader. You want to be avant-garde. You want to shatter old paradigms. You want to challenge conventions. You want your ideas to be considered revolutionary. This is the whole idea behind our awakening.

We live in an incredibly exciting time, as we are just on the cusp of collective consciousness starting to make a huge shift. People are starting to wake up and look at their lives in ways that they haven't before. They're making attempts to get to the core of who they are. They're not only evaluating their lives by superficial criteria related to "success" anymore, but by indicators related to "happiness" and "fulfillment." We are witnessing paradigms that served prior generations quite well for decades start to break down. The whole energetic landscape is changing and we must make changes in our daily lives to keep up with it and play a part in propelling this collective expansion. We see these shifts starting to take place across the entire spectrum of humanity, from relationships to the food choices people are putting in their bodies. They are starting to do things with more mindfulness and introspection, and as they make more conscious decisions, they are impacting not only their own lives, but their shifts in consciousness, insignificant as they may seem, have a ripple effect that reverberates its way through the collective consciousness.

The divorce process is densely packed with several decisions to be made in a short period of time. While it can be challenging to make decisions, especially when you're feeling emotionally compromised or physically depleted, it is important to remember that **you** are the only one in the position to make decisions for your life. I'm going to state that again — it bears repeating because it's that powerful — **you** are the only one in the position to make decisions for your life.

Along your journey, you will encounter other people who give you advice, guidance and ideas to consider. They can tell you what other people have done. They can tell you the data that the research has put forth. But what nobody else can tell you is what your truth is. Only you know that. The real growth occurs when individuals are empowered to make choices that are congruent with who they are. It is only through the process of aligning ourselves and reconnecting to Source Energy that we may step into our truth, shine our light into the world and encourage others to do the same.

You are the only one living your reality. **You** are the only one walking in your shoes. **You** are the only one navigating this human experience from your vantage point. **You** are the only one who is intimately familiar with your belief system. **You** are the only one who truly knows your desires, preferences and intolerances. **You** are the one who has to live with the repercussions of your decisions day in and day out, regardless of what they may be.

Getting into the business of doing you and staying there is not easy. There will be growing pains along the way as you will be shedding things that no longer serve you, like toxic relationships, fears, doubts and feelings of self-doubt and worthlessness. As you learn to overcome the barriers that hinder you from living your authentic life, it will become easier and more natural.

As you find your voice and learn to speak your truth, you will find that this new way of living takes some getting used to. Do not be disheartened or discouraged; it's a normal response of the human condition to cling to old ways of operating, for that is what is comfortable and familiar to us. People often feel compelled to stick with what is known rather than risk that comfort and familiarity and trade it in for uncertainty. Dealing with change is not easy, and can be downright scary unless we rewire our minds to process it in a new, more progressive way.

Your answers aren't on the internet. They're not found in the well-meaning advice of friends and family who might think they know what's best for you. Remember that all advice from others, even when given with the purest of intentions, is filtered through their own life experiences, beliefs and culturally-accepted norms. They're not found solely on the basis of hours and hours of research, and your answers are not discovered via pros/cons lists.

You already have your answers, and you've had them all along. The fun part is discovering them. It requires quieting the mind so that you can sit quietly with yourself and hear your inner voice as it speaks to you.

Learning to speak your truth can be scary, as our ideas may be counter to what others are doing. We may feel like we're going against the grain. What we are doing may be considered revolutionary. It may look bold. It may be unconventional. We may be bucking trends. It may be avant-garde. But that's the point. It's no longer about conforming to mainstream culture. It's about doing **you** and not worrying about how it fits or doesn't fit the mold of what others are doing. It's not about getting others to understand it, and everything to do with living your truth.

I can assure you that this is where life really starts to become magical. You will start to feel liberated. Empowered. Untethered. Limitless. Unstoppable. Bold. Avant-garde. Joyful. It will be so awesome that going back to your old way of living won't even be a fleeting thought.

Whatever your truth is, the time to step into it is **now**. The

Universe is ready and excited to co-create your new reality with you.

Discovering Your Authenticity

- Have you ever become so exasperated with a situation you're in and said, "I can't live like this anymore"? Why are you? What is holding you back?
- What blocks and obstacles are preventing you from stepping into your truth?
- In what areas of your life are your thoughts, actions and behaviors misaligned?
- What is a change that you have been contemplating but are too fearful to make?
- Have you thought about the very real possibility that your new life could be infinitely better than your current reality?

For a special bonus on stepping into your authentic reality, visit https://liveauthentically.today/soar-resources to download the guide.

3

THE EGO AND THE SOUL

Our underlying motivating factors begin to change radically when we operate from our Higher Selves.

What is the ego and what is the soul, and why is it crucial to give both some airtime? It's not enough for me to give you ideas for executing the "how." For any idea to have staying power over the long haul, we need to explore the "why." We need to get to the root of why we are taking this approach, which will then enable us to take a deep, exploratory dive into the depths of our psyche and operate from our Higher Selves. When we move from navigating our way around this world from an ego-based perspective and shift into living with intentionality from a soul-based existence, we begin to experience a depth and richness that would not have otherwise been achievable compared to when we were letting our egos continue to direct the sails. We begin to make decisions that fulfill us and bring us inner peace. Our underlying motivating factors begin to change radically when we operate from our Higher Selves. We naturally begin to crave different things than we used to. We start pining after certain "feelings" such as joy, peace and freedom and arrive at a point where we can't tolerate feeling any other way.

First, we must explore the dichotomous nature of our being. We don't have souls; we are souls. We are souls that are housed in our physical bodies that serve as their homes during the time spent here on Earth, which I affectionately call our "Earthly Classroom." I call it a classroom because we are here to learn and to grow, and of course to give and receive love. Everything else in our world: other people, our physical belongings, our resources, how we choose to spend our time, among other things, can either serve to support our growth or deter it. It is our job to sift through that which we encounter in our physical world and make the determination as to whether or not it serves us. We can find this out by asking if something is enhancing our growth or impeding it. We need to discover and cultivate our self-awareness so that we can learn to recognize what is in our highest good and empower ourselves to make the appropriate choices and necessary changes to keep us on the path of our evolution.

The Higher Self helps us stay focused on the true meaning of life and our purpose in it. It's the part of us that is focused on the eternal nature of our being, and not what is happening on the physical plane. It's what gives our lives depth and richness. It allows us to connect directly to Source Energy, and is always striving to deliver to us what is in our highest good. Source Energy has several names that can be used interchangeably, such as Universal Energy, the Divine, the Universe, God, etc., and provides the never-ending life force energy that runs through each and every one of us. Why is it important to connect to this lifeline and work to keep the connection active and vibrant? This is where our true power is realized. It's where we begin to realize that we are limitless and feel unstoppable, untethered and liberated. The soul is concerned with concepts such as happiness, fulfillment, spiritual growth, transformation, evolution, compassion, kindness, forgiveness, peace, generosity, selflessness and other similar ideas. These are all incredibly powerful virtues, and ones that I would contend are woefully undervalued and under-practiced in today's society.

To take this journey in an authentic way, we must recognize and explore the soul's counterpart, the ego. The ego is focused on matters of the physical world, like how we perceive and measure up against certain physical-world barometers. It's that voice inside our heads that tries to tell us who we are by using certain "control levers" such as fear, doubt, stress and negative self-talk. It's the force that keeps us wanting to measure ourselves against self-imposed expectations which may or may not be realistic and prompts us to compare ourselves against other people.

There are certain things that try to impede or block our connection to Source Energy, and things rooted in egoic fundamentals play that part. The ego can have a loud voice and it is important to harbor a sufficient level of self-awareness so that we can realize when it is trying to overtake us and take measures to limit it, or in some cases, silence it altogether. The ego likes to initiate power struggles with our Higher Selves, but we can quickly temper these struggles by learning to disengage from them or by transmuting the unproductive energies of our ego into fuel that burns within the fire of our Higher Selves.

The ego is often made out to be the "bad guy" or the villain in the story and often has a negative association, but I've come to realize that when used appropriately, it can play an extremely influential role in the growth process. There is a fascinating interplay between the soul and the ego, which often results in a strong push/pull dynamic. The perpetual dance between the ego and the soul can play a huge role in fueling our growth and transformation. Learning to keep the ego in check can be accomplished by having a dialogue with yourself. Every time the ego speaks, it is offering a rich opportunity for tremendous growth and transformation. View each word uttered by the ego as illuminating various undiscovered aspects of yourself and inviting you to reach higher.

I've come to accept that virtually every project I undertake requires the need for a productive, healthy tension-infused dialogue between my ego and my Higher Self to achieve the result. I think of every project or process that I engage in as being broken up into three parts: beginning, middle and end. The first stage and last stage are always easy for me; I'm always brimming with enthusiasm and energy during the first third, and during the last third I pick up speed as the finish line is within sight. The middle third is where I have a tendency to struggle. Here is where I have a long-standing pattern of losing momentum and having thoughts of doubt creep in. Sometimes there is so much inertia that I have thoughts of throwing in the towel altogether. This happens in varying degrees in virtually every project or activity, from treadmill sessions to domestic projects, and truth be told, even in this book-writing process. Every time I have to coach myself through it by first identifying the source of the stagnation followed by powerful language from my Higher Self. I have to channel Universal Energy and say things like "You are stronger than this. You are capable of pushing through. The world needs this."

Each time, I receive affirmation that the voice of our Higher Selves is louder than the voice of the ego. Every time I push through the period of frustration and stagnation, I draw from my inner strength and am infused with a level of energy and enthusiasm that would not have been realized without the ego's role, as I reconnect to my Higher Self and hook into my personal power.

Ego is concerned with what others think. It's the little endorphin rush we get when someone else validates what we are doing. It's called an ego boost for a reason. It's the fleeting surge of "feel good" emotions, and as soon as they are gone, we start craving more. It's like the process of becoming addicted to a drug or anything else that our bodies becomes behaviorally or chemically dependent upon. At first, just a little gives us the rush that we're seeking. Before too long, the small bit no longer quells our craving and we need to take more to satisfy ourselves. It's a vicious cycle that continues for as long as we continue to give in to the ego. The ego is never able to achieve and sustain happiness because it is always coming from a place of lacking and needing and wanting and desiring. By prompting us to continually resist a current situation and seek validation outside of ourselves, it keeps us in a place of suffering because we are never satisfied with and grateful for what we have.

We live in a society where we have been conditioned to focus on the physical aspects of our own human experiences, such as the houses we live in, the cars we drive, the possessions we own and our financial status. We are conditioned to focus on achievements and titles, and success is defined by how many degrees you have, the letters behind your names, how many employees report to you or whether or not you have a corner office. None of that matters when we leave this Earth. Social media fuels this culture of external validation, as some people equate their feelings of fulfillment and happiness with the amount of "likes" they get on a certain post. The ego wants us to take selfies; the soul wants us to operate from our Higher Selves. Social media has its merits, it allows us to share our lives with people and provides a place to reconnect. However, it may also condition us to look for happiness in all the wrong places. The limitations of the ego keep us in the "shallow end." Ego has no depth. The ego is concerned with materialism and consumerism and attaching self-worth to those items. It tries to keep our identity wrapped up in those things, but that is not where fulfillment and happiness are found.

There are certain activities that promote inner peace, and we can intentionally and mindfully make decisions to engage in those activities that promote connection with our Higher Selves. Such activities include those that promote our overall well-being physically, mentally, emotionally and spiritually and will be explored further in the self-love section of this book.

In every moment, you are either feeding the ego or feeding the soul. They are two mutually exclusive aspects of you and both require different "fuel" to sustain it. The ego relies on feelings of fear which come in many shapes and sizes, like fear of failure, fear of change, fear of abandonment, fear of rejection and fear of death to name a few, and is also fueled by doubt, insecurities, stress and anxiety. The soul, however, relies on more wholesome growth and transformation-focused initiatives that expand and enrich the mind, body and spirit.

There is a perpetual sense of emptiness and numbness felt when we live purely from an egoic position and allow it to overtake our existences. Unbeknownst to us, some of the go-to activities we partake in and categorize as "relaxation" mechanisms are in fact fueling the ego. They are only temporary relief modalities that silence the ego for a brief period of time. The ego is persistent and tireless, and it is just a matter of time before the ego is asserting its demands again. Ego-fueling behaviors such as addictions to recreational drugs, excessively drinking alcohol, gambling, some forms of entertainment, certain sources of distraction and anything else that keeps one externally focused, mask issues and inhibit an internally-focused, soul-based existence. I am a big believer in balance, and while I am not suggesting that we strip away all forms of enjoyment that may not fuel the soul, we must be mindful of the extent to which we are engaging in certain activities and exercise self-control and self-restraint.

Of course, we cannot turn a blind eye to the practical considerations of day-to-day life, as we all need a stream of income to provide the means for our physical existence. We need a place to live. We need transportation. Life can get so complicated, and fast. Everyday living can be overwhelming while we attempt to juggle the responsibilities of jobs, families, take care of personal needs and attempt to have some fun along the way.

Start asking yourself, "Does this action feed my ego or does it feed my soul?" The soul promotes a feeling of wholeness and contentedness, whereas the ego promotes a competition mindset and tries to keep us distracted and unfulfilled. Your intuition and the way you feel in each moment are the best indicators of how a particular experience is or is not serving you.

Life is our greatest teacher, and the ego is a necessary part of our human experiences. It's one of the mechanisms that, when paired with a growth-based mindset, allows us to dissect our life experiences and find more profound meaning and purpose. Our life experiences afford us the opportunity to deconstruct the ego and develop the self-awareness that is necessary for our spiritual growth and evolution.

The ego tries to keep you powerless, whereas connecting to your Higher Self allows you to access your true power by drawing directly from Source Energy. Your true power is realized when you learn to sit quietly with yourself. Acknowledge and observe your thoughts while simultaneously understanding that they don't define you. Get comfortable with who you are, adopt a growth-based mindset and create an environment that facilitates your evolution.

Any life experience is a scenario of abundant lessons and gifts. Times of transition and those that encompass massive change, such as divorce, are rich in growth opportunities. There is no shortage of lessons and there are hidden gems everywhere just waiting to be discovered. Like anything else in life, you have a choice as to how you approach divorce. You can either subscribe to antiquated ways of thinking and do divorce the way everybody else does it, or, your can embrace the experience, complete with all of its transformative potential and use it as a springboard to catapult you into a higher realm of existence.

Discovering Your Authenticity

- What experiences have provided you with the greatest long-lasting happiness and fulfillment? Why do you think that is?
- In what areas of your life are you doing things to please others or to maintain a certain image or status?
- What motivates you to maintain a growth-based mindset?
- What barriers prevent you from maintaining a growth-based mindset?
- List the top 20 most important aspects of your life. It can be anything, including particular relationships, possessions, hobbies, values, etc. Does each feed your ego or your soul?
- What are the top three areas that require the most work in order to shift from an ego-based perspective to a soul-based perspective?

4

DIGGING DEEP

The Universe always has grander plans and our highest good in mind, and if we surrender and trust the Universe's infinite wisdom, knowledge and process, we are catapulted to unprecedented levels of spiritual growth.

My Background

First and foremost, let me make it clear that I am not a professor with a doctorate in psychology. I'm not a licensed social worker. I'm not a therapist. I'm not a yoga teacher, and I do not come from a family of Shamans.

What I am, though, is like you. I am a parent. I am a child. I am a sibling. I am an aunt. I am a friend. I am someone who has experienced the heights of joy and the depths of despair. I have experienced loss. I have experienced pain. I have experienced triumph and I have experienced defeat. I have experienced the birth of a child and I have experienced the death of a child. I have experienced marriage and I have experienced divorce.

No one is exempt from hardship. No one is exempt from

disappointment. No one is exempt from challenges. The one thing that life guarantees is that there will always be challenges to navigate. Challenges don't discriminate based on gender, race, religion, sexual orientation, financial standing or social status. We don't always get to choose our circumstances, but we most certainly do get to choose how our experiences can shape our current realities. I have made a conscious choice to use my life experiences as opportunities to dig deeper and become more acutely in tune with my own self-awareness and I am using these experiences as tools of transformation to enrich my life and the lives of others.

Spirituality is an Individual Journey

I used to think spirituality was a term that was used to define the lifestyle of a small subset of people who had extraordinary gifts that they used to access the divine.

Now, I understand that we are **all** spiritual beings who are having a human experience. This Earth is our classroom and our life experiences are our teachers. We come here with predetermined lessons, and during our human experience we subconsciously call in people, experiences and circumstances so we can learn the things we have come here to master. Everything, including human interactions, relationships, experiences, hardships and disappointments have been divinely orchestrated and play an important role in propelling us along our own personal journeys. Life is both beautiful and complicated because we are all inextricably involved in various relationships. Often, the decisions we make for ourselves inevitably impact others, but we must always be mindful of the fact that the journey through spirituality is first and foremost an individual endeavor. Sometimes we hesitate to make changes because we fear disrupting anyone else's life. That is understandable, but you are not doing anyone any favors if you are not honoring yourself and living a life that is true to who you are. I now define spirituality as a lifestyle whereby we use our own personal life experiences to craft our own belief systems and propel our own growth and transformation.

Significant Personal Experiences/Catalysts

According to my definition of spirituality, technically every life experience is a catalyst that propels each of us along our own journey and has the potential to usher us into higher levels of self-awareness. A catalyst can be anything that moves us or shakes us up a bit, resonates with us at a deeper level and causes a stirring in the soul. It doesn't always have to be a mountain-moving, life-changing experience like a death, illness, struggle with an addiction or a loss that shakes one to the core. It can be something as seemingly minor as a piece of music that you find inspiring. It can be a piece of artwork or a poem. It can even be a conversation with a perfect stranger. While every experience I've had has played a part in delivering me to my current level of evolution, there have been a few life experiences that have been particularly poignant.

The Power of Prayer

One hot and humid August night when I was 16, I was working at a local, family-owned Italian restaurant. It was nearing closing time and one of my co-workers asked if I wanted to go out with her and her friends after work. I would usually say "yes" without hesitation to this type of invitation, but this time was different. I immediately got a very heavy, sinking feeling in my core. Without thinking, I briefly paused, then muttered, "I can't. Something really bad is happening in my family right now." She asked what I meant and I answered, "I don't know, but I know it's really bad." Within moments, my mom's best friend scurried into the restaurant, completely frazzled. She walked up to the counter where I was standing and told me that I needed to come with her. She said that my dad had been riding his bike on a path in a local forest preserve and was hit by a car. She was there to take me to the hospital.

When I got to the hospital I could immediately energetically sense the heaviness in the room. It was, in fact, as bad as I had thought. Nobody said anything, except for my mom who turned to me and told me that my dad loved me very much. The fact that she used the past tense jolted and shocked me. My eyes welled up with tears, and I asked if he had died. She told me that wasn't the case, but I knew by the way she phrased her message, the prognosis was grim.

The following few days were highly tense and uncertain, and my dad was given the sacrament of last rights. We all assembled in the hospital chapel to say final prayers. I'll never forget the sight of my mom collapsing and sobbing hysterically, as the love of her life was gradually slipping away. Somehow, through the perfect blend of the power of prayer, God's grace, my mom's strength and refusal to give up, the support of so many people and my dad's will to live, he hung on. The next several days were fraught with many touch-and-go moments, exorbitant uncertainty, a wave of hope, loss of hope, followed by another wave of hope. At one point, the doctors came to us with a particularly solemn look on their faces and told us that it was unlikely that he would live, and if he did there would only be a 10 percent chance his brain would be functional.

The one thing that remained constant throughout this situation was my mom's faith in God. She carried the torch of faith in one hand, clutched her rosary in the other, and invited us all to join her. We spent days, which turned into weeks, which morphed into months, on the couches in the Intensive Care waiting room, alternating between an upright seated position and a half-reclined position as we drifted off from time to time from the emotional and mental weight of the situation. There was a steady stream of family who came to keep us company and help us keep the faith. But, nestled within the stress and the uncertainty and the despair and hopelessness was a glimmer of hope. A few fleeting seconds of sheer peace and serenity that would serve to be the bedrock of the hope that we so desperately would need to rely upon in the weeks and months to come. Through all the challenging moments that would ensue over the next several months, we would always anchor back to those pivotal moments.

My mom always prayed to St. Therese. She even carried prayer cards that contained this prayer:

> St. Therese,
> The Little Flower.
> Please pick me a rose
> From the Heavenly Garden
> And send it to me
> With a message of love
> Ask God to grant me
> The favor I thee implore
> And tell Him I will
> Love Him each day
> More and more.
> — Author Unknown

Except for the few brief moments of the day when we were allowed to step into my dad's hospital room, we recited this prayer over and over and over again. There was nothing else to clutch on to. My mom was moments away from losing her husband. My brother and I were moments away from losing our dad, at the tender ages of 14 and 16. None of us could fathom a life without him. None of us could envision saying goodbye. We clutched our prayer cards and gripped every last shred of hope with all our energy and continued to pray. My dad spent weeks in a coma, completely unresponsive and all the while we continued to pray.

One afternoon as my mom and I were sitting on the couch in the waiting room, she suddenly turned to me and asked if I smelled what she was smelling. I did. It was the most beautiful, potent scent of roses I had ever experienced. With bewildered looks on our faces, we both scanned the room in an attempt to find the origin, but no roses were anywhere in sight. I even got up and looked down the hallway to see if anyone had walked by with a flower delivery, but there was no one around. By the time I got back to the couch, the scent had dissipated. No traces of it were left. I looked at my mom and no words were necessary....we both knew. It was a divine intercession by St. Therese, the saint we had been praying to every waking moment. We took this as a sign that we would make it through this ordeal, somehow, some way, and in the months to come we would always draw upon the energy and the serenity and the peace and hope and comfort that these few fleeting moments offered.

Over the weeks and months to come, my dad started to gradually regain consciousness. There would be fleeting moments of somewhat coherent exchange, and then he would drift off again. When he reached a point in his recovery that he was able to articulate what he remembered from his experience, while we were all watching and waiting and praying, he shared this account: A knight on a horse approached him and asked if he wanted to come with him or go back. "Coming with him" meant that my dad would leave this physical world, and transition to the next phase of his journey into the spiritual world. My dad responded that he wanted to go back. The man said he could do so, but it would be under certain terms. At that time my dad was unaware of what those terms were, but he accepted the challenge.

There were many hurdles over the next several weeks and months, including multiple surgeries, therapies, doctor visits, etc. He would need to relearn the basics of daily living, including simple self-care activities such as walking, feeding himself, getting dressed and writing. As the weeks progressed, it was becoming abundantly clear what "the terms" of the agreement were. He would come back to this Earth with the challenge of a disability. My dad was left-handed, and no matter how much therapy or stimulation was performed on his left arm, he still had no movement or feeling in it.

In times like this, it's normal to feel alone, abandoned, hopeless and reliant upon and limited to what we are exposed to in our physical world, but it is this experience that keeps me deeply rooted in my faith. It was the first experience that truly shook me to my core and showed me an up-close and personal account of how fragile life is and that nobody's tomorrow is guaranteed.

You can call it prayer, meditation, invocation, devotion, worship or something else, and you can call the interceders angels, saints, spirit guides or divine helpers. The terminology doesn't matter. The important thing is that there is a whole other realm out there with an unlimited amount of resources and helpers to help guide us through our darkest moments. In our desperation, we were summoning the support of religious and spiritual aides and tightly clinging to every shred of hope, because that's all there was left. I remember asking my mom several times how we were going to get through this ordeal. I needed to know how we could keep going even when we were drained and full of so much despair. Her answer was always the same. She always replied that we needed to trust that God is going to take care of us and get us through it. She always encouraged me to think positively. In her mind there was no room for negativity or doubt.

This was my first experience of learning to rely on faith. Learning to rely on a power greater than we are. Up to this point, my experiences with religion had been routine and rehearsed and perfunctory, like learning about religion in class, attending weekly mass and attending sacramental celebrations for family members. Prior to this incident, I never had to dig really deep and completely surrender my situation to a higher power.

The way in which my dad overcame his challenge over the years still blows me away. He is a shining example of tenacity, perseverance and old-school determination. He never allows his disability to deter him from pursuing his passions. Engaging in home improvement projects has long been a hobby of his, and to this day he still tackles projects of any size, even without the use of his left arm.

The years progressed and I continued through what one might classify as the normal, expected course of events. I went to college, got a job, got married, bought a house, focused on my career and became a mother. Everything seemed to be progressing according to my plan, until my world was turned upside down on September 11, 2005.

An Angel on Earth

It was a beautiful September day in 2005 and life was good. I was 29 weeks pregnant and had just spent the day celebrating my 31st birthday with my husband, one-and-a-half-year-old daughter, parents and brother. We spent much of the day excitedly talking about the baby-to-be, and people were submitting their guesses on the gender and trying to figure out the names we had picked. All this baby talk reminded us that the big event was not far off, and it was now time to start counting down the baby's arrival in weeks, not months.

On the way home that evening, I told my husband that I didn't remember feeling the baby move that afternoon and I was very worried. But, we had been busy before the party and my mind was so preoccupied while they were there, so I kept telling myself that I probably just didn't feel any movement because I wasn't paying close attention. I decided to wait until 8:30, which was the time of evening when I would always feel the baby move — *without fail.* If I didn't feel anything then, we would go in to be checked. The right time rolled around, and I started chugging orange juice like there was no tomorrow. I sat anxiously awaiting a movement as I watched the clock: 8:31…8:32…8:33, still nothing, and it didn't take too long for sheer panic to set in.

The minutes seemed like hours at this point and I paged my doctor and told her that I was very concerned. She tried to alleviate my obvious panic by saying that it was quite possible that I just didn't notice movement, and it was a bit early in the pregnancy to expect to feel movement on a predictable basis. Despite her words that were so comforting and hope-filled, I couldn't shake the sinking feeling that I had. In my heart, I knew what I needed to prepare myself for.

I called my parents to tell them what was going on and they immediately came over to stay with our daughter. We drove to the hospital in complete silence. When we arrived, the nurse immediately ushered us into a room with an ultrasound machine and they immediately began trying to find the baby's heartbeat. After several attempts, she looked at me and delivered the somber news.

We were told to return to the hospital the next morning so they could deliver the baby via C-section. After they prepped me for the delivery, they asked if I wanted to walk to the delivery room, but I just couldn't. I was completely deflated physically, mentally and emotionally, and barely even had the strength to reply to their question. At 11:01 a.m., our baby girl was delivered into a room that was silent. Loudly silent. She was perfect in every way; pristinely sculpted tiny fingers and toes, and a face that looked like a porcelain doll. The only thing that wasn't perfect was that I wouldn't get to take her home with me.

We got to spend some time with her in the hours after delivery, and one by one, close family and friends arrived and grieved with us during this devastating time.

The part of me that lives in the physical world was in complete shock. I couldn't get my mind around how this could have happened. It was completely counterintuitive that we suddenly found ourselves in a position where we needed to say "goodbye" before we even had the opportunity to say an official "hello." I couldn't fathom how we could go from excitedly picking baby names and preparing the nursery to sitting in a family room full of sympathy flowers, all in the blink of an eye. It seemed like a bad dream, and I wanted more than anything to just wake up and make it all go away.

There was a small piece of me that was prepared for it. In the two months prior, I dreamt the same scenario three times. Each time, my husband and I were in a hospital room and I was holding the baby. The mood in the room was quite opposite the mood that you would normally expect upon the arrival of a baby. Our parents were there, as were a few close family members and friends, and everyone was very quiet and somber. After I had the dream the first time, I tried to pretend it didn't happen and thought that maybe it was a fear playing out. Maybe it was something from the external environment that my subconscious mind picked up without me realizing it. After the second time I had the dream, I was somewhat successfully able to convince myself that my mind was just trying to purge whatever remnants of the first dream that were still lingering. But, the third time I had the dream, complete with the exact same details and an overwhelmingly strong feeling of impending doom and despair, I knew it was time to start preparing myself. The way in which it played out in real life was uncannily similar to the dreams I had experienced.

After the initial shock wore off, it was time to figure out how to live with our loss. Unfortunately, healing from a loss doesn't heal the way a broken bone does. You don't gradually get better each day until you are fully healed, at which point you've almost completely forgotten that it happened. Grief is a strange animal – just when you think you're doing okay, anything can trigger your sadness. The rawness definitely softens over time, but the scars are always there.

Anyone who has grieved the loss of a loved one knows that the grieving process is a roller coaster. The emotional turmoil seemed endless, and as I was struggling to process this loss I spent many nights unable to sleep. I would lay there contemplating the concepts of life and death and everything in between. I thought a lot about religion and the associated beliefs and tried with all my might to turn this over and simply trust. I couldn't get there. I couldn't handle the finality. I couldn't handle the thought of going through this life without sharing it with someone with whom God had entrusted me for a brief period in time, but then took her back so abruptly. I was angry and questioned my faith, God, and everything else about religion. Well-meaning people would say things like God needed another angel in heaven, and my response was always to ask, what kind, loving, merciful God would choose to inflict such unimaginable pain on someone? I wondered if anyone realized how excruciatingly agonizing this was. I found that the traditional religious ideologies weren't providing the comfort and peace and closure that I was so desperately seeking. I was grasping at straws in an attempt to find an explanation that resonated with me. At this point, I was non-discriminatory and was completely open to any belief system that could provide me with what I needed. During my processing, I spent a lot of time on the internet learning about the medical aspects of what had happened to me, as my logical mind was trying to make sense of the physical side. I wanted to know what causes stillbirths, if I could have prevented it and what it meant for any future pregnancies.

In the midst of my attempts to make sense of what had happened, I was continually unsatisfied. My soul was craving more. I was totally unfulfilled. Empty. Hopeless. Despondent. Fearful. Stifled. Crushed. Through my research, I stumbled upon the concept of Spirit Babies. In short, every woman has a circle of spirit babies above her, and if a baby dies in the womb prematurely, its soul re-enters the circle and there exists the possibility that the soul may return in the body of a future baby. Call it denial or the inability to accept it. Call it whatever you want, but it was **the only** explanation that gave me any shred of hope. It was something to cling to, and helped me get out of bed and put one foot in front of the other in the hopes that we would eventually see brighter days. I didn't realize it at the time, but it is the discovery of this theory that opened up my eyes to an entirely new way of thinking, expanded my mind and took my belief system into completely uncharted territory.

Still deeply immersed in the depths of our pain and in complete fear-mode, we began discussions with my doctor about the possibility of future pregnancies. For us, the decision to try to have another baby was not a matter of if, but rather a matter of when. Our desire to have another baby far outweighed our fears, which were nothing short of monumental, but nonetheless, we decided we were willing to try it again. Granted, we knew the next pregnancy would be fraught with worry, but in our minds, the joy a child can bring to your life is still so much greater than the pain we had experienced. So, in early February (four-and-a-half months after our loss), I went back to the doctor with the hope of getting the okay to start trying again. I was nowhere close to being fully emotionally healed, but felt that being pregnant again would give us a reason to be joyful and to look ahead. Much to my surprise, the doctor said it was fine to start trying again. Although I got the answer I was hoping to hear, it still evoked feelings of sadness along with the excitement. Many questions kept running through my head: Have I given myself enough time to grieve the baby we lost? Am I ready to handle this? Am I just trying to replace the baby we lost? I barely held it together emotionally while we were in the office, and burst into tears the second we stepped out of the building. What was I thinking? I'm so not ready for this. I quickly realized that thinking was not the answer. Trusting was the only way through it.

The Next Pregnancy - Hope in the Midst of Fear

For as long as I live, I'll never forget the words of the doctor who released me from the hospital after we lost our baby. He was clear that he had seen many women miscarry babies and go on to have healthy babies. He told me that it was crucial for me to believe that this was not going to happen again. While we were still distraught over our loss, his encouraging words cast a glimmer of hope that we would be parents to another child someday.

I wasn't even close to being fully emotionally healed, but I felt that being pregnant again would give us something to look forward to. Deciding to try again felt as if I were skydiving. I was just going to take the jump and cross my fingers that my parachute would open. I didn't know what I was getting myself into but knew that it was the only way we'd achieve our dream of having another baby. Little did I know that at the time we got the okay from the doctor, that I was just days away from what would be the official start of 40 extremely significant weeks.

I was indeed pregnant. Finding out this news was, in a word, overwhelming. To make hearing this news even more emotional, my due date was November 13th, just 11 days before my due date the previous year. Even though it was a brand new start, in my mind, the experience was still incredibly closely linked to our loss. I was still grieving the loss of our baby. What on earth were we thinking by deciding to layer on the stress of another pregnancy? How would I ever survive the remaining 36 weeks of this pregnancy? What if we lost this baby, too? How would we deal with two consecutive losses? What if it happened after we decided to tell our daughter, who might actually be old enough to feel the pain this time?

I quickly recognized that I was relapsing back into "month at a time" mode when my new mantra was supposed to be "one day at a time." It was time to stop playing out hypothetical scenarios in my mind and deal with the here and now. It really is a discipline of the mind and not something that used to come naturally for me. But I quickly recognized the power in constantly challenging myself to remain in this mindset, as it helped to make otherwise insurmountable things seem to be less daunting.

My doctor warned me that the next eight months were not going to be easy emotionally and psychologically, which of course was no surprise to us. They said that they were willing to do anything to help give me the extra reassurance I'd be looking for. Medically, what happened to us was regarded as a random event (i.e. bad luck), and while they certainly couldn't guarantee a perfect outcome, the odds of having a healthy baby were in our favor. They were able to guarantee something, though – any day I was feeling particularly anxious they'd squeeze me in to be checked, no questions asked.

At this point, we were anxious to get through the first trimester. We announced our first pregnancy at seven weeks, and unbeknownst to us at the time, we had already lost that baby. We had forever been stripped of our naivety about what could go wrong and were anxious to get any form of reassurance we could get. We had an appointment at five weeks, an ultrasound at eight weeks, and another appointment at 12 weeks. Between appointments, I was feeling sicker by the day, which was just fine with me, as I viewed it as a sign that the pregnancy was progressing.

We were relieved to make it to Week 13. I just kept trying to focus on the numbers. At this point, there was only a one percent chance that we could lose this baby, which meant that there was a 99 percent chance that we wouldn't. This time I was going with the numbers. I made the decision not to live my life obsessing about an event that was statistically extremely unlikely. I didn't obsess about it the last time, and even if I did, all the worry might not have translated into anything productive or favorable. It would not have made our loss any easier to bear, and it would have just taken away from the excitement along the way, and I wasn't going to let that happen. I knew there would still be some worrisome moments here and there, but I decided to deal with those when they came up.

Now that we had reached this significant milestone, we decided it was probably time to start sharing the news. We told our daughter, parents, families and friends, and everyone was overjoyed. I was surprised by the fact that no one expressed surprise or asked questions that would seem typical in situations like this. Instead, they expressed joy and excitement, and it was contagious.

The highlight of the second trimester was definitely the Level 2 ultrasound that we had at 20 weeks. We were delighted that everything went without a hitch. There was nothing of even the slightest concern. I had heard of so many people going for "follow-up" ultrasounds for one reason or another, and I joked that God knew that even just a simple "double-check" might put me over the edge.

We decided not to find out the gender of the baby. We knew that we would love this child unconditionally, and at this point honestly felt that the gender didn't matter to us. And since the baby would be delivered by a scheduled c-section, we wanted the delivery to have one element of surprise.

There was a brief time after our loss when I had a strong preference for the gender of our next baby. I remember thinking about a month or two after our loss that if I were ever to get pregnant again, I could only see myself with another girl. I think I was just trying to trick myself into thinking that having another girl would take all the pain away, but in my heart, I knew that if we had 10 girls, we would still miss our daughter just as much. Having a child of the same gender certainly wasn't going to ease the pain. Each of our children is first and foremost a unique and precious individual, and their gender is a distant second. Fortunately, though, all of these thoughts regarding gender preference were fleeting, and I was relieved that by the time I became pregnant again, we honestly didn't have a preference.

Seeing the precious baby during the ultrasound reaffirmed our feeling that the gender just didn't matter to us. The baby was so amazingly perfect, and I remember wishing that I could lay on the ultrasound table and just watch him or her frolic around in there for hours, days, even weeks. We already loved this baby so much and longed for the day that we could hold the baby in our arms. Toward the end of this trimester, I began non-stress tests on the baby that continued throughout the pregnancy.

By the time the third trimester of pregnancy arrives, most women are on auto-pilot, simply needing to pass the time before the big day arrives. But not for me; my work was just beginning. I was now at a point where I should be able to feel movement consistently, and my doctors gave me specific guidelines for tracking movements. I didn't need to be a slave to the kick counts, but paying close attention to the baby's activity was something that I needed to be doing consistently throughout the day.

My weekly non-stress tests continued throughout this trimester, and I even popped in for a few impromptu visits on the days I needed a little extra reassurance.

The middle of the night was the hardest time for me, as most of my panic-stricken moments came then. I'd wake up and all would be quiet, including the baby. I'd lay there and watch the clock, waiting for a kick, flutter, roll, anything. I usually generously gave the baby a good 30 seconds until I flew down the stairs and chugged a juice box, only to have the baby begin a 20-minute gymnastics routine a few seconds later. That was just fine with me, though. More kicks meant more reassurance for me, which was exactly what I needed. I used to joke that our family single-handedly bolstered apple juice box sales for a few months.

I was reminded of how much attention pregnant women get. Perfect strangers would gaze at my obviously pregnant belly and ask the typical questions about which number pregnancy this was for me and if I knew the gender. Although most pregnant women hear questions like this regularly and they are seemingly light and innocuous for most impending mothers, for me, both had extremely profound answers. Of course, I would politely smile and give the appropriate answers, but the thoughts that were running through my head were more along the lines of, "No, this is actually my fourth pregnancy, and I don't know if I'm emotionally ready to find out the gender because last time we lost a girl." I, of course, appreciated everyone's excitement, even strangers, but the first few times those questions were sprung on me were difficult. Over time, these questions got easier to answer and even helped to get us even more excited about the big day quickly approaching.

The hardest two weeks of the pregnancy from an emotional standpoint came during this trimester. First, I hit the 29-weeks mark, the point at which we lost the baby last time, and on the heels of that milestone was the first year anniversary of our loss. There were times during Week 29 when I thought history was repeating itself, not because the baby didn't pass the kick counts test, but because I felt extra-vulnerable during this week. But then I'd think of it from a numerical and more objective perspective. What are the chances that I'd lose two consecutive pregnancies during week 29?

For us, the build-up and anticipation before the first-year anniversary of our loss was more difficult than the day itself. I expected to be emotional the entire day, but as it turned out, there were only a few hard moments, and the rest of the day was relatively normal.

As I approached the end of this trimester, we scheduled the C-section for 7:30 a.m. on Monday, November 6th. In advance, I requested a different operating room, recovery room and hospital room so that our experience this time would be as different as possible from the last time. I could hardly believe the big day was almost here.

Little did we know that the big day was sooner than we had planned. In the early morning hours of Thursday, November 2nd, our first son decided to make an early appearance. He had the sweetest little cry and was amazingly perfect from head to toe. I could hardly believe he was here. All those months of waiting, wondering and worrying were over. I remember wishing I could freeze time and live in the moment when we first met him. It was beautiful.

I was awestruck and speechless about how beautiful moments such as these are only made possible when we surrender and trust in a higher power. I was blown away to experience how quickly life can turn around. On November 2, 2005, I attended a mass at our church on All Souls Day which, for Catholics, is a day that is dedicated to the souls of loved ones who have passed on. It was one of my lowest points, as I bawled my eyes out, mourning the recent loss of our daughter and wondering if we'd ever be parents again. I was still so immersed in my grief and wasn't sure when or even if things would get better. Then, exactly one year later, November 2, 2006, there we were holding our perfect newborn son. If that wasn't a little slice of heaven, I'm not sure what is.

People who have gone through tragic events often say that it never makes sense at the time, but over time some of the "pieces" may start to fall into place. Over the years, I have kept my mind, my heart and my life puzzle open to any of these pieces anyone is willing to send my way. Was it purely by chance that my husband and I happened to drive by the cemetery at exactly 11:01 a.m. (the time our daughter was delivered) on September 12th one year later, on the way to pick up our daughter from school, or an attempt by the divine powers to let me know she's okay? Was it purely by chance that our son was born on All Souls Day, or yet another message that she's okay? I believe that everything that happens has significance and meaning, and if we look hard enough, we will find it.

Experiences like the loss of a child resonate at such a deep level and are forever a part of who we are. There is simply no degree of busyness that will crowd out the memories and thoughts about the way in which those whom we love have touched our lives. I will always think of her as part of our family and while we can't hold her in our arms, I will always hold her in a special place in my heart.

Reclaiming My Identity

The next several years were full of hustle and bustle and we were blessed with the treasured gifts of two more children, and with those additions came everything that is part and parcel of being a full-time mom. Sleepless nights, endless trips to the pediatrician, knee-high piles of laundry, homemade baby food and homemade playdough, to name a few. After the dust from the baby and toddler years was finally starting to settle, I went on a mission of reclaiming my identity and reinvesting in myself. I remember looking in the mirror one day and barely even recognizing myself, physically, mentally or spiritually. While I was in the throes of motherhood, I had completely lost sight of who I was. I joined a gym, completely overhauled my eating habits and totally revamped how I lived. Through this process, I connected with other like-minded individuals, all of whom were making daily investments in themselves across the spectrum. I had an epiphany. Life doesn't have to be all about work with no time for play. It doesn't have to be about sacrifice 100 percent of the time, and I realized that I had been trying to pour from an empty pitcher for years.

As I started to reinvest in myself, I felt a spiritual pull. I started to meditate, do yoga, practice mindfulness and built my tribe, which included like-minded people with similar belief systems.

I had a conversation with my husband and told him that I was feeling a pull spiritually and that I was going to do a reading with a spiritualist, just to prepare him in advance in case he noticed the charge on the credit card. He was okay with it, as long as I didn't spend too much money on it. I snickered, but I did float the idea as a cryptic invitation of sorts. Part of me was hoping that he would have jumped on this wagon with me. At this point, I didn't quite understand the individual nature of the spiritual journey. It's all about the self. Everyone is on his or her own individual journey and awakens at different times, and at different speeds, depending on what situations and people are placed in their own personal reality. There's really nothing that can be done to accelerate someone else's evolution to bridge the gap between where they are and where you are. It needs to happen on its own time and in its own way. All forms of change and transformation need to come from within. Trying to force someone else's transformation with some extrinsic factor is like trying to force a rose to bloom by prying the petals open. You'll crush it. We must sit back and let the flower bloom in it's own time. Everything in nature happens according to its own schedule. Some flowers bloom in early-spring. Some bloom in mid-spring. Some bloom at various points in the summer. In much the same way that we sit back and observe nature, the best thing we can do for someone else's journey is to become a silent observer in his or her reality.

Aura Photography and Crystal Reading

Acknowledging the individual nature of our personal journeys, I continued down the path of mine. In October 2015, I attended an aura photography and crystal reading at a health and wellness spa. This place truly is an oasis. It is a hidden gem that is tucked away in a quaint little one-story complex of offices, and doesn't have even a hint of the production-line feel of larger, more commercial spas. It had just opened the previous May, and every time I go there, I think about how it's just a matter of time before they outgrow their space. If love at first sight can exist between a girl and a spa, it surely exists here. It sends out such awesome vibes. From the moment I walked in the door the very first time I was captivated. I immediately had a feeling that the place would become my home away from home. The owner is delightful and the kind of person you can easily sit and talk with for hours because you feel like you've known her forever. We have gotten to know each other very well and have exchanged many anecdotes about our experiences and belief systems.

The first service I had there was a chakra balancing. Chakras are spiritual energy centers within the physical body. It is important to ensure that our chakras are open and balanced because they serve as a portal for accessing Universal Energy, and govern various aspects of our physical, emotional and mental well-being.

One evening, the spa hosted a spiritualist who specializes in aura photography. She started by explaining her background and experiences and then ushered each one of the guests into the area where she would be taking the photos of our auras. After she took everyone's pictures, we waited until they were developed, at which time she called each person back individually to discuss the results.

When it was my turn, I entered the room and quickly scanned the individual pictures, anxious to see if I could identify mine. I couldn't see the faces in enough detail, but I did notice that one of the pictures was distinctly different from the rest. Most of them had a rainbow effect, containing most of the aura colors in various proportions, but one was purely indigo. Bright indigo. Unmistakably bright indigo.

I sat down. Without hesitation she plucked my picture out of the group. It was the bright indigo one. I sat there for several seconds in complete silence.

She looked at the picture, glanced up at me, looked down at the picture again. I could practically hear her thoughts stammering around in her head as she struggled to find the right words. I just sat there quietly and waited, all the while stifling a smirk because I knew exactly where she was going.

The woman with the bold presence and resolute confidence finally pulled herself together and started to speak. She explained that in the 26 years she had been performing these readings, she had never seen a monochromatic bright indigo quite like mine. She wanted to know if I understood the significance of it. She told me I was highly intuitive and have a deep level of understanding everything. She knew I was creative and a writer and told me that I should consider writing children's fiction. She also could tell that I am deeply spiritual, that I know things before they happen and that I have strong psychic abilities. She then asked if I was aware of all of these things. I laughed as I told her that I had known it for about 25 years.

She continued to tell me that Indigos are guided by a third eye, and we can see "mental movies" when we close our eyes. I knew exactly what she meant, as I call it the "timeline in my mind." I can see future events in as much detail as I see the past. That's why I don't force anything — ever. This foresight has always enabled me to truly live in the present, soaking up every experience, whether it be positive or negative. What a tremendous gift it is to be able to just sit back and enjoy this ride called life completely faith-filled and relatively fearless.

She asked if I had any questions, and I didn't. Nothing was a surprise to me. I already knew my aura color, but I couldn't pass up the opportunity to have it validated by way of a physically tangible modality. As for the other stuff, I had no questions about any of that either.

Again, she reiterated how rare this aura presentation is and proceeded to hand me a sheet that contained a description of Indigo personalities that she doesn't often give to people. The last paragraph was most noteworthy, as it gave me some clarity on what I could shift my focus to next. The timing was pristine, as I had been contemplating my next steps along this journey and was having thoughts ranging from philanthropic initiatives to business endeavors, as I have a deep desire to share these gifts with a more expansive group. Energy work in the healing capacity is what interests me most.

Our meeting ended and I walked back into the room of women comparing their multicolor results. I was totally not interested in discussing mine but knew it was a matter of time before someone asked me what mine looked like. I said nothing and just opened up my folder and showed them. Most people commented about what a "pretty color" it was, but one lady's reaction was different from the rest. It was from the woman who had done my Reiki chakra balancing five months before. She asked a few questions that were all calling direct attention to my spiritual gifts. I just smiled and interjected, "Yes, I know." She quickly launched into a persuasive monologue on how I should do something with these gifts. She gave me the contact information for her mentor, and encouraged me to talk to her because she'd be able to pick up on my energy right away. She also recommended that I seek out institutions that have a large menu of offerings in the spirituality/ metaphysics fields.

It is on this evening that I realized that my calling was to play an active role in awakening others. I didn't know how or when it would unfold, but continued to march along the path that enhanced my spirituality and trusted the process and all of its divinely orchestrated perfection.

Discovering Your Authenticity

- What does being spiritual mean to you?
- What internal and external influences affect how you process life events?
- What were some significant life experiences that served as catalysts on your journey?
- What did you learn about yourself from those experiences?
- Did you seek comfort and peace through looking inward, or did you turn to external sources to ease your pain?

5

THE UNIVERSE DELIVERS

The Universe always knows the magnitude of the catalyst that is necessary to shake up our current realities and launch us into our authentic realities.

March 8, 2017, 6:18 p.m.
While I was in the midst of making dinner for the kids, I heard a text come in, so I checked my phone. It was from my husband. It complimented a meal choice and asked about an accompanying wine.

It was totally out of context, and I knew it wasn't intended to be sent to me, so I immediately responded with "Who is this for?" No response. I escaped to my bedroom so the kids wouldn't overhear the conversation, and I proceeded to call him. He didn't pick up. I called again. He answered and I immediately asked who the text was for. He answered that it was for a colleague who was having a dinner party with wine.

My intuition told me otherwise. With all the spiritual work I had been doing on myself, I had gotten incredibly clear on who I was and what felt right and what didn't. I had become so confident in trusting my gut and had gotten to a place where I had completely relegated away fear to the point where it no longer has a place in my life. With complete brazenness, I said "I don't believe you. You're having an affair, aren't you?" There was a long pause, and he finally exhaled and said I was correct. I very calmly said, "We will talk about this when you get home."

I went back downstairs and continued with the dinner and homework routine until he got home. While I was contemplating this crushing blow and the associated shock and complexity, I suddenly realized that this was the day for which the Universe had been preparing me for three years. I had been seeing the code 1118 relentlessly for three years. I remember the first time I saw these numbers. I was at a stoplight and the license plates of the first and only cars in front of me were "IGNITE1" and "1118". Prior to this point, trying to crack the code on license plates was not one of my hobbies, but this combination was particularly attention-getting. Over the next several months, which eventually turned into years, I would see the code frequently. My oldest daughter, who is with me often, even noticed. She called it to my attention and we both agreed that it had a very ominous feeling to it. She would ask me repeatedly what I thought it meant and what was going to happen. I told her that I didn't know but didn't have a good feeling about it. I never pass up the opportunity to validate intuitions even if they are unsettling or negative. I strive to continue to cultivate that awareness for myself and always validate my kids' intuition because the first step in finding your voice and stepping into your truth is getting really cozy with what your gut is telling you.

I rarely left the house on weeknights except to drive the kids to their activities, but one rainy Wednesday night several months earlier, I had a case of cabin fever and decided to run out to buy a baby shower gift for a friend. On the way home through a torrential downpour, I saw this code twice. The Universe is always intentional in its messaging and its attempts to communicate with us, but it was at that point that I realized it was going above and beyond what it normally does in an effort to shift me out of my current mode of operating and launch me into a space where I desired to seek out more answers, so I decided to visit a spiritualist. I explained the messaging I had been experiencing, and she said that on March 8, the Universe would send me a very clear message and it would be obvious what my next steps should be. She made it clear that everything would be up for change. I asked her if I needed to meditate to receive the message. She said that I should just go about my daily activities and it would come to me when I least expected it. I was happy to hear that she agreed that the messaging had spiritual significance and it was helpful to have some clarity on what to expect.

Now nearly three years later, on March 8, 2017, I was sitting squarely in the middle of the scenario my spiritualist had alerted me to three years prior.

After we completed the evening routine and tucked the kids in, we sat down. There really wasn't much to discuss. I think we both knew the writing was on the wall. You can only operate on auto-pilot for so long before something has to give.

The moment the Universe had been preparing me for had finally arrived. Everything was, in fact, "up for change," just as the spiritualist said. I had a decision to make.

I called a friend and told her I found out that my husband was having an affair. She told me to come over immediately. I headed to her house and surreptitiously tiptoed into her basement so I wouldn't wake her family, as it was close to midnight. We sat on the couch in her basement, she looked at me and in a calm yet direct manner, and laid it out for me. She said I had two choices. I could either get a divorce or work on the marriage and make it stronger than it ever was before.

Little did she know, I had already made my decision. We had already worked on the marriage. In my opinion, we had already given it the old college try. We had been in counseling for five months at this point, and with each session came more and more clarity about the direction in which this would go.

When we entered counseling, although I didn't realize it at the time, I was still very much in fear mode. I still embodied the negative associations of divorce that society has imprinted on us. Just hearing the word "divorce" would conjure up images of separatism, animosity, failure, defeat, contentiousness and every other negative connotation imaginable. Both of us came from traditional Catholic backgrounds, and divorce was something that you just didn't do. Both of our parents had been married for decades, and all of our siblings were in long-term marriages. How could we be the only ones to do this? At that point, I was still totally committed to figuring out how to remain an intact family unit. What I was totally discounting, however, was how much of my happiness and fulfillment was being compromised in achieving this objective.

I really did go in with the hopes that someone would magically be able to fix our marriage and would help us achieve our happily ever after in the house we had built to serve our family, including future generations, for decades to come. After all, that would be easiest. That would be the approach that would allow us to slalom around the idea of making massive changes. I think there was a small part of me that was hoping there was some magic bullet list that the therapist could give us that could take us from disconnected and unfulfilled to connected and fulfilled. Sometimes you can get there, but in our case it was too little too late. I didn't anticipate the self-discovery component of the sessions, and with each session I gained a lot of clarity about who I was and what I embodied, and it became clearer and clearer that we had become two totally different people over the years. The disparity was masked by the daily hustle and bustle of all the things that go into taking care of a house and family, and while I was operating on autopilot, I had effectively completely lost sight of my individuality and everything I embodied.

My friend gave me the name of a high-powered family law attorney in Chicago who I called the very next day to set up our first meeting. The next call I made was to my therapist. We already had a couple's session scheduled for that evening, and I wanted to talk to her beforehand to inform her of the recent events. She was in shock. I calmly told her that I had already decided I wanted to get divorced and that she should prepare to help manage any fallout that may occur when I communicated the decision that evening.

The logistical details of completely reorganizing and restructuring our family were daunting. Every aspect of our lives that we had so tirelessly and meticulously curated over the last 20 years would need to be reworked. Just the thought of how we would manage four kids across two households was dizzying, to say the least. I couldn't help but think that we could barely keep track of all the appointments and pieces of hockey gear with all of us under one roof much less manage it across two households, with half the resources in each. But, I wouldn't give that thought permission to sway my decision.

I knew that this undertaking was going to be a huge task, and the number and complexity of the decisions we would need to make would be consuming our time and energy for quite some time.

One of the thoughts that used to give me pause when I contemplated my own personal views on divorce was how it would be perceived by others, including the overarching stigma that society places on divorce. I needed to first mentally overcome that hurdle before I could face the world with the resolve and the confidence that this divorce was going to be done a new, progressive way.

Initial reactions from others were fear-based and wholly reflected what **they** wanted for us, not what we wanted. We often hold ourselves back from what we truly desire in an effort to uphold a pristine image that is congruent with what things **should** look like, according to societal conditioning or others' beliefs that have been imprinted on us. I was no longer going to let that inherited programming impede the direction in which I would go.

I didn't realize it at the time, but March 8, 2017 was not only the day our physical realities would embark on a different trajectory, but for me personally and spiritually, it was the day I stepped out of fear mode. It was the day that what was left of my ego officially began to burn off at warp speed, as I committed to embracing a soul-based existence. I no longer cared about what anyone else thought. I was no longer scared of change. I was no longer afraid to step into the unknown and I was no longer willing to compromise who I was for the sake of maintaining an image. Yes, during this process there would be plenty of moments of apprehension, indecisiveness, and uncertainty, as those are all normal reactions of the human condition, but all of these moments would be still pale in comparison to the gravity of being stuck in a situation that wasn't in my highest good or my family's best interests. The situation felt much like jumping off of a plane with a parachute. You just have to take the leap of faith and trust that your parachute will open. I was no longer on the plane afraid to jump. I decided I was going to leap, and view it as an adventure.

This was, in fact, the beginning of a huge paradigm shift for me. The way in which I navigate life would be forever changed.

I very quickly got to a place of "This has nothing to do with them. This is about us." It has nothing to do with how this is perceived by the outside world. It has nothing to do with how perfect the Christmas cards look, and has nothing to do with the size of the house. It has everything to do what's going on in our minds and hearts and whether or not we are happy.

Well-meaning people anxious to weigh in and offer suggestions would make comments that questioned my thought process and people wondered if I had thought about my kids before I made my decision or thought about waiting until the kids were older to make this move. Others suggested we seek out the help of a specialist. At one point I distinctly remember telling someone, "This is not a democracy. We aren't taking a vote here. The decision has already been made. If you would like to do anything, please give your love and support to the kids."

This was the moment of truth. I quickly realized that we had the power to directly influence how this process would unfold. If it was infused with animosity and fighting and contentiousness and separatism and stress, everyone around us, particularly our kids, would absorb that energy and react accordingly. On the contrary, if we resolved to navigate this with a commitment to respect, kindness, compassion and collegial problem-solving that balanced everyone's needs and desires, we would arrive at an outcome that was in everyone's best interests much more quickly and smoothly.

We were the pilot and copilot. We were flying this airplane. Everyone else is a passenger. While going through turbulence, the tone and demeanor of the pilot or co-pilot making the announcement sets the tone for the entire cabin. If they come on with a frazzled, frantic tone and announce "Everyone, hurry, get in your seat immediately and hold on; it's going to be a wild ride," that conveys a very different energy than a calmly-proclaimed, "Ladies and gentlemen, we've hit a little turbulence but in no time we'll be on to sunnier skies." Our goal was to have a calm cabin.

There is obviously a complex and deep emotional component to this in addition to all of the logistical considerations, but I knew that our mindset and our willingness to recognize that how we conduct ourselves will have a direct impact on the process as well as our post-divorce reality.

As much as I knew we were making the right decision, my thoughts were swirling. I felt as if we were at the bottom of a mountain looking up, and we had an incredibly steep ascent ahead of us, in sweltering heat. Writing has long been my go-to modality when I need to process my thoughts, so on March 15, 2017, I sat down at the desk in our office and put a pen to paper in an attempt to organize my thoughts.

My notes were as follows:

Meditation

Focus on Grace, Compassion, Forgiveness

- *Grace* - be a role model to the world on reverence.
- *Compassion* - the only way to forgiveness. There is no room for judgement. Consider the feelings involved for all parties that lead to this point in the journey. All events are interconnected across space and time and play a role.
- *Forgiveness* - the ultimate goal. There is no place for anger, it only hurts me. Be patient, as this is the hardest to achieve. Grace and compassion are the building blocks.

Think about how I would want to be treated if this were me. One can never truly judge another unless we have walked in the other's shoes.

Feel Gratitude

- All day, every day.
- Be grateful for our kids.
- Be grateful for the courage to do this now rather than wait.
- Be grateful for all the happy times.
- Be grateful for all he has done for our family over the years.
- Be grateful that this situation, despite the intense pain, will ultimately launch all of us to a happier place.
- Be grateful for this catalyst.
- Be grateful for this opportunity to transform. With each event/emotion ask "What is the lesson here? What can I learn from this? How can I use this to become a better person?"
- It is hardest to practice gratitude in challenging situations where you have no control, have been betrayed or trust has been broken. You need to find a way.

Visualizations About the Future

- Envision everyone happy when there is harmoniousness, laughter, fun, kindness, respect and we are living a life based on authenticity.
- Envision qualities of a future conscious relationship. This can only occur after healing is complete.
- Envision the best version of myself.
- Envision everyone supporting us and the kids emotionally and consistent with the tone we set.
- Envision a smooth transition.
- Envision being better parents separately than we were when we were together.

I read this meditation daily as we embarked on the early stages of this process. I read it until it had been woven into every stitch of my tapestry. I resolved to make it my mantra and navigate this process with grace and integrity and respect and with everyone's highest good in mind. During the tough moments, I would anchor to these tenets I had set for myself and revisit them when I felt the need. During my strong moments it gave me more strength. During my weak moments, it was my guiding light that would provide the peace and tranquility and trust-filled knowingness that I so desperately needed. While only time would tell how this would truly play out, unbeknownst to me, I was literally manifesting my future.

We must always strive to align our outer world to reflect what is going on in our hearts. It is not until that occurs that what is truly meant for us will effortlessly and organically come into our existence. We will exude a different energy and therefore attract the people and experiences that are a vibrational match. The Universe will meet us there. It is not until that quintessential alignment is achieved that the Universe can begin to actualize what is truly meant for us. When we are aligned with what our own spirit wants, there is no hesitation. There is no doubt. There are no pauses. And there is no limit on our power and the impact we can make on the world.

I knew where I was and knew where I wanted to end up. I knew the endpoints. The in-between could follow any number of paths and I possessed the power to pave those any way I saw fit. Embarking on this process felt a lot like skydiving. You just have to jump and **trust** that your parachute is going to open and that you will have a soft landing. I knew that I had to take a leap of faith. Going in, I knew there was no roadmap through the divorce process. No one hands you a blueprint that you follow verbatim. Yes, there are guidelines; yes, there are laws that need to be followed and yes, there would be professionals to help us along the way. But each situation is unique and comes with its own set of considerations and needs and desires and challenges in a number of different arenas: logistical, emotional, etc. Each situation is as unique as the individuals themselves, and the opportunities to creatively design your post-divorce reality are limitless. This was the moment I realized that our post-divorce reality didn't need to look like anyone else's. We had the license to be as creative as we wanted to be.

It was at this moment that I realized I had a choice. I could have chosen anger. I could have chosen resentment. I could have chosen bitterness. I could have chosen separatism. I could have chosen animosity. I could have chosen grief. I could have chosen fear. I could have chosen judgement. But I didn't. Those are all feelings associated with suffering. That's not me. I don't suffer. I don't wallow in self-pity. I don't play the victim.

I could have chosen to let my ego lead, but I didn't. I chose to let my spirit lead instead. I knew that it was my spirit that would guide me through this process with the compassion, grace and forgiveness that I aspired to embody. I knew that it was my spirit that would allow me to transcend the unproductive emotions and feelings that would keep me stuck and disallow me from doing greater things. I knew that it was my spirit that would keep nudging me toward expansion to the states of acceptance, empathy, love and peace, which was where I needed to be.

For the first time in years, I felt totally empowered, energized and untethered. It was in this moment that I realized that I could shatter antiquated paradigms. I could test boundaries. I could be totally bold. I could take an active role in raising collective consciousness. I could blaze new trails so that others could overcome fear and step into the essence of who they are. It was in this moment that I knew that all of this would be possible **only if** I consciously and purposefully chose love.

This was the beginning of a huge paradigm shift for me personally and had the potential to send reverberations out into the Universe that would have a ripple effect throughout collective consciousness. I realized I needed to partner with the Universe. We needed to co-create. I wanted to expand. I wanted to transform. I wanted to stretch for greater things. I wanted to allow this process to guide me to my purpose. I vowed to view every moment of this journey as an opportunity to learn and grow, and by letting my soul illuminate my path as a lightworker, I will help others find their light.

I had long felt the pull to direct my energy into an endeavor that benefited the greater good, but I never knew how or when I would discover it. I just trusted the process and knew that it would come, but on the Universe's timetable, not mine. I always marvel at the brilliance of the Universe and all of its infinite wisdom. It always knows the magnitude of the catalyst needed to launch us into our authentic realities. I had a choice. I could have succumbed to the powerful forces of fear, resentment, hate, regret and all of the other negative feelings commonly associated with divorce and allow this experience to break me down, or I could declare this moment as my breakthrough. The choice was easy...I chose breakthrough.

This specific scenario, complete with all of its divinely-orchestrated details put into place by the Universe, was never going to be presented to me again. I knew I needed to strike while the iron was hot. I knew this journey promised richness and depth from a personal growth perspective, and had tremendous potential to reverberate far and wide as I imprinted progressive thought patterns and instituted a new paradigm. This was, in fact, the moment I had been waiting for.

There were so many jewels here waiting to be discovered and I was hell-bent on discovering them. I decided I was going to do this differently. I was going to turn this sequence of events into a transformative spiritual journey and let love lead the way. We were going to have to navigate a lot of rules and formalities over the next several months, but I just kept relegating anything that didn't squarely fall into the "spiritual journey" category to a separate category that I affectionately call "Earthly nonsense."

There is always room for love. Even in the midst of divorce, there is always room for love, but you need to be willing and committed to creating it. I knew that if I did this right, I could redefine what divorce looks like. Smashing antiquated patterning and encouraging conscious thought is truly what sets my soul on fire.

I knew that the only way through this was to choose love every single day. I knew that parts of this journey were going to be challenging and downright arduous at times, and during these moments, I would have a choice to either let fear take over or consciously choose love. I knew that to truly embody love, during this process and beyond, I needed to weave it into every thread of my being. I needed to act like love, think like love, talk like love, walk like love and be love. I looked up one of my favorite Bible passages, Corinthians 13, wordsmithed it with a spiritual twist, and incorporated it into my daily practices:

> I am patient
> I am kind
> I do not envy
> I do not boast
> I am not proud
> I do not dishonor others
> I am not self-seeking
> I am not easily angered
> I keep no record of wrongs
> I rejoice in the truth
> I always protect, trust, hope and persevere

As unique and magical as this sounds, I'm not alone here. We all have a story. We all have challenges placed before us that have the potential to put us on the brink of a breakdown. Events that strip us to the core and make us wonder how we'll ever put the pieces back together and move on. We all have the power within us to transform our own lives and impact the lives of others in a positive and very powerful way. We have a choice, though, we must consciously and actively **choose** to access Universal Energy and exercise the power that resides within all of us. It is often our toughest situations that launch us into the purposes we are each meant to fulfill.

Discovering Your Authenticity

- What signs, or "synchronicities" have you experienced?
- How has the Universe reassured you that you were where you're meant to be?
- What life experiences have you had that prepared you for something greater?
- Have you ever taken a leap of faith, knowing and trusting everything would work toward your highest good?

6

CHOICE

View every aspect of your life as a menu, and then ask yourself if you would still make the same choices.

We often drift through life without realizing that everything we do is a choice. How we spend our time is a choice. Who we spend our time with is a choice. The food we put in our bodies is a choice. Whether or not we workout is a choice. Making time for self-care is a choice.

It is easy to limit our thinking about the choices we make to "big" decisions like what to study in school, where to work, who to have a relationship with, where to live and what car to drive.

What can be difficult to realize is that each day presents us with a steady stream of opportunities to make choices. How do you respond to life? Do you lapse into more unconscious modes of operation and stick with what is safe, comfortable, routine and what feels easiest in the moment or do you take a moment to pause and strategize about how you will best respond? Every challenge, every human interaction, every disappointment, every frustration, every misunderstanding is an opportunity for each of us to roll up our sleeves and do the work that is necessary to become a better version of the person we each were yesterday.

Challenging ourselves to respond to life differently by shifting our perspectives and asking ourselves the right questions will help us make the shift out of unconscious modes of operation and elevate our own awareness. View every opportunity as a gracious invitation from the Universe to ascend on the elevator of consciousness.

The one caveat that you must bear in mind is that the consciousness elevator only goes up. Once you get on, there is no going back down. As you ascend from living purely in a physical state into a realm that is governed by the spiritual essence of your being, it can become increasingly challenging to operate in a space with physical world limitations. But, life also becomes simpler and more fulfilling as you engage in activities that prioritize growth and transformation.

It took me years to realize that how we spend our time is a choice. For years, I thought I was "too busy" for certain things, and I didn't have the time. What I didn't realize, is that I wasn't making the time. We make time for things that are important to us. If something isn't important, we make an excuse. It really comes down to that basic truth. Several years ago I had a love/ hate relationship with working out, and I would go for several weeks at a time without working out and would keep telling myself "I'm too busy." I had to get really honest with myself and coach myself by asking if I really was too busy or if I was subconsciously prioritizing other things. By spending my time doing other things, I was effectively making the choice to not work out. I was stuck in a certain routine that didn't involve working out, and I didn't know how to shift out of it until I started to change the dialogue I was having with myself.

Each individual is wired a certain way, and your behaviors and patterns are a result of your predispositions that are largely affected by your interactions with caregivers in your developmental years. Throughout our lives, we summon various relationships to give us an opportunity to heal the unhealed parts of ourselves.

Shifting from an unconscious state to being fully conscious is not a linear process. It doesn't work that way. It's a natural part of our human condition to experience the full range of emotions and to honor and validate them, as experiencing them is an instrumental part of the process. We must grant ourselves compassion and grace and understand that all of our emotions are welcome and play a vital role in our growth.

We often can't control everything that happens to us in life, but we **can** control our responses to what happens. How we respond is a choice, and the choice you make has a strong correlation to the amount of stress you feel in addition to the range of outcomes you are able to achieve. When you understand that everything is a choice and then take steps to turn the unconscious patterns into conscious choices is when you start to claim your personal power and learn how to craft your reality. Are you choosing to flow with the direction in which life is taking you or are you resisting?

Discovering Your Authenticity

- Think about the most important areas of your life, and ask yourself if you would still make the same choices.
- In what areas of your life can you make more conscious choices?
- What is your internal process for when you need to make a choice?
- How do you flow with the direction life is taking you?

For a special bonus on designing your life with conscious choices, visit https://liveauthentically.today/soar-resources to download the guide.

PART II

STRENGTHENING YOUR WINGS

Strength comes from continually challenging yourself to interpret your life experiences through spiritual lenses.

7

CREATING A NEW PARADIGM FOR DIVORCE

Any situation that challenges us has the potential to be highly transformative if we let our soul lead the way.

Divorce. Ugh. The "D" word. The word that makes people cringe. The topic that causes many people to tip-toe around out of fear that they'll say the wrong thing or make someone uncomfortable. Why? Because we've been conditioned to think that divorce is full of contentiousness and separatism. The old relationship paradigms are no longer sustaining relationships the way they used to in prior generations. People are looking to their primary relationship for a deep sense of fulfillment and connection more than ever before, and it stands to reason that we should also be updating our ideologies on divorce to keep pace with the change in the relationship landscape. I'm here to shatter antiquated beliefs and modes of operation and show you that the divorce process and post-divorce landscape doesn't have to conjure up images of contentiousness and separatism like they used to. We can consciously reframe what divorce is through our mindset and through a commitment to spiritual growth.

Divorce has the potential to be highly transformative for everyone involved. It's a golden opportunity for you to take inventory on the respective contributions to the breakdown of the relationship and use that new-found awareness to craft an even better version of yourself. The reality is that you can design your post-divorce reality to look any way you want it to. You have creative license. There are no rules.

In the spirit of being authentic, I'm not going to paint a picture of divorce being all rainbows and butterflies. After all, it involves disentangling a life that is closely intertwined with another individual and the number of considerations can be many, particularly if there are children involved. There is inevitably a lot of change involved in divorce but how do you know that your new reality isn't going to be substantially better than your prior one? Therein lies the beauty and the magic of trusting the process.

Divorce is an opportunity for both individuals to step into their respective authentic realities and live more congruently with who they are. I did it, and so can you.

Changing Landscapes

We are on the cusp of collective consciousness starting to make a huge shift. People are starting to awaken and are starting to examine their lives and their choices with more mindfulness and more depth than ever before. In prior generations, if there was food on the table and the bills were paid, life was good.

The landscape of romantic relationships is changing and the model that worked well 50 years ago is no longer valid. In prior generations, roles were much more gender-delineated. In general, the patriarch was responsible for providing the financial resources for the family while the matriarch was responsible for all things related to the house and children. There was very little overlap, if any, between the respective roles and responsibilities. People are relying on their primary relationship for a sense of fulfillment and connection more than ever before, and if those ingredients are not present, they are more willing to consider embarking on another trajectory. This is just one area of life where we are starting to see people "wake up." As the nature of relationships makes a shift, we must adeptly respond by accepting that relationship breakdowns and redesigns are a natural by-product of global shifts in consciousness.

Divorce is a vehicle that allows us to undo antiquated programming and reprogram ourselves and future generations with the coding that prompts us to honor our soul's purpose and play a role in elevating the collective consciousness of the planet.

We are beginning to witness these shifts on a global scale, and these broad shifts are the results of efforts made on an individual level. The path from going from being totally unconscious to becoming fully conscious is a fascinating non-linear process of self-discovery. We don't go directly from point A to point to point B. Sometimes there are detours. Sometimes there are hiatuses. Sometimes there are full-blown breakdowns. But every twist and turn and stall is an important part of the process. Metaphorically speaking, I view the process of becoming conscious much like the process of an artist painting a mural. After spending time painting up close, the artist steps away in an attempt to see the painting from a different perspective. Then the artist continues painting another area, steps away and moves in again to paint another section. This process continues until the artist is fully-satisfied with the masterpiece.

I'm a firm believer that for something to be sustainable, one must go through his or her own process of self-discovery and arrive at the answers independently. While it may sound more efficient to follow someone's advice, that is the unconscious route. There is significant growth that takes place when we ask ourselves questions like "What are the underlying motivating factors?" "What makes sense for me?" " Am I really comfortable with this?" "Is this in line with my values and beliefs?" Through asking ourselves deeper questions along the way, we continually make the unconscious parts of ourselves conscious.

Honoring and Transmuting the Pain

I'm not here to give you a sugar-coated version of a divorce story and tell you that after you follow a bunch of simple steps that you'll be on your way to a picture perfect reality. While that would be a positive spin on divorce, it wouldn't be an authentic representation. It is completely normal and expected that pain is experienced and honored during and after the process, and turning a blind eye to the amount of pain a divorce inflicts would be doing a disservice to ourselves and to humanity. Putting on a happy face and pretending that everything is fine only defers the pain and delays the healing process.

People often associate displays of pain, such as crying, with weakness, but in reality it is much the opposite. Not allowing yourself to feel pain is avoidance. Not allowing yourself to be vulnerable is the quick and dirty way through. Not allowing yourself to SCUBA dive into the depths of your human emotions is like continuing to sweep stuff under the rug and expecting the rug to be able to hold all the debris forever. There will come a day when there won't be any more room under the rug and you'll find yourself in a cold and harsh reality. It takes tremendous strength to be vulnerable, take off your mask and allow any challenging life experiences to meticulously craft you into the best version of yourself.

I recognize and validate that there is pain associated with divorce because I have experienced it and witness it as we learn how to navigate our newly-structured reality in a progressive way. Acknowledging the pain gives rise to the opportunity for you to choose what to do with it. Do you allow the pain to keep you stuck, weighed down in a reality that promotes a victim mentality and stifles your true potential? Or, do you allow it to energize you and prompt you to do some deep soul searching so that you can use it to access your personal power, optimizing not only your own life but having a positive impact on the world around you? Your struggles don't define you. What defines you is how you respond to life.

Divorce introduces many areas that require healing. Healing requires that we first make ourselves aware of our feelings, honor and validate them and accept that they are a very normal and real part of our human experience. It is crucial not to rush the healing process. Everybody's timeline is different and there is no cut and dried answer for how long it takes to heal from a divorce. The rate at which you move through the healing process is directly correlated to your willingness to roll up your sleeves, get your hands dirty and get real, get vulnerable and own your stuff so that you can emerge as a more refined version of yourself.

Nothing prompts you to take self-inventory quite like the breakdown of a committed relationship. Divorce is a golden opportunity to pull back the curtain of your psyche and explore how your various life experiences have played a role in shaping who you are today so you can learn how to make conscious choices and be perfectly positioned to embark on a trajectory of transformation and self-actualization. Some of the hardest things in life are meant to help us learn and grow and evolve to our own Higher Self, and divorce is no exception.

Your life may not be playing out as you once planned, but the good news is that you can still have your Happily Ever After, and it could quite possibly turn out to be your Happiest Ever After. This doesn't come easy but it is well within the realm of likelihood. By learning to partner with the Universe, you can co-create a reality that supersedes your prior reality.

Divorce Involves a Series of Choices

The divorce process can be challenging because it involves a significant amount of change in a relatively short period of time. We have to make short-term and long-term decisions about logistics, finances, potential moves, parenting issues and many other things and attempt to weigh both parties' needs and wants, all while various intense emotions are swirling. Virtually every aspect of our lives is affected. We often dive in head-first and follow the patterns and trends on how divorce is "supposed to be," as dictated by society at large, or the influence of various people in our lives.

Before we make any of the aforementioned decisions, we must first ask ourselves some very important questions:

- What do I believe about divorce?
- How do I envision the post-divorce landscape?
- Do I want to follow society's views of divorce?
- How can I use this as a catalyst for my own personal

growth?
- How can I help others view divorce from a healthier perspective?

The decision to use the divorce process as a tool for growth and transformation is a choice made at the individual level. Even though you are in the process of trying to disentangle your life from the life that has been closely intertwined with another individual, the way in which you navigate this journey is your choice. Sure, it would be ideal if both parties decided to embark on this initiative together, but what's important is that you remain on your path. Even if the other person is not willing to navigate the process with a growth-based mindset, you can still show up and use this experience as a tool for growth and transformation.

It is important to remember that everyone is doing their best from his or her respective level of consciousness, and each person's thoughts and reactions and behaviors are filtered through the lens of one's own life experiences, past and present, and from one's current state of evolution. Everyone is precisely where they need to be at every moment in time. As much as you may love to see the other person sign on to this growth-based initiative, it is important to remember to stay in your lane and remain steadfast in your commitment to growth. Your soon-to-be former spouse will navigate this process from whatever state of evolution he or she is currently at and there isn't anything you can do to accelerate the growth if there is no willingness to do the hard work. This isn't the time for you to be preachy or try to "teach a lesson" - either retaliatorily or didactically. Just as you can't force a flower to bloom, your former spouse will bloom at his or her own pace. But, don't underestimate the impact that your example can set. Regardless of whether or not you realize it, your soon-to-be-former spouse is observing what you do, and your actions speak decibels louder than words.

We are all operating at different planes of consciousness. Some of us have been sent here to serve as lightworkers and play a role in awakening others, while others have yet to experience their awakening. Metaphorically speaking, some people's worlds are highly illuminated and objects are crystal clear, and for others, their worlds are dimly-lit and they are searching for the light switch. They're doing their best. The best thing we can do is to meet everyone with compassion, empathy, kindness and love and help them find their own light.

The tone and spirit of your divorce is a choice that has a direct impact on the outcome and on all of the lives affected. Through committing to a growth-based mindset, we can empower ourselves to navigate the process as a conscious endeavor and set a new precedent about how divorce can and should look.

Discovering Your Authenticity

- Examine all areas of your life and ask yourself if, based on the person you are today, you would still make the same choices regarding your career, relationships, geographical location, etc.
- In what areas of your life are you living according to societal conditioning, and in what aspects have you made conscious choices?
- What aspects of your life no longer serve you? What aspects are past their expiration date and are holdovers from an outdated version of yourself?
- Have you thought about disengaging from certain activities and relationships so that you can better align what you think, do and believe?
- What is holding you back from making different choices?
- What are your views on divorce?

8

EARTHLY MECHANICS OF THE DIVORCE PROCESS

In the spiritual world, everything always unfolds in a divinely orchestrated manner, and the people and experiences that are meant for us are placed in our path at the perfect time.

We decided that the approach that made the most sense for the dissolution of our marriage was the collaborative process, a team-based approach to divorce whereby the two parties are empowered to craft a post-divorce reality with the help of professionals. That was important to us. Nobody knew our family situation and the people involved in it better than we did, and we wanted to retain the power, autonomy, creative license and the flexibility to craft our new realities rather than allow someone else to do it for us.

We spent several weeks assembling our team and then it was finally time for kick-off, for real. It wasn't until the start of the first meeting that the first wave of reality set in. All the people dressed in professional business attire assembled into a conference room in a downtown high-rise made it feel like a throwback to my

Corporate America days, except this time we were there to put our heads together about how to best split up our family. I remember that my head spun for a moment and then everything felt surreal. At the beginning of the meeting, one of the professionals gave some opening remarks and eluded to the fact that we were giving our kids a gift by doing this. My eyes welled up with tears, and as much as I was trying to stay in my space and sit in this moment, I looked across the table at my soon-to-be-former husband. I had wished for years that our respective outward displays of emotion could have been more closely aligned and that he could meet me on some things with even a quarter of the emotion that I would express in any given situation, and even he was moved to tears. That sight alone reinforced the emotional heaviness that this journey promised to deliver. As much as I invested in my self-care and tried to remain in a positive headspace, sometimes the emotional and mental and physical fatigue would get the best of me. The gravity of the process that we were about to embark on had officially made itself known.

Over a period of roughly 18 months, our legal professionals ushered us through all aspects of the divorce process. We explored financial scenarios, parenting plans and finalized all other agreements that needed to be made. The purpose of this section is not to provide an exhaustive summary of all such topics and considerations though; every situation is highly unique and there will be plenty of resources and guidance from professionals who will help you balance your needs and desires. I have selected some highlights from the process and have included commentary on how I coached myself through from a spiritual perspective.

Deciding on Living Arrangements

The not-so-trivial task of deciding our respective living arrangements and determining which one of us would remain in the marital home was a major issue we had to tackle. This wasn't just any marital home. This was a huge home that we had custom-built just three years earlier. It was the home that we had poured our blood, sweat and tears into for years during its creation. It was the home for which we had meticulously appointed every single square inch to match our tastes and preferences and dreams. It was the home that we built with future generations in mind, and it was the home that was intended to be our forever home. Early on in our discussions, I had to come to terms with the fact that "forever" would no longer be the time horizon for us in this house.

In my heart, I knew I wanted to move at some point. I just didn't know when. Maybe a year down the road. Maybe two. Maybe three. I didn't have a plan, but fortunately, the Universe has an uncanny way of knowing what you're feeling in your heart, and often without us realizing it, is already orchestrating plans behind the scenes, eager to honor our heart-centered requests.

The Universe is always ready to honor heart-centered requests.

The harsh reality was that the home reflected who we were and what we thought we wanted at the time we embarked on the mission of creating it, but was no longer congruent with who we were at the time we were divorcing or in line with the direction in which either one of us wanted to take our respective futures. For me, significant growth had been taking place over the last few years, and I was a completely different person than the person I was when we moved in. Practically unrecognizable, my entire belief system, the things I value and the way in which I approach life had been radically transformed in the time we were in the home. There's nothing quite like a pastoral, tranquil setting that exposes every nook and cranny of your psyche. It was completely void of external stimuli, and my thoughts crystallized and were clearer than ever.

To untether myself and freely move in the direction I was supposed to go, I had to part with the idea of what was "supposed to be" and dive into some more serious soul work to decide how to best move forward. I had to reflect on who I had been previously, who I was at that moment and articulate what I valued and why I valued it the way I did. I realized that subconsciously building this house was the idiomatic Hail Mary pass and maybe it would be what we needed. More space. A pastoral setting. Countless modern-day luxuries. In hindsight, we were still grasping onto egoic measures for happiness.

During my period of intense growth, I spent a lot of time thinking about happiness and what it stems from. I discovered that, for me, happiness is deeply rooted in freedom. Freedom from doubt. Freedom from judgement. Freedom to speak my truth unabashedly. Freedom from societal expectations. Freedom from roadblocks and obstacles. Freedom from antiquated programming that doesn't serve me anymore. Freedom from all types of fears like the fears of failure, rejection, pain, death, disappointment, worry and the egoic barometers that promote a shallow existence. Untethering myself from all of these things that were weighing me down would allow me to soar, and I needed to figure out the best way to do that.

We're conditioned to think that happiness is always somewhere else. Never where we are. It's easy to get into the habit of expecting happiness to be ushered in with future events and think things like, "I'll be happy after I have a place of my own after I graduate" or "I'll be happy when my kids are older and life is easier," or "I'll be happy next year when I get the promotion and the corner office." The ubiquitously uncovered truth is that happiness can be found precisely where we are, but we have to choose it. Happiness is what happens **along the way**. It's the experiences we have. It's the people we meet. It's the connections we deepen. It's the self-awareness we discover. Happiness is always right here, right now, but we need to find it and choose to cultivate it.

Life-long, sustainable happiness doesn't come in the form of houses. It doesn't come in the form of cars. It doesn't come in the form of jewelry. At the end of the day, it's all just stuff, and we can't take any of it with us when we leave this Earth. During my journey, I came to the realization that relationships alone cannot be the sole source of our happiness. It comes when we find our own truth and live it out. It comes when we honor ourselves. It comes when we honor our authenticity rather than trying to satisfy what other people want for us.

We often underestimate how much we are compromising our own level of happiness until we have a significant catalyst dropped into our lives. These catalysts are divinely orchestrated and strategically placed and are meant to shake us up and prompt us to revisit our beliefs and take inventory on our lives.

After the dust settled after building our house, literally and figuratively, there was nothing left on the horizon. No big projects. No more distractions. We had been operating in turbo mode for years and had drifted apart as we were each burning the wick at both ends in our diverging realities. We finally had a chance to catch our breath and it was time to start metabolizing all that we had consumed over the last several years.

One Saturday afternoon, my husband and I were discussing some of the many changes that would be occurring over the next several months, and we decided that I would be the one to stay in our marital home, for an undetermined period of time. As much as it no longer reflected who I was and my current state of spiritual evolution, I was willing to stay for a period of time in an attempt to keep at least one thing constant for the kids during a time that was fraught with so many other changes. I envisioned myself moving someday but was far from attempting to assign a timeframe to it. I started to check the real estate listings in a quest to reacquaint myself with the real estate market and instill a degree of preparedness for the day I would begin to seriously consider moving.

Unbeknownst to me, the Universe had surreptitiously been curating plans for me behind the scenes to honor what I was feeling in my heart. That evening, a house came on the market, and it was a house I knew quite well. The owners were very close friends of mine, and I had spent countless hours at their house over the years for get-togethers and late-night scrapbooking sessions. It was just a stone's throw away from the home that we brought all the kids home to when they were babies.

This house hit the market on a Saturday evening and I didn't hesitate. After a tiny bit of negotiating that lasted for all of about 10 minutes, we reached an agreement on that Monday morning. Logic and reason told me that I should stay in our marital home, and my gut told me the complete opposite. It was time to get up and go.

If someone would have told me 15 years ago that someday I'd live in the house I bought, I never would have believed them. I walked past this house daily for nearly a decade, before we moved away for a few years. Even before I met the owners, I was drawn to the "vibe" of this house. There was always a sort of "buzz" and it was kind of like Grand Central station with lots of hustle and bustle with comings and goings, gatherings and an unparalleled sense of warmth, hospitality, and tradition. On my daily trips to the park during the dreaded bewitching hours when the kids were babies and toddlers (full-time moms you know what I'm talking about!), they would always be out back grilling and inviting perfect strangers to join them for dinner.

I admired their perfectly-balanced and symmetrical family with two boys and two girls and how the matriarch always made family management look so effortless, as she always handled the chaos with such grace and solemnity. Whatever was ensuing around her, she always remained grounded and centered and tranquil, and everyone around her followed her lead.

She has long been a faith-filled mentor of mine in this game of life and we've hit on just about every topic over the years, from "here are some ideas for how to get out of pajamas before noon," to ruminations about God's plan as she helped me cope with a devastating loss years ago.

I love that the spirit of this home has remained unchanged after we moved in. I love the hustle and bustle. I love the circle drive full of cars. I love the impromptu conversations with neighbors. I love the neighborhood kids, some of whom walk into our house without ringing the doorbell. I love going to the store and stocking up on snacks in preparation for the next round of get-togethers. I love the sound of the snowplows whizzing by. I love our parties. I love carrying on the tradition of handing out the King Size candy bars on Halloween, which the neighborhood kids have grown accustomed to over the years.

It was a bit surreal to think that I uprooted and moved, just like that. I could have overthought the situation and talked myself into staying. I could have convinced myself that not moving was the option that made the most sense. Over the years I've come to realize that the best way to kill the magic is to overthink, so I've learned to listen to my heart. Overthinking is so incredibly exhausting and cumbersome. Listening to my heart is precisely what I did in this moment, and in true divine fashion, my heart led me home.

Energetically, I feel so much more at peace and full of joy and contentment. Every day feels like a celebration. Shortly after we moved here, I was sitting at my kitchen island and my daughter commented that I seemed so much happier than I had before, and commented that we'd had more parties in the three months that we'd been here than we had in the last three years. The heart always knows the way.

In the Spiritual World, Nothing is a Mistake

In our discussions about the house and in the process of deciding who would stay there, we both shared our reflections. At one point my husband commented that building the house was a mistake. I said nothing in response to that. We both had wildly polarized views of how the world works, so at this point, any last-ditch efforts to ask him to see the world through my lenses would have futile. Of course, I agree that the whole undertaking didn't play out as we planned, but in the spiritual world, **nothing** is a mistake, ever. Everything that happens is orchestrated in a pristinely and divinely orchestrated manner, and everything serves a purpose. Every house purchase. Every house sale. Every oversight. Every delay. Every altercation. Every victory. Every missed phone call. Our conscious minds may think something is a mistake, but embedded in that statement is an implicit assumption that we are all-knowing. What we must recognize is that our conscious minds are so very limited, and cognitively they can only process what is available to us through our five senses. Living in the physical world often stifles our ability to bear in mind that there is a whole other dimension at work and that the Universe is always in the business of delivering what is in our highest good. It's like a game of chess. The Universe can see 10 moves into the future, but our visibility is limited and blurry at best. We must trust the process and surrender to the infinite wisdom of the Universe.

My perspective on how this was playing out was so very different than his. I remember thinking about how organically everything was unfolding. There were so many lessons there for all of us, kids included, and I needed all of my fingers and toes and then some to quantify all of them. I was sitting on the edge of my seat in eager anticipation about what the Universe would serve up next. The purpose of this undertaking was abundantly clear, and I was excited to continue along this path.

I don't regret any of the time we spent building or living in our marital home, even though we decided not to stay. Every moment has led me to where I am today and has given me tremendous clarity on who I am, what is truly important to me and has given birth to my purpose.

The kids will bring up our prior homes from time to time, and say that they miss them and I capitalize on the opportunity to shape the way in which they process change and grief. We have deeper discussions about processing the events of life and managing change in a healthy way. I help them enumerate and appreciate the things we can do now that we couldn't then. We talk about how a house is just a house, and it's the people and the love that make it a home. Where we live now is our home. We will always take the memories with us wherever we go.

It is completely normal to miss and pine for the way things used to be, and any of us can do that in any situation. How often do we look back and miss the time when our kids were little, the sweet smell of a baby fresh out of the bathtub, cuddling under the blankets with bedtime books, or the way their tiny hands felt in ours as we ushered them to the park? How often do we long for the carefree days from our college years where friends were just a dorm room away before we got saddled down with responsibilities of the real world?

It is completely normal to long for prior experiences but we must balance it and make sure it doesn't rob us from enjoying what is currently in front of us and prevent us from living in the now.

I love that this experience has allowed us all to experience contrast. Every experience we have puts yet another item on the menu in each category, and we have a broader range of options from which we can choose.

Learning to Trust Your Intuition

Intuition, inner voice, gut, heart... I use these words interchangeably to represent the pull that we feel when we are faced with a decision. Natural instinct more often than not leads us to the right answer. It's often hard to put into words because it's a feeling, and the language of the soul can't easily be translated into Earthly language.

I've found that the easiest way to tune into what our souls are trying to communicate to us is to pay close attention to how the dynamics of a particular situation are unfolding, as well as how the dynamics make us feel. Does it feel like you're trying to fit a square peg in a round hole? Does it feel unnatural? Does it feel choppy? Forced? Stressful? Or conversely, does it have a fluid, natural, organic feel? The key question to ask yourself regularly is, "Am I forcing this or is it flowing?"

I've found that the things that are meant to be unfold effortlessly and organically. There is an unmistakable feeling of naturalness that is pervasive in just about every aspect of a situation that is meant for us. For example, in an interpersonal relationship, whether it is a friendship or romantic in nature, there is a mutuality of investment on both sides. No one person is doing all of the heavy lifting all of the time. There are ebbs and flows with regard to what each person is able to contribute at any given time due to several other external factors that are either within or outside of their control. But, the dynamics will always gravitate back to the equilibrium that keeps the relationship fair and balanced. When there is a chronic one-sidedness with regard to which person is putting in more effort, it's time to start asking yourself the right questions: "What is the nature of this relationship?" "Does it serve me?" " Is it in my highest good?" " Is it meant to teach me something?"

During the divorce process, I relied on my intuition and awareness of what it feels like when something is being forced and consciously chose to follow what my gut was telling me to do.

The story of how we sold our marital home exemplifies this. After spending a few months getting situated in our respective new and separate realities, we finally felt ready to put our marital home on the market. We were fortunate that we had the logistical and financial flexibility to pour all of our attention and energy into building our new lives but it was finally time to release the past by directing some of our attention to selling our marital home.

We put our home on the market in January. We were still in the midst of the divorce process, and during one of our meetings, we had to decide for how many months we wanted to pre-fund the ongoing expenses associated with this home. According to market averages, the expectation was that it could take at least 18 months to sell. This house sale wasn't going to conform to the statistics. I was going to make sure of that. I knew there was a way to take an active role in making sure the house sold faster than that by working behind the scenes through energy. We had to decide how many months to put in the contract. Despite other people's opinions, I said that the longer timeframe we put in the contract, the longer it will take to sell. That idea was met with silence, as everybody left that comment alone. Thinking like this was so routine for me at this point, but if somebody would have said that to me five years ago, I probably would have looked at them like they were speaking a foreign language backward.

By March, we accepted a cash offer. My real estate agent and I were planning a trip to Mexico for spring break with our kids, and we were envisioning ourselves toasting and celebrating the sale with margaritas by the pool. While we were there, we were trying to finalize our decision about requests made during the inspection, which should have been nothing more than a formality on a recently-built house that had been pristinely maintained. After some back and forth, energetically I just didn't like how it was starting to feel. It felt very heavy and forced, and just didn't have that feeling of flow.

Bringing the transaction across the finish line would have come down to one minute detail, which, in relation to the entire transaction, was like a drop in the bucket and was irrelevant to me. After all, this was **our** house and **we** would be the ones to decide if and when and to whom we sold. I was totally resolute in my willingness to walk away from the transaction, but I had one not-so-small challenge ahead of me....convincing my soon-to-be-former-husband.

I left a message for him, and he called me back while we were at dinner. I left my real estate agent with the kids at the restaurant and engaged in a 45-minute long persuasive speech as I paced by the pool and attempted to plead my case. I recognized that what I wanted to do was bold. Really bold. I mean, who walks away from a cash deal over an amount that was negligible compared to the scheme of the whole transaction? But, after all, when you do bold things and take risks, that's when the magic happens. I asked him to trust me, and with extreme confidence assured him it would sell quickly. By the end of the call, he was in my camp, albeit somewhat reluctantly.

I was grateful that he was open-minded enough to consider my perspective and that he trusted me enough to let me take the risk. This point is significant not only because he was willing to step into a situation that was fraught with uncertainty, but because he doesn't speak the language of the Universe. He has seen me operate like this and deferred to my intuition a number of times in the past, and after seeing how it had played out over and over and over again, he was willing to let me do "my thing," yet again.

Communications of closure abound in my world, so I followed up with this text to him:

> *"I'm glad you finally shifted on the house sale. Shutting it down is absolutely the answer. When a situation feels forced and someone or something is not in integrity with*

> *who I am, I walk. Simple as that. They're not the only buyer out there and someone who is reasonable and in touch with the value of what they are getting will drop in as quickly as they did."*

My agent called her office and asked her assistant to prepare the documents that would terminate the contract. She asked her assistant to change the garage door code, and then she leaned over and asked me what I wanted the code to be. I had no immediate idea. After my agent and her assistant chatted for a few more seconds, I leaned over and said "0518 - the house is going to sell in May. And probably around the 18th." I told my agent we were going to manifest it to happen that way.

The house went back on the market, and just as I had promised my co-seller, another buyer did drop in quickly. Everything about the transaction was smooth, from the negotiations through the inspection, and as co-created by me and the Universe, we closed in May, within a week from the date I predicted.

This incident is significant for several reasons. First, I trusted my intuition and knew how to listen to my inner voice. Secondly, I was able to recognize when it was starting to feel forced and had the courage to walk away. You don't have to stay in that space. Give yourself permission to walk away without guilt. If it doesn't feel right, it isn't. You don't owe anyone any explanations. Lastly, I employed extremely powerful manifestation techniques to achieve the outcome we desired.

You have to be willing to clear the space and trust that the Universe will replace it with that which is in your highest good.

Digital high-fives and celebratory emojis were exchanged after the offer was finalized. I said, "Who knew selling a house could be so much fun? That went so flawlessly that I bet we could go back and ask the buyer for another $10,000 to fund another trip to Mexico." My agent and I handled negotiations while my soon-to-be-former husband was out of the country. When he returned, he sent a text asking about the final manifested result.

My agent and I celebrated his acknowledgment of a spiritual concept, albeit in a lighthearted manner. What a breakthrough moment! I replied, "You're starting to dabble in the language - nice!!" His reply indicated that he was actually envious of my ability and indicated that if he could manifest things that it would dramatically cut down on his stress level.

That simple text elicited a flood of thoughts and emotions for me. First of all, he said the word "manifest." You can manifest anything, I thought. Anybody can. Manifesting isn't a skill that only a select few can cultivate. Accessing Universal Energy and learning how to incorporate the laws of the Universe to shape your human experience is something that we can all do. Like anything else, the more we practice it, the better we get. The reason I can manifest things the way that I do is because I work at it every single day. When you master it, life feels like magic.

Secondly, he referred to his stress level. That implied that it was greater than zero. He's not alone in this. I would expect that the vast majority of people are walking around feeling like they're weighed down by stress in varying degrees. It made me sad to think about that, particularly because I am all too familiar with that feeling. For years, I was constantly stressed. It was more or less the "rule" for me, and any time I wasn't feeling stress of some kind was the "exception."

The game totally changed when I learned to take a soul-based approach to my human experience. Since I started to truly live in the spiritual realm and learned how to co-create my reality with the Universe and surrender and trust the process, I hardly ever feel stressed anymore. Sure, I may experience fleeting moments of stress here and there, but now I've learned how to coach myself out of it. Someone could lose their temper at me and now I know how to disallow myself from meeting them in that low-vibrational place. I used to feel stress because I would allow boundaries to be blurred and took on others' problems, but now I am more astute about recognizing that we are on individual journeys and without the lessons, there is no growth.

Craving Simplicity

The breakdown of my marriage prompted a huge paradigm shift that caused me to think about every aspect of my life from a completely different vantage point. Shortly into the process, I found that I started to crave simplicity in a big way. I was feeling a strong pull to be in an environment that fostered peace and simplicity. I wanted to downsize and streamline everything. I wanted to feel totally unencumbered. I wanted one furnace, not three. I wanted one-quarter of an acre, not eight. It was a little preposterous to think that I was choosing to walk away from something that we had created. At one point every decision we made for that house was so incredibly important, and now none of it mattered to me. I was suddenly craving experiences, not things. I had no problem parting with custom-made furniture we ordered for a custom-built house. I wanted our day-to-day living to be low-maintenance and I wanted to minimize the time I spent taking care of a house. I felt like I had been so weighed down for so long by the day-to-day operations. I was ready to free myself from all that no longer served me, and this was the perfect opportunity to do so. I wanted to be in an environment that gave me peace, and I wanted to align myself energetically so that I could step into the purpose that I have come to this Earth to fulfill.

The Beginning of Our New Realities

I dropped the kids off at my parents' house so they would not have to experience the psychological distress of seeing their dad's belongings, and some of theirs, loaded into a moving truck and being hauled away. That is a childhood memory I didn't want them to have.

The slow steady beeps of the moving truck as it pulled into my driveway is assuredly something I will never forget. My heart sank. For the last twenty two years, more than half of my life, every moment of every day was spent building this empire, working toward goals together. Memories flooded my mind and it felt like there wasn't any force on this Earth that could stop them. All I could think about were the vacations we took, bringing our kids into the world and all of our other shared memories. I thought to myself that it seemed like the worst day of my life. Everything we worked so hard for was imploding. As the movers loaded boxes onto dollies and hauled away his personal belongings, I decided against staying to watch every last item be loaded. I left to go to the gym, my happy place, but on a whim first decided to stop at my new house. I kept stalling by coming up with "just one more thing" to do. The stalling was the Universe's way of ensuring that I would I receive the message I needed to hear when I got to the gym. As with everything, there would be a divine timing element. So, after I finally accepted the reality that it wasn't feasible to work out with my sunglasses on, I dried my tears and headed over to the health club to warm up on the bike. As I was adjusting my settings, a very powerful song came on, "Best Day of My Life." The day my soon-to-be-former husband was moving out and the day our kids' lives would be officially split between two households is the best day of my life? What an odd thought. But, the Universe always gives us precisely what we need in each moment, and in that moment it gave me this song to help me get back in the right headspace. It was the day we would all finally begin to step into our authentic realities.

The kids' dad wanted to have them with him the weekend that he moved, so the practice of alternating the kids between weekends officially started. I went out with friends that night and will never forget coming home to the eerily and starkly quiet house. Nobody was there. I had pined for silence for a period of time long enough to hear myself think for years. Now I had it, and I didn't want it. The previous 14 years had been a flurry of constant controlled chaos as I bounced around between my various roles of playing unpaid Uber driver, short-order cook, family historian, homework helper, nurse, bedtime book reader, and every other mom-job on the planet. Somebody was **always** home. But not this time.

I went up to the master bedroom closet to change my clothes. His side of the closet was barren. Not one thing remained. I stood there. For the last few months we had been straddling two totally disparate realities, one where we maintained a business-as-usual front because it wasn't yet time to communicate the news to the kids and another reality where we were surreptitiously curating our blueprint to decouple our lives. Now, it was beginning to feel real. It was really happening. For several minutes, I was flooded with memories. It's over. It's really over. This is it, the beginning of the end. We poured our blood, sweat and tears into this regime for years. Decades, actually, and now it's all imploding. I stood there for a few minutes and took it all in, and I felt like I was watching a highlight reel from our time together.

I wasn't as concerned about the kids' well-being as much as I was concerned about the fact that I felt like I was missing out. They're out having fun and I wasn't there with them? How could that be? We were accustomed to all of us doing things as a family for years. I had to allow myself to feel all the emotions that accompanied the feeling of missing out, but after I honored them, I coached myself by telling myself, "I have a choice." I can either remain in a negative mindset, sulk and remain stuck **or**, I can recognize that this is, in fact, the inception of our new reality, and in this reality there are times when we will all be together and times when we are not. This is my opportunity to invest in the areas of my life that do not involve the kids, like reclaiming my identity, doing my growth work and investing in other relationships that are important to me.

Suddenly, with a fleeting yet potent surge of undoubtedly recognizable Universal Energy, I found these feelings of lacking and incompleteness and self-pity to be hastily replaced with feelings of abundance and gratitude and adventurousness and celebration. I had to dig deep. Really deep. I had to shift from viewing it as the "beginning of the end" to the "beginning of a new beginning." So, I pulled myself together, curled up on the couch under a cozy blanket with a cup of tea and enumerated all of the things I had to be grateful for in this moment of peace and solitude.

A Sea of Christmas Ornaments

We were approaching our first Christmas under our newly-structured reality and I had the poignant task of splitting up our Christmas ornaments that we had accumulated over the years. I had put it off for as long as I could, and given that Thanksgiving was approaching, the time to face the music, and the bin of ornaments, was suddenly upon me. I gently scattered them all out on the family room floor and sat in the middle of them. One by one, I mechanically started placing them into one of two piles. Mine. His. Mine. His. Then I picked up the "Our First Christmas" ornament. Followed by a "My First Day of Kindergarten" ornament. Followed by a "Baby's First Christmas" ornament. Followed by a "New Home" ornament. There was no end to the steady stream of Christmas ornaments and associated memories, and a steady stream of tears were soon to follow. I fell apart emotionally. "This totally sucks," I remember thinking. I was sitting squarely in the middle of a sea of Christmas ornaments, and felt like I didn't have a life float.

I had no choice but to regroup and reframe. I needed to allow myself to honor the emotions as they emerged, while not letting them overtake me by forcing me to board a runaway train. It's a delicate balance. I paused, gained my composure and went back to the highly underutilized and highly-underestimated relaxation technique, breathing. I started to coach myself. "These memories aren't contingent upon whether or not you are still married. You still have all of them. You carry them in your heart and they will always be very much a part of who you are."

I jumped online, and ordered some duplicates so each of us could preserve the memories and keep them alive in our own hearts and our own respective homes. These were, in fact, memories that were an extremely important part of our past, and could and should still be cherished, marital status notwithstanding.

Navigating Milestones with Acceptance

We were approaching the first family milestone and celebration since we had announced the divorce, and I was worried that I would experience an overwhelming sense of sadness on the occasion. Our oldest was coming up on her graduation from eighth grade and we should have been celebrating it as an intact family. It was sad to think that we squarely in the middle of splitting up our family. What about pictures? Could we all still take a picture together? I quickly decided that there are no rules in situations like this. Nothing says that you can't take whatever pictures you feel moved to take to capture whatever moment you want to capture. As far as I know, no rules exist about the relations of people who can pose in pictures together.

In preparation for this milestone, I did a lot of work to help reframe my thoughts in a more celebratory and positive light. This day was about **her**. It was **her** milestone. It was a celebration of her accomplishments to date and was filled with excitement and anticipation about her next steps on her individual journey. We might not still be an intact family unit, but we would all still be there. Her mom, dad, siblings and grandparents were all present to partake in the ceremony and celebration that followed.

Like many other things in life, often the anticipation and associated worry and anxiety is far worse than the events that actually transpire. For us, the day was filled with smiles, laughter, many pictures and reflections on her life and accomplishments. There might have been a few tears, but not at all stemming from sadness associated with the divorce. I'd classify them as expected, "My baby's growing up" tears and were nothing dissimilar from what various other parents were experiencing.

Creating our Parenting Plan

We reached the point in the process where it was time to put a dry-erase marker to the white board and start sketching out various parenting plan options. It was insane to think that we were about to set sail into a phase that involved carving up the week so that we could each spend time with the kids separately.

It was crazy to think I would have them every other weekend. It was crazy to think that every Thursday night they would be at their dad's house. It was crazy to think that we would no longer all be vacationing together. As crazy as all of this sounded, it was part of what needed to be addressed as we crafted our post-divorce landscape.

We were fortunate to have divorce coaches to help us navigate the decisions that would usher us to a place that balanced everyone's needs and desires to the greatest extent possible. We wanted to construct a new reality that preserved our respective pre-divorce roles as closely as possible. Prior to our divorce, my husband had been the one working outside the home and I was a full-time mom and therefore responsible for the day to day logistics of managing the family. Because I had the logistical flexibility to take care of them before school and after school, we decided to construct a schedule that kept the school week as intact as possible. We visually laid out various options on the whiteboard until we reached a schedule that felt fair and balanced to both of us. The schedule that we ultimately decided upon was that they would be at their dad's house every Thursday night and every other weekend.

We both agreed that it was important to us that the kids see their dad more frequently than that and I was absolutely committed to facilitating that relationship. On Monday, Tuesday and Wednesday nights he helps with driving the kids to and from activities, helps with homework and is welcome in my house to visit with the kids.

We both remain as flexible as we can to cover for each other when we have a conflict so that the kids can remain in the care of one of their parents rather than hiring nannies or babysitters more than we need to.

Learning to Live in the Present

The divorce process can be so emotionally and mentally exhausting because it requires an astronomical amount of mindpower all at once. There were times when I felt like a high-speed computer central processing unit as I was reflecting on the past and the future concurrently. On an emotional level, I would replay all the highlights and from time to time a flicker of doubt would creep in as I would ask myself if we were doing the right thing. Then I'd have to switch gears and shift back to the future and review financial projections as we contemplated different scenarios. It became overwhelming fast, and I would need to reign myself back to living **today** because anything more than that was just too much to process.

One of the most powerful lessons the divorce process taught me is to truly live in the present moment. The one thing that we all share ubiquitously, regardless of status, race, age, gender or any other delineation, is that we all only have this day. Any of our lives could radically change from one day to the next or from one moment to the next. We could spend all day ruminating on the past or obsessing about the future. But, if we spend all of our time doing either one of those, we miss out on what's right in front of us, right now. Our kids are this age only once. The time to enjoy them being this age is **now**. The people who are currently in our lives now aren't guaranteed to be in our lives forever, as moves happen and life happens. The time to enjoy them is **now**. Although we may want to fast-forward through the divorce process and get to the other side, it would mean missing out on all of the other things in our lives that we have to be grateful for. Don't put celebrations and milestones on hold just because you're in the midst of a divorce. Do it anyway. Even if you're going through the motions. If it's bittersweet because the celebration doesn't look like it used to, do it anyway. If you're hesitant to host a gathering because you might get emotional, do it anyway. If you're worried that someone else might not approve of the way you're handling things, do it anyway and do it your way. The people who love you and care about you will show up, meet you where you are and walk with you through this journey. The ones who don't weren't your people to begin with, so thank them for showing you who they really are, and redirect your energy to the ones who reciprocate your love.

The cumulative effect of the emotional stress over an extended period of time undoubtedly takes its toll on a person, and some days I felt like I was merely in survival mode. Meeting days were especially exhausting, and I would be mentally and emotionally exhausted for the rest of the day and into the next. It's so important to remember to meet yourself with compassion, grace and forgiveness during these times of peak stress. Some days I barely even had the energy to partake in activities that I usually love. I love to cook, and even the thought of menu planning didn't appeal to me, and the thought of grocery shopping felt exhausting.

When you feel incredibly physically, mentally and emotionally compromised, it's easy to cascade into a downward spiral of negative thoughts. It can be hard to transition out of a place of negativity into a mindset of positivity, hope and gratitude unless you have a strategy and a few go-to mindset rewiring techniques. There are a few things you can do to work through that.

Privileges, Not Obligations

One approach that will help you transition into a more positive and grateful mindset is to view everything you do as a privilege rather than an obligation. It's easy to get mired down in all of the responsibilities you have and get overwhelmed by to-do lists. Try to find deeper meaning in what you do, even the little things, and strive to find little morsels to celebrate. For example, you might replace, "I have to cook dinner every night" with "I'm going to ask my kids what they would like me to cook and will enjoy making them their favorite meal." You might replace, "I have to exercise" with "I'm excited for this opportunity to invest in my health and wellness."

Any time you find yourself complaining about something, immediately ask yourself how you can transmute it into something to celebrate. For example, replace, "I'm annoyed that I got the farthest-away parking spot in the lot" with, "I'm grateful that I'm healthy and strong enough to walk this distance." Rather than focusing on what you don't have, focus on what you do have. The more you train your brain to think like this, the more natural it will become and the less tolerant you will be of anything that makes you feel lower-vibrational emotions and will quickly make the necessary adjustments so that you feel good in that moment.

Pick Your Mantra

Another approach that is especially helpful is to pick a mantra and recite it to yourself several times a day. It can be something you heard or an original saying that you make up. Either way, the most important thing is that it resonates with your soul. Paying attention to the feelings it produces is a great indicator for how well it resonates with you. Through this process, you are rewiring your mind and reprogramming your new belief system. The way your future turns out is heavily influenced by the thoughts you are thinking right now. So, it is important to choose words carefully, to say them with intention and feel the feelings you want to embody.

Whatever phrase you choose, say your phrase like it's a fact. Say it with conviction. Say it so unwaveringly that you'll smile at the memories you have from the past but quickly and naturally shift your gaze to the future, as you are flooded with anticipation and excitement about what is to come.

The phrase that was my anchor during the divorce process, and still is, is, "The best is yet to come." I still recite this phrase and always will because I believe that despite one's circumstances, the Universe always has surprises in store for us that keep making life sweeter every day.

Discovering Your Authenticity

- What things in your life bring you happiness?
- Have you ever tried to force something that wasn't meant to be? What was the outcome?
- Can you think of an instance where you didn't follow your intuition, and regretted the decision later on?
- If you were to assign percentages to your thoughts, categorizing past, present and future, what would they be? How can you shift them so that the "present" category is as high as possible?
- How can you reframe your obligations as privileges?
- What mantra that makes you feel empowered, energetic, etc. resonates with you?

9

NAVIGATING DIVORCE ENERGETICALLY

The best gift you can give your children is two happy, fulfilled parents living in their authentic realities. Whether or not they are married to each other is secondary.

Our thoughts play a huge role in creating our own realities, and the good news is that we can choose our thoughts like we choose anything else.

When you focus on the negative aspects of any situation by dedicating your thoughts to them, you activate more negativity in your vibration and thus become a magnet for more negativity. By rewiring your mind to choose more positive thoughts, you are signing up to be an empowered deliberate creator with the Universe. Give negative thoughts less air time by replacing them with positive thoughts.

It's pretty clear that the old model of divorce isn't working. Just the word divorce conjures up images of contentiousness, animosity, separatism, blame, guilt, awkwardness and a myriad of other feelings that make us feel not very good. They don't make us feel good in the moment and unless we are able to figure out a rock-solid way to overcome them and embody emotions that make us feel good on a sustainable basis, we will remain stuck and stifle the ability to move on.

I am here to tell you that by deliberately creating with the Universe, we can paint a completely different landscape. The issue is that with divorce and so many other situations in life, we are conditioned to accept the image or the imprint that someone else hands to us.

I refused to accept the image of divorce that society wanted to hand to me because I didn't like how that felt. I don't like how I feel when there is tension, animosity, contentiousness, blame, guilt, superiority complexes and separatism.

I like how harmoniousness feels. I like how I feel when things are flowing and there is ease. I like how I feel when people are happy and there is congeniality. I like how I feel when there is love. I like how I feel when I have mental clarity. I like expressing love and appreciation and kindness, and I know that taking the path of least resistance is in everyone's highest good and is immensely powerful in allowing all of those touched by this process to come into closer alignment with their own inner being. I knew the old paradigm wasn't going to get me there so I embarked on a new trajectory and made it my mission to do it a new way.

I've come to learn that that is where the power is. It's when you are aligned that you are able to draw directly from Source Energy, and it is from that place that we will always be in the best position to receive what is in our own highest good. There is no better gift you could give to yourself or to your loved ones than the gift of aligning to who you truly are. We will take a deep dive into the concept of alignment later in the book after we have taken a backstage tour of the laws of the Universe.

This scenario is not unrealistically lofty nor unachievable. An entirely new world opens up to you when we dream big and do things that others aren't willing to do. You buck certain systems. That's how you shatter antiquated programming. Not by staying within the bounds of what's been culturally and socially deemed as acceptable. Not by staying where you're cozy and comfortable. Not by limiting yourself by fear or doubt. I'm a dreamer, and I like it that way. I like when I feel creative and limitless and unstoppable and aligned and energized and feel like the world is my oyster. It's not just **my** oyster; it's all of ours. We all have it within us and it is well within the realm of your power to achieve this feeling and state of being. Living in alignment with Source Energy is the best place from which to experience this Earthly journey.

The good news is that anyone can get there. You just have to bring a healthy dose of self-awareness and open-mindedness to the table coupled with your creativity and willingness to roll up your sleeves and do the work. Most people who are handed a coloring sheet and a box of crayons, would start to color the picture. I want you to get to a place where you turn the paper over and draw your own picture.

Don't be discouraged by any backlash or opposition you may receive from others. There will always be others trying to test the waters and infuse doubt in the process. Remain unshakeable. That is a ubiquitous and normally expected part of any situation that involves a huge upheaval and is infiltrated with change. There is an unconscious tendency to resist change, and the underlying factor is fear, all kinds of fear: fear of the unknown, fear of failure, fear of what others will think and the list goes on.

Get to a place where you are so sure of yourself and so committed to your decision that you brush off the unsupportive commentary as effortlessly as you brush a gnat away from your face. There's no way to totally avoid the doubt from external sources, but you can get to a place where you transmute the doubt into fuel for your mission. Dazzle the naysayers.

When you make a decision for yourself that is in alignment with your inner being, don't look back. Pour all of your energy into building your new reality.

How many times have you witnessed that the "vibes" totally transform in a room when your former spouse walks in? The energy immediately shifts and everyone seems to start observing others for how they will react. You might even hear whispering and observe a level of awkwardness and apprehension. Energetically, everyone is pulled down because the focus is on the outcome of the relationship, and in today's society, so many people equate divorce with failure. There can also be chatter that involves blaming, guilting, finger-pointing and shaming.

Instead consider your former spouse to be a person who was highly instrumental in shaping you into the person you are today and helped to deliver tremendous clarity on the direction you want to move going forward. The fact of the matter is that the relationship played a huge role in molding both people into who each of you are today, and has helped both of you further sculpt the reality you want to create for yourselves going forward. There is no room for blame in this situation. There is no room for guilt. There is only room for gratitude and appreciation and kindness and love and for all of the other positive aspects that the relationship produced. Every relationship is a gift, no matter what the details were and regardless of how it ended. Every relationship holds the potential to illuminate parts of ourselves that we didn't even know existed. Expressing joy and gratitude and appreciation and all of the other "feel good" feelings is most assuredly the pathway to alignment.

The principles discussed in this book apply under any set of circumstances. Regardless of one's external circumstances, the primary objective is to deal with whatever issue you are facing from a place of alignment. The old paradigm won't get you there. Approaching divorce through this revolutionary, totally avant-garde, think-outside-the-box type approach will serve you not only through this process, but will pay dividends for the rest of your Earthly journey.

It is important to remember to meet yourself with compassion on your path to alignment. It is more challenging to fully achieve alignment during a process of such heavy transition because you are still trying to disentangle yourself from your old life. The only way out of a situation is to move through it, and you must push through all the messiness and the pain and the discomfort to arrive at a place where you have the best chance of operating from your Highest Self.

For the concepts in this book to be applied effectively, you will need to part with the old way of operating. This will require a more active, conscious way of living. The foundational element of this approach is energy. Vibration. Taking steps toward mastering alignment will allow you to unlock the secrets of the Universe. This is where your true power is unleashed.

Statistics

I think it is especially important to provide a backdrop here because it will illustrate the radical shift I made over time in the way that I approach life.

Truth be told, every aspect of my life used to be riddled with fear. In my younger days, I was a master at the craft of worrying. If there wasn't something readily available to worry about, then I'd worry about not having anything to worry about. That's how extreme it was. I would quickly fill in the space and create a situation to stress over. I remember sitting on my bed as a child and worrying about going to school the next day. I didn't have a test or a quiz or anything else beyond the realm of a normal school day, but I always assuredly created something to worry about. In high school I played softball, and before my games I'd worry that I'd make an error and cost the team the game. My life was dictated by fear and I felt powerless.

In college, I was an Actuarial Science major, which is a field heavily concentrated in mathematics and statistics. As I went through life, I would always measure my situations up against the statistics and had the unconscious expectation that I would just fall in the majority because that's what the numbers dictated. I just assumed that if I maintained my status quo, the outcome would be more or less predictable.

I didn't realize it at the time, but all along I was living in a very disempowered state. I was crippled by fear and I was allowing statistics to play the starring role in causing me to feel tethered and bound. I wasn't willing to take risks because the statistics told me otherwise and I would always focus on the scenario that would not be to my benefit. I wasn't willing to step outside of my comfort zone because the chance of something unfavorable happening was greater than zero.

Up to this point, I had zero idea that it was possible to take an active part in creating my reality. I thought life just happened. I thought you just drifted through and took it as it came and just hoped and prayed that nothing bad would ever happen.

Now, I've come to the realization that by choosing to live consciously, we can actually influence the statistics rather than letting them influence us by lulling us into a state of complacency and unconsciousness. Choosing to live consciously allows us to harness our true power, as the Universe always loves to partner with a creative and conscious mind that is determined to operate from its Highest Self. From this place, everyone wins. As people start to wake up and make more conscious, mindful decisions that honor who they are, over time the results of new paradigms will be reflected in the statistics.

We hear tales of people defying odds every single day. How do they do it? Mindset. They refuse to give up. They pour all of their energy into their passion and refuse to let any doubt creep in. They cling onto their vision tenaciously and will stop at nothing to bring it into fruition. They don't do it by sitting on the sidelines and expecting that they will be yet another statistic.

Because of the life events I experienced and the way in which I taught myself to transmute pain into power, I no longer subscribe to statistics the way that I used to. I've come to learn that we are immensely powerful in the roles we play in the way in which our lives unfold and that no idea is too crazy or too "out-there" or too cutting edge.

The statistics on the aftermath of divorce can leave a person downright shaking in his or her boots, fraught with negative thoughts about all of the unpleasant short-term and life-long repercussions we would experience and be thrusting upon our kids. The statistics are staggeringly high and you don't have to look very far to find doomsday statistics for any negative effect including lower grades, school drop-out rate, psychological issues, suicide rate, etc., each with many factors that could be controlled.

I quickly realized that all of these factors have fear-based undercurrents. They all point to the "gloom and doom" worst case scenarios and perpetuate a feeling of fear. While it is important to entertain the potential considerations, they in no way, shape or form dictate your outcome. Statistics can play a major role in keeping people stuck.

I found it somewhat irritating that nobody talks about the potential benefits of divorce. Why is the spotlight not being shone on the upside? Why is nobody highlighting how immensely transformative the shift can be and how it can launch everyone involved to a higher place? Why isn't anyone getting excited about the fact that the life you're stepping into can be immensely better than the past? Why isn't anyone talking about the fact that the situation, if done right, can teach kids life skills and introduce concepts that they never would have been exposed to otherwise. What matters most is how the landscape looks, and you can play a huge role in designing that. That was precisely the moment I decided that I am going to take this by the reigns and do this differently. It was in this moment that I felt like someone had poured lighter fluid on the spark that flickered within me and I was ready to embark on this mission. My spirit took the helm and I placed my complete trust in the infinite powers and wisdom of the Universe.

Man-Made Agreements versus Soul Contracts

The pull of our souls is much more powerful than any man-made contract. We lose sight of the fact that our souls have pre-planned experiences and pre-scripted meetings orchestrated well before we incarnate to this Earth. The terms and conditions of such man-made contracts and agreements are often based on the information we have available to us in the physical world at a particular point in time and we make decisions based on what our conscious minds tell us to do. When what transpires in our physical reality is not in congruence with the terms and conditions that these man-made pacts have set forth, we often panic and go into fear mode. Understand that while everything may not always make sense on the surface, underneath it all is a predetermined and divinely-orchestrated plan and every moment is unfolding perfectly. Sometimes experiences are dropped in and completely shatter the plans we made for ourselves in the physical world. It may feel as if our lives are turned upside down and we are sitting squarely in the middle of a million little pieces, contemplating how we should move forward. Any time we are grappling to make sense of a situation, there is tremendous opportunity for growth and transformation.

Our souls call in the experiences that we need for our own evolution, and free will is the mechanism that allows us to call in those experiences so that we can master what we have come to this Earth to learn. Sometimes these experiences are not in alignment with the terms and conditions of man-made contracts. Our souls want to be free. They want to be free to move about this Earth and drift from experience to experience so they can learn the lessons they have come here to master. Our souls are the students, life is the teacher and this Earth is our classroom.

In my situation, the purpose of my marriage was to bring these four children into the world. Once our soul contract had been fulfilled, the well was dry in terms of what we could give each other in a romantic, committed relationship. The terms of our contract were up, and we had the choice to either resist the expiration of that contract by forcing ourselves to remain in a stagnant reality that no longer served us, or flow with where life was taking us and embrace the change. Our marriage was undoubtedly a huge success because we carried out the mission our souls sought out to fulfill.

Formulating Your Ideal Version of Life

As we go through life, we are in a constant state of observation. We observe other relationships. We observe other families. We observe other people's lifestyles. We observe different jobs. As we soak up different personal experiences and observations, we are constantly formulating a mental image of what the ideal scenarios are for any given part of life.

The image that exists in your mind and in your heart embodies all of the aspects that you desire, as developed through your observations and experiences, and you are the only one who is intimately familiar with all elements of it. Even if you tried to articulate them to someone, you would be attempting to recall them from your conscious mind and would be leaving those which reside in your subconscious out of the equation for the moment and therefore would not be relaying a complete representation of what your ideal image is. It is not until you make another observation or have another experience that the element is activated in your memory. Furthermore, the list of ideal components is forever growing because each day you make new observations and have new experiences and imprint more elements that you desire into your image.

As you go through life and are formulating your ideal image, you are picking and choosing certain elements from a wide variety of different situations and incorporating them into what you deem to be your perfect scenario. The more contrast we experience, the more information we have to work with and the more elements we can incorporate into our mental image.

Take a romantic relationship for example. It's something we can all relate to. Everyone has a highly-individualized and unique mental image of what a perfect romantic relationship is. Some of this will come from observations you had and some will come from personal experiences. Growing up, you observed the interactions of your primary caregivers, whether they were in a marriage, a committed relationship or any other romantic arrangement. You likely observed things you wanted your ideal romantic relationship to embody and you likely observed things you didn't want to emulate. For example, if there was a lot of disharmony and tension, you may envision a relationship that encapsulates harmoniousness. If you observed two disconnected parents who were living two separate and parallel realities with little interaction, you may crave a sense of connectedness. On the other hand, if you observed a lot of physical affection and kind, loving words of affirmation, you may wish to bring those elements to your own romantic relationship.

It is highly unlikely that one example will deliver all of the elements that you desire. We subconsciously place the burden onto others to deliver us our mental image and are often disappointed when they aren't able to. Measuring our own current realities against a perfect mental image leaves us in a state of disharmony and dissatisfaction and compromises our chances of aligning with Source Energy because we are coming at it from a place of lacking and are focused upon the disparity between your current reality and perfection. We are often disappointed when no one person or entity can match the image that we've created, but it is unreasonable to expect any one person or any one thing to be the sole source of our happiness and fulfillment.

Above all else, the ultimate goal is to align with Source Energy and then ask yourself how you need to arrange your physical environment to support that. Sometimes you can get there by making minor adjustments in your current situation and other times it means completely shaking up your physical reality and turning your life upside down temporarily and then rearranging the pieces so that you are living in a place that is authentic to your spirit and promotes your alignment with Source Energy. Again, we will explore the concept of alignment more thoroughly later in the book.

The real question comes down to which scenarios in your life can help you achieve alignment. In what scenario can you operate from your Highest Self?

At this point you may be thinking that you're not the only one affected by your decision. There are other people involved and there is a chance that you may affect their lives unfavorably as a result of getting yourself to your higher place. Rest easy knowing that there's no such thing as "messing up someone's life," as any situation can be navigated from an empowered state by flowing with the laws of the Universe.

Regardless of whether you decide to stay in your marriage or leave, you need to make sure your energy is whole and your focus is not split. There are places in life where the sweet spot is in the grey area by finding that perfect blend of black and white, but this is not one of them. You need to get to a place where you are all-in or all-out. That place looks different for everyone. Wherever you heart is, is where that place is. Wherever your spirit is whispering for you to go, is where that place is. Wherever your soul pulls you, is where that place is. The worst thing you can do is say things like, "I'm going to stay in the marriage, but my heart's not really in it." or, "I'm going to stay for the kids and compromise my own happiness." or, "I'm divorced but I'm constantly wishing that our family were still intact." or, "I'm divorced but I'm feeling guilty about making the decision that I made."

Once you make a decision, it's important to rally every aspect of your being, mind, body and spirit and make sure they are all congruent with and supportive of your decision. Focus on the goodness of whatever scenario you decide upon and reframe your self-talk to celebrate the joyful aspects. Unless you concentrate your energy, you'll be living in a constant energetic quagmire and your ability to live authentically will be unattainable and your true potential will be hindered significantly. Pick which high diving board you want, take the plunge head first and don't look back.

Let's explore a situation where there are children involved. The best gift you can give your child is the gift of being an aligned parent. Kids are astutely observant of and highly responsive to the energy a parent is emitting, even if they aren't aware and aren't able to articulate exactly what they're feeling. Children are highly intuitive and energetically sense when parents are operating from their Highest Selves and when they are not.

Shortly after we moved into our new house, my daughter commented that she could tell I was happy now. Despite the fact that we were still in the middle of the divorce process, she could already energetically sense that I was in a better place. My energy was already starting to make a huge shift.

Above all else, our job as parents is to give our children the gift of our authentic selves. Sometimes that can be accomplished within the marriage and sometimes it can't. In the case where authenticity and alignment with Source Energy is not able to be accomplished within the marriage, you need to look at the scenario and find the hidden gems and the gifts that are waiting to be discovered.

When someone is not approaching a situation from a soul-based perspective, it is so easy to go down the rabbit hole of all types of non-productive emotions that, simply put, don't feel good. Blame, guilt, doubt, resentment, anger and regret are all ego-based. It is normal for these emotions to come up during the process, and each time they present, it is an opportunity to go deeper within and direct it toward the purpose of our expansion. The less we are moving in the direction of alignment, the more likely we are to succumb to these emotions and let them direct the process. It's a slippery slope. Once you start going down the path of these negative emotions, you quickly pick up speed and before you know it, you're moving at a blazingly-fast pace and the chances of a graceful and peaceful outcome are less likely.

On the other hand, if you are committed to a growth trajectory, then you realize that you can consciously replace emotions that don't feel good with emotions that do. You make a conscious effort to choose gratitude, joy, contentment, peace and other high-vibration emotions in every moment. Once you start to embody these "feel good" emotions, they spread like wildfire and you become magnetic for more positivity. Rather than condemning the other person and blaming them for making your life miserable and causing disruption to your family, you're in a much better position to maintain an attitude of gratitude. You'll think and say things like:

- "Isn't it wonderful that this relationship helped highlight what I **do** want in a future relationship?"
- "I'm so grateful for all the things I learned about myself."
- "I'm grateful for the role all of this is playing in my expansion."
- "I'm grateful that we have found harmoniousness and authenticity."

It can be easy to get stuck on the thought of "We aren't a family anymore." That couldn't be further than the truth. That thought assumes that there is only one definition of family and that it is a rigid construct. Families are defined by relationships, not by pieces of paper. When two adults make the decision to go separate ways on an emotional level and incorporate new partners into their lives, the opportunity for more perspectives and love to flow in expands quickly. The key to navigating this thought is to reframe it and process life as it is. If we are constantly comparing our lives as they are to what we thought they should look like at this point in time, we will remain stuck.

The Opportunity to See Contrast

Many parents who decide to separate feel guilty about the fact that they weren't able to deliver a totally flawless, intact family experience to their children. They feel guilty that they weren't able to show them the perfect version of family life, as defined in their minds. Remember that every person has an individualized version that is based on life experiences and observations of the world.

This way of thinking can be reframed in a healthier way. As a result of a divorce, the children will be exposed to two different realities and as a result will have even more options for elements they can incorporate into their own version of what family life embodies.

When children experience two different realities, one at Mom's house and one at Dad's house, they witness and partake in two different ways of doing things for each aspect of living. They may witness options at both ends of the spectrum and as they formulate their own image of what family life is, may choose to emulate one of those or pick any other point along the spectrum. For example, we follow a plant-based diet in my household. We rely largely on fruits, veggies, nuts and seeds for our nutrition and sustenance. Dairy is offered in small amounts, and meat is never an option. In the kids' dad's house, an omnivorous diet is served, including meat, chicken and fish as options. As a result of the different diets in the households, the kids are exposed to two different ways of eating and are in a position to more consciously choose the path they will take.

I will even go so far as to say that children affected by divorce have advantages and opportunities that aren't available to children who are not exposed to such diversity. They are being prepared for life and are learning life skills such as flexibility, compassion, forgiveness, and effective problem-solving to name a few. They are exposed to different ways of living at a younger age and are positioned to more consciously ponder how they may want to live their lives, rather than feeling like they need to replicate a model of how family life is supposed to look.

There is tremendous benefit for kids to witness two parents making the decision to honor who they are individually, and cooperatively working together to provide the same degree of love and guidance in their parental roles. Kids are highly perceptive of how co-parents interact with each other. Recently, my daughter came up to me and out of the blue commented that having divorced parents is totally fine. She highlighted that she has two of everything...two bedrooms two bikes, etc. But more importantly, she made a profound observation that transcended any materialism, and said she was happy that she gets to see both of us so often. Lastly, she excitedly shared that she perceived me and her dad to be friends with each other. That part resonated with me deeply. We didn't sit down with the kids and assert our commitment to maintain an amicable relationship. While harmoniousness was absolutely the spirit and the tone we strived to display, she just observed it based on the way in which we interacted (and still do), and her observations validated that we were doing this right. We are both free in our new realities and are in a much better position to bring our best selves to every aspect of our lives. Kids always pick up the energetic vibrations, so it is crucial to put yourself in a place of authenticity.

It is normal for parents to want to protect our children from hardships or challenges. We don't want to see them struggle. However, we must not lose sight of the fact that the purpose of our existence is not to deliver a totally flawless and sheltered existence for our children. It is more important that we empower them with a mindset of growth and gratitude and usher them to a place where they can align with who they truly are and live a life that is authentic to who they are. It is from this place that everything else like happiness, abundance, peacefulness, gratitude, appreciation, kindness and compassion flow freely. The best way to usher them into a place where they can connect with their Higher Selves is by blazing the trails and being the first to take the leap into your authenticity and showing them how you can stand in your truth unwaveringly regardless of what's going on around you. You can't get there any other way than by taking the pathway through the self. The best thing you can teach them is how to find peace in the midst of chaos. How to find happiness in the midst of heartbreak. How to find hope in the midst of despair.

The qualities and skills our kids have gained from this experience are incredibly valuable. At the tender ages of 15, 12, 11, and eight, they are prepared for life. They have just lived through a period of massive change and upheaval, and I'm confident this experience has empowered them and has laid the groundwork for them to navigate anything life throws their way with grace and confidence. They will adeptly transmute any challenges they encounter into stepping stones as they climb their individual mountains of growth and transformation.

Part With the Objective of Being Right

In a situation where there is the potential for high conflict and stress such as divorce, there can be a tendency to blame, and it is easy to fall into the trap of making it your mission to be right. This is **not** the path that is in your highest good. Blaming, guilting, controlling are all low-vibrational states of being and inevitably lead to not feeling good, because they lead us to resentment, anger and animosity. The Law of Attraction promises that we always attract what we are, so when we embody negativity, we attract more of it. Furthermore, as you bring emotions like this to the situation, you will experience resistance because the other side will naturally feel the need to push back and defend themselves.

It's normal to want to feel good. It's normal to want to feel happy. What we don't realize is that learning to feel good can be natural and easy; we just need to teach ourselves how, and practice feeling good on a constant basis. We don't realize that we are the ones holding ourselves hostage to negativity and that we've created a Catch-22 dilemma for ourselves that we can't find our way out of. We first want things to be easy so we can be happy, but we don't realize that we need to make ourselves happy first and then ease will follow. Happiness assuredly does not come from insisting that you are right, controlling, resisting, blaming, guilting or forcing. It comes from flowing with the current. It comes from moving about freely in the direction life is taking you. It comes from expressing gratitude. It is not until we learn to let go and release negativity and assert our intent to be happy that things will start flowing with ease.

Discovering Your Authenticity

- How can you be a rebel and shatter antiquated programming that no longer serves you?
- How can you play an active role in helping others become more consciously aware of their belief systems?
- How can you become a pioneer in adopting new belief systems and encourage others to do the same?
- How do you take an active role in creating your reality?
- Think about certain relationships you have in your life and try to identify the soul contract. Is it readily apparent what your souls have come together to fulfill?

10

BETRAYAL

The pull of our souls is infinitely more powerful than any man-made contract we could create.

Betrayal. Infidelity. It's one of the topics people tip-toe around because it's ugly and messy and uncomfortable to discuss. The time has come for us to crack this topic open. I've learned that we don't get anywhere by sweeping things under the rug and talking about issues behind closed doors. Growth and personal expansion can't happen in a place that is void of transparency and vulnerability. You need to be willing to put yourself out there and take a deep dive into the topics that others tip-toe around.

Infidelity has touched my human experience and has undoubtedly shaped who I am. It would not be authentic if I didn't address it and usher you through my evolution of thoughts as I progressed through the healing process. We don't get anywhere if we aren't willing to crack open and dissect the not-so-pretty parts. In avoiding the real issues, we only defer our healing and make it more difficult to move forward in a healthy and productive way. By sharing our stories with each other, we each set an example for others to share theirs too.

I knew the old-paradigm view of infidelity wasn't going to get me anywhere productive. Measuring one human's actions against a man-made contract of any kind is pretty black and white: you either comply or you don't. If you would have asked me about my views on infidelity a few years ago, you would have witnessed some very black and white thinking, much like this. There's right and there is wrong. There is good and there is bad. After a lengthy period of deep soul-work and introspection, I have arrived at a place where I have been able to meet the situation with compassion, grace, understanding and forgiveness. I didn't get there overnight, and one should apply a healthy dose of self-forgiveness and self-compassion as they move through this process, as there is no "normal" timeframe through which to move. Whatever speed you are going is the right speed for you, and while there are support systems in place to help usher you through the process, the vast majority of the heavy lifting will need to be done by the individual whose human life experience this has touched.

Let me start by saying that discovering that you've been cheated on sucks. Plain and simple, it sucks. It doesn't matter how old you are, how evolved you are, whether or not your are enlightened or whether you've been together with someone for one year or 30. We all have the human element governed by our ego that wants to pull us into emotions and reactions that embody anger, resentment, blame, retaliation and hate.

As much as I was committed to taking a self-preservation path through this experience, I felt the same human emotions that one would expect in the aftermath of discovering infidelity. Shock. Horror. Despair. Anger. Grief. Sadness.

Various scenarios kept running through my head as I tried to make sense of everything. I would fall asleep at night, anxious to get a break from the barrage of thoughts that would run through my head during the day, only to be greeted with a dream that it didn't really happen. I enjoyed the dream while it lasted, until I awoke in the morning, at which point the nightmare began over again. I'd find myself replaying the past, as if it were stuck in an infinite loop. I couldn't help but wonder if he was really where he said he was on occasions he was gone. Thoughts along those lines haunted me for months, until the shock finally wore off and I was in a place to internalize the experience and incorporate it into my healing process.

For years I think we both recognized that our marriage was in a state of disrepair, and we each had our own coping mechanism for dealing with it. During that time, I was running my life on autopilot. I was caught up in the day-to-day operations of running a big and active family and was the one responsible for all things house-related, which for us was no small undertaking.

Although I wasn't sleeping in somebody else's bed, my heart wasn't fully invested in our marriage either. I was so bleary-eyed for so many years of our time spent raising the four kids we had within seven years, that I really think I was lulled into unconsciousness and was putting one foot in front of the other, just trying to keep the ship afloat. Some days I felt accomplished simply by virtue of getting out of my pajamas before noon or because I was able to unload the dishwasher within five minutes with no interruptions. Day-to-day life was definitely not easy, and I was barely even conscious about where I was putting my energy. I'd go to playgroup with the kids and the dialogue exchanged among all the other moms was more or less the same, so I figured this is just the way married life is. I felt stressed much of the time and felt like I was a single parent, not because he wasn't willing to pitch in more, but the demands of his job often kept him away from home due to work or other obligations.

Given that we had two totally disparate jobs (he worked outside the home and I was a full-time mom), I experienced the disconnect, but always assumed that connection was something that would automatically make a grand entrance at some future date when life got easier, like when the kids were older, or at least when they were more self-sufficient. We were each burning the wick at both ends, pouring our energy into our respective jobs, and I never took the time to stop and realize that no real investments were being made in our primary relationship.

I don't think I would have ever categorized our marriage as a rock-solid, connected relationship. Maybe we were when we were in our early twenties, when we were just married and we were in that illusory invincible stage where you think you're the ones calling all the shots in your life (hello...wake up calls ahead!), and life was about all things 20-something like the wedding, the first house, new cars, careers, materialism, consumerism. There was no deep soul searching happening in those days, that's for sure. Shortly into our marriage we experienced profound losses together but somehow they didn't pull us closer together. In many respects, cracks in the foundation started to appear at that point, as we coped individually and in our own ways. Those cracks permeated the foundation for what would eventually be a house of cards.

I of course had always felt the heavy weight of our disconnect, but never developed an action plan as to how this would be addressed. I oscillated between "that's just the way married life is" and "maybe we should explore this at some point." Sometimes part of me thought it was a significant issue and sometimes part of me would dismiss it. I had given thought to the notion of divorce from time to time and would contemplate where I stood on the issue, and every time I did, I would quickly be launched back into the old-paradigm, fear-based way of thinking. "Divorce is a failure. Divorce flies in the face of our religious beliefs." "The kids would never be 'okay' with it." I thought about continuing to trudge through, staying in it "for the kids." But were we really doing the kids any favors by putting on a happy face and pretending to be happy? Is this really the mental image of marriage that we want to give them? Do we grin and bear it until the youngest moves out, at which time we move our separate ways? I was having these thoughts, but never shared them openly because it made me feel too vulnerable. It felt scary. It invited fear and doubt and uncertainty and several unknowns and stressful thoughts and a whole host of other feelings that I didn't want. The quick fix was to continue to ignore it and focus on my responsibilities or other distractions, so auto-pilot mode ensued. But that's survival mode. That's not living. That's existing.

It was necessary for me to take this retrospective, longitudinal account back through our married years to attempt to piece together the events sequentially that lead us to this point. No events in our lives happen in a vacuum; in each and every situation, all prior events in our lives play a part in delivering us to this precise moment. I needed to explore this at a much deeper level if I wanted to have any chance of moving through it. I contemplated the concept of betrayal at unprecedented depths and arrived at a newly-crafted definition, as I feel the concept is deserving of a much more expansive and all-encompassing interpretation. One that extends beyond the physical realm in which we are accustomed to living into one that envelopes matters of the heart. The idea of infidelity often causes people to focus on the physical violations, but the concept of betrayal encompasses so much more. The concept of betrayal is not just limited to marriage, as it permeates all areas of our human existence.

When the life you are living on the outside is not congruent with what you hold in your heart, there is betrayal. When what you say, do, think and feel are not in harmony, dishonesty and betrayal are taking place somewhere. Any time you are withholding information that affects someone else's life, there is betrayal. Any time you are misleading someone intentionally, there is betrayal. Any time you aren't sharing your deepest, darkest secrets, fears and anxieties with those whom you have close relationships with, those who are deserving of that information, there is betrayal. Any time your outer world doesn't reflect what's going on in your heart, there is betrayal. Sometimes this means you are not being honest with yourself and sometimes it means you are not being honest with another person. Sometimes it means both. Either way, anywhere there is a misalignment, we need to dig deep and ask ourselves some very important questions. In our most sacred relationships, we must show up with the courage to be vulnerable and put ourselves out there, even if it means that we run the risk of a reaction that we didn't expect.

The purpose of this chapter is by no means to condone or encourage extramarital affairs, nor is it to shame anyone who has engaged in such an act. My hope is that your eyes will be opened to a new and progressive way of viewing the concept of betrayal, and by reframing it in this way, realize that what initially feels like your greatest pain may in fact be the pair of scissors that allows you to cut ties with your unfulfilling past and launch you into a reality that allows you to soar.

When evaluating affairs within the construct of the physical world, on the surface they represent complete devastation. Complete and utter defiance of the terms and conditions of a contract to which two parties once agreed. But, the chaos is just an illusion. The way this story is playing out is the perfect exemplification of how, on the surface in the physical world, it may appear that chaos is ensuing, but behind the scenes everything is unfolding in a divinely orchestrated manner. Without the discovery of the affair, I very well may have continued living in an unfulfilled reality. An extramarital affair is a prime example of a catalyst. Catalysts are meant to shake up our current reality. They're meant to jolt us out of our unconscious modes of operation into higher realms of consciousness.

It's an example of how a soul contract overpowers a man-made agreement. Remember, the pull of our souls is infinitely more powerful than any man-made agreement. Before we incarnated, we chose the lessons that we want to focus on during this phase of our incarnation, and our souls will move mountains to call in the experiences that we need to have the opportunity to learn these lessons.

People are often quick to point the finger at those who were involved in extramarital affairs; after all, that is the easy route. It's the route that involves the least amount of soul work and allows us to fall back on the very black and white, old-paradigm way of thinking. Where is the compassion, grace and forgiveness in that? Where is the room for growth and transformation? It is each individual's job to dig deep and perform the transformative soul work, and whether or not someone does that is that person's choice. It's not anyone's job to "teach someone a lesson." We must always stay focused on our own individual journey and ask ourselves what we can learn from each experience.

Discovering Your Authenticity

- In what areas of your life are you not being honest with yourself?
- In what areas of your life are you not being honest with others?
- How does the thought of stepping into your truth make you feel?
- Is your physical reality congruent with what you hold in your heart? If not, what is holding you back from aligning them?

11

FEAR

Transmute your fears into personal power.

Fear is hands down one of my favorite topics to talk about, mainly because I spent years, decades actually, in fear mode, and have finally gotten to a place where I simply no longer create space for it in my life.

One of **the best** compliments that someone can give me is to tell me something I did was bold because, to me, it signifies the recognition of the absence of fear. I'm super-addicted to the feeling of fearlessness. It reminds me of that feeling of invincibility we all had when we were kids. The best kept secret is that we **can** get that back.

Love and fear simply cannot coexist. The concepts are binary and mutually exclusive (sorry that's the actuary geek in me!). Fear is what keeps us tethered to antiquated patterns. Fear weighs us down. Fear fuels anxiety. Fear causes us to clutch on to antiquated belief systems. Fear causes us to resist change. Fear stifles us from gaining the courage to step into our authentic realities. Fear ultimately crowds out love.

The degree to which we embody fear is directly related to our ability to give and receive love, and when we are in fear mode, our ability to give and receive love is hindered significantly.

In the spirit of total transparency, our time in counseling wasn't the first time I had ever thought about what life would be like if we were divorced. I realized that I was living in fear mode and it paralyzed me so much that I would shudder at the thought of making a change. Questions about how to orchestrate the logistics of everyday life so it would run smoothly, the effect the divorce may have on the kids, what the long-term implications would be and whether I might ultimately regret the decision constantly plagued me. The list of things to worry about was lengthy, and fears of all of them disabled me from making a change.

I contemplated the tradeoff between keeping our family intact and my own personal happiness, and for a long time, I sacrificed my individuality. I realized that by tethering myself to physical-world considerations, I was denying myself significant spiritual growth, and was denying my kids the gift of having a truly aligned, fulfilled, happy parent. But, I didn't have the courage, strength or confidence to address the issue and make a conscious decision about what would be in my highest good.

The issue with fear is that we relinquish our power over to it. Fear is not the enemy, but handing your power over to it is. We let it cripple us and stifle us in a reality that disallows us from claiming our personal power and prevents us from tapping into the Universal Energy that is available in unlimited quantities. Nobody benefits when we feel smothered and stifled.

Sometimes the fear originates within us and sometimes we acquire a fearful mindset by observing the fear-based behaviors and commentary of others. "What if I fail?" "What if I don't make the team?" "What if I don't get into the college I want to?" "What if I struggle socially?" The list of things to be fearful of, and therefore worry about, is lengthy and expansive, and it can spiral out of control quickly if you don't have a mechanism to reign it in and process it in a healthy way.

From a Law of Attraction perspective, we attract what we think about. The more we obsess and perseverate on negative or unfavorable outcomes, the more likely they are to come to fruition. Energetically-speaking, fear is a low-vibrational emotion and is not where we want to be on the spectrum of vibration. These concepts will be explored later in the book.

I've come to realize that fear can be an incredibly empowering and motivating force and can usher us to a level of action that would have not been achievable in the absence of it. Without it, we may become complacent and continue to let life happen to us without taking an active role in creating our own realities. Fear illuminates that which we do not want, and thereby gives us an opportunity to do something about creating a reality that we do want. It's an invitation to identify exactly what we fear, what fuels that fear and what needs to be done to transform the fear into power.

Here's a very real example of something most of us deal with in order to illustrate this concept: Most of us worry to some degree about our well-being and the well-being of those we love. In fact, in my younger days, I think I was a full-blown hypochondriac because with any minor ailment that I or someone I know would have, I would worry that it was the start of something serious. Even when everyone was healthy, I would worry about them getting sick or dying. My fears were usually totally unfounded and contrived and would bear no correlation to the current reality. I was, in fact, creating something to worry about.

I am still concerned about the well-being of the people in my life, but I no longer let it rule my thoughts. I have totally reframed and transformed this way of thinking and now channel that energy into more productive and enjoyable initiatives. Instead, I enjoy today. I celebrate what we have and who we have in our lives in this very moment. I like to view every day as a party because I know that today is all we're guaranteed. I used to reserve the dining room in our house only for special occasions, and now I view every day as a special occasion as each day offers many things to celebrate. So, now instead of worrying, I get up, dress up, and soak up all the amazingness each day has to offer.

Go easy on yourself and don't blame yourself for fearful thoughts. It's totally normal to have these thoughts, particularly when you are facing a situation that involves a lot of change. Start having an internal dialogue that sounds something along the lines of, "Universe, thank you for making me aware of what I do not want. Help me direct my energy into co-creating a reality that is in my highest good." The manifestation chapter of this book will help you put into place effective modalities for partnering with the Universe to co-create your reality.

Discovering Your Authenticity

- What do you fear?
- How might you be able to transmute your fear and allow it to motivate, rather than paralyze you?
- Look back on your life and try to recall things you feared in the past. Go back five years, 10 years ago, etc. Did any of those fears come to fruition?
- Document your fearful thoughts and replace them with faith-filled action items.

For a special bonus on transmuting your fears into personal power, visit https://liveauthentically.today/soar-resources to download the guide.

PART III

ADJUSTING YOUR WINGS

Life unfolds with ease when we learn to glide in the direction the wind is taking us.

12

NAVIGATING CHANGE: FOCUS ON STEPPING INTO THE NEW

The secret to navigating change in a healthy way is to stay focused on what you are stepping into and view the future as an adventure.

Once you make peace with the idea that life is a steady stream of changes, the way you handle change can be radically transformed. Rather than resisting it, learn to flow with it. We have a natural tendency to want to bask in the moments when life is wonderful, stress is at all-time lows, and resist change because we don't want to see that phase of life come to an end. But, there is a natural rhythm to life. There are good times, followed by challenging times and eventually the good times return. That same ebb and flow continues ad infinitum. You must get to a place where you soak up whatever is in front of you right now, accepting that wherever you are is where you are meant to be. The secret is learning to flow **with** the change rather than resist it.

For most of my life, I used to resist change and had a really hard time processing it. I always had a really hard time leaving whatever phase I was in, out of sadness that I would miss certain things. When the kids were little, I would never welcome the exercise of filling up their dressers with the next biggest clothing size because it symbolized the end of a certain developmental phase and I was sad to see it end. As I reflected on my emotions further, I realized that I was always so focused on what I was stepping out of and giving insufficient attention to what I was stepping into. It didn't even occur to me that the next phase we were about to embark on could be even more exciting than the last.

Divorce comes with a significant amount of change and at times it can feel downright dizzying. Depending on the complexity of the situation, times of transition mean that potentially every aspect of your life is touched by change at varying degrees and that is understandably overwhelming. Regardless of how harmonious the situation is or how committed both parties are to navigating the situation with minimal conflict, there are still several decisions that need to be made within a short period of time. It can feel incredibly overwhelming emotionally because we are processing the past and future all at once and our minds tend to be pulled in a million different directions.

Processing Life as IT IS - Not as You Thought it Should Be

I can confidently say that nobody's life turns out exactly as planned. I don't think anybody would disagree with that. Regardless of who you are or how skilled of a planner you are, everyone experiences things that are unexpected. When this happens, we always have a choice to either resist the change or flow with it. The goal in any situation should be to make peace with where you are and flow with the current. Until you have learned how to accept that where you are is precisely where you should be, you will be living in a constant state of resistance. You will never be able to absorb and enjoy the present moment because your mind will always be preoccupied with where you thought you should be. Resistance is exhausting and drains us of energy that could be directed into more productive and enjoyable initiatives.

Instead of giving attention to the gap between your current reality and the one that exists in your mind, take a moment to look around and appreciate all that you have. The goal is to close the gap. The point where each of us is in this very moment is precisely where we are meant to be. Nowhere else. Shifting into a gratitude mindset often is the point that starts the tsunami of positive thoughts. The more positive thoughts you think, the more momentum they will garner and you will eventually start to notice that energetically you feel lighter and happier and more accepting that where you are is where you are meant to be. Flow with the current of life and let the waves carry you.

Consciously Choose Where You Direct Your Energy

We all have a finite amount of mental and emotional energy to expend each day. What you may not realize is that you have a choice in where you concentrate that energy. Start by developing an awareness of where your thoughts are naturally gravitating. Are you ruminating on the past? Worrying about the future? It takes an enormous amount of emotional energy to ponder various future scenarios, and you can easily end up worrying about the most catastrophic outcome. What if I run out of money? What if I am lonely? What if I regret the decision I'm making today? Whenever you find yourself ruminating on the past, or worrying about the future incessantly, ask yourself how doing so is serving you. How are those thoughts helping you in this day, in this moment? I think you'll be surprised to learn that most often they are not. Make a conscious effort to redirect your thoughts by replacing any unproductive thoughts with expressions of gratitude for what you have right in front of you in this moment.

Live in the Present

It is often not until you are spread so emotionally, physically and mentally thin that you realize that for your own sanity and well-being you are left with no choice other than to make a choice about where to concentrate your energy. In the past, you may have tricked yourself into thinking you can process everything all at once, but that only delivers situations of split energy and that never leads to anything productive or fulfilling. The Universe always knows what it will take to cause us to change how we live. Living in the present used to sound like a cliche to me. It was one of those phrases that sounded great but I never really understood how to effectuate it in my own life or why it was even necessary. Up to this point, I had prided myself on the idea that I could rival any high-powered computer central processing unit by being able to run several programs at once. Well, any situation that leaves you feeling overwhelmed and fraught with worry at times will teach you exactly how to live in the present. Trying to process the past, present and future contemporaneously was exhausting and never lead to me feeling good. I realized I needed to simplify and concentrate where I was focusing my energy. Yes, there are times when being in a state of transition may call for you to make certain decisions that affect your future, but it is important not to dwell there and make a conscious effort to pull yourself back to the present.

Regardless of what our own current situations are, the one thing we all share is that we only have this day. Nothing is guaranteed and everything is temporary. Everything is transitory, everyone and everything, and this moment you have in front of you right now is the only moment that will be exactly like it. Marvel at its uniqueness. Recognize the blessings. Find the silver lining. Express gratitude for the abundance. Any one of our lives can change with a phone call or with a decision somebody else made or another's actions. We must make it our mission to immerse ourselves in what we have in front of us and soak up all the goodness. It is often not until we look for it that we realize the abundant blessings we are surrounded by. When we focus on all the good, the good gets better and the thoughts of lack and limitation and negativity quickly start to fade away.

Celebrate What Hasn't Changed

It's easy to get swept up in all the changes that a divorce scenario brings. One might feel inclined to focus on all the changes and potential stress that comes with them, but in the midst of a time of such upheaval, it is important to anchor to the things in our lives that we value that haven't changed as we consciously design our lives the way we want them to be going forward.

Take a conscious approach to deciding what will change. Don't assume that just because a certain aspect changed for someone else or for most people that it will necessitate a change for you. An example is relationships and friendships after the divorce. Just because people have been repeatedly exposed to a "delineation" mindset when it comes to divorce, which includes separating belongings to disentangle their realities, understand that relationships need not follow the same trend. If it's important for you to continue relationships with people on your former spouse's side, by all means make the gesture to do so.

Your social circles also need not change. People express concerns about their friend groups changing as a result of a divorce. It doesn't necessarily have to change dramatically, or at all. But, if it does, as a result of whatever factors that are out of your control, there are 7.6 billion people in the world, so I'm pretty sure there's no shortage of like-minded people, or better yet, people who can introduce you to new ways of life.

While the primary relationship between the parents has changed, the children can still have two parents who care for them and love them. They can both be intimately involved in their children's lives and can have as much day-to-day interaction as both people can agree to have.

The Best is Yet to Come

It is normal to resist change because of the underlying fear that the past is better than the future will be. I'd have to challenge that sentiment with the questions, "How do you know that your best days aren't yet to come? Why do we always cling onto the past as if our best days are harbored in our memories? Why can't our best days be alive and well in our dreams? Our hopes? Our visions for our future?" What you are thinking at each moment plays a critical role in shaping your future, as we will explore in the chapter on manifestation. The key to navigating change in a healthy way is to focus on what you're stepping into and get really, really excited about it. Embody the emotions that you want to feel now. Start expressing gratitude for them now. Envision yourself in a completely different life and start believing that you are deserving of it and it will happen.

Channel Your Inner Adventurer

Comfort and familiarity can feel like a fuzzy, warm, cozy blanket, but on the couch isn't where the adventure is. Change can offer tremendous opportunity to expand your horizons and discover parts of yourself that you didn't even know existed. We live in a vast world where opportunities for life experiences are limitless. So, get out there and try something new!

Discovering Your Authenticity

- How do you typically respond to change?
- Do you seek or avoid change?
- Do you have fears associated with change?
- How can you challenge yourself to process life as it is?

13

CO-PARENTING: CREATING YOUR NEW REALITY

Open-mindedness is a critical component of the negotiating and decision-making process.

Our reality prior to the divorce had been predicated on very traditional roles and responsibilities. The majority of my husband's responsibilities were outside the home, as he provided the financial means for our family. Mine were concentrated inside the home and encompassed all things kids and house-related. We were now charged with the task of delineating our respective contributions and reallocating our roles and responsibilities in a way that was fair and balanced across two different households.

Every situation is highly unique and has various considerations across the entire spectrum of categories, from logistical and practical to emotional or spiritual. It is neither reasonable nor possible to evaluate all categories and the constituents of each. Instead, I will provide some overarching ideas that can be applied to any situation that is highly complex and that requires in-depth problem-solving. Various situations bring various degrees of complexity and can leave one feeling overwhelmed with too many decisions to be made in a concentrated period of time. That is totally normal. Depending on the situation, there may be certain legal considerations and emotional implications that are outside your realm. Remember that there are professionals available in any area where you have a need to give you guidance and direction. At the end of the day, though, remember that you are the only one who is in tune with what feels right to you. Make sure you articulate what resonates with you and don't settle on something if it doesn't feel right. It's better to invest the time and energy up-front to design a reality that is congruent with who you are and balances everyone's needs and wants contemporaneously to the greatest extent possible than to have to go back to the drawing board later because you didn't listen to your gut.

From the get-go, I anchored to my unwavering belief that our reality doesn't need to look like anyone else's. We had a blank slate and therefore had the latitude, flexibility and autonomy to design it to look any way we want. That's pretty much how I approach every aspect of my life. I don't need my anything to look like anyone else's anything. In fact, if everyone is doing something one way, I'm usually the one looking to break the mold by brainstorming revolutionary and avant-garde ways of doing it. Just because something has always been done a certain way doesn't mean that it's the only or best way of doing it. Sometimes what the world needs most is for someone to blast a mega-dose of creativity and shatter the old paradigm so that the new can be constructed. Name yourself Director of Creative Solutions and get excited about designing your new reality your way.

Several people asked me how we were going to delineate our friends and family. Each time I heard the question, my reaction was to wonder why they had to be delineated at all. This wasn't some sort of draft for which we were team captains who would alternate choosing who we wanted on our teams. The only thing that was changing relationally was the relationship between him and me. We would both still serve in our role as parents and both still be very present in the lives of our children. There was no reason for us to not have the same friends. We both cultivated relationships with various people, irrespective of which family tree they fall under or whose circle they originated from. The change in relationship between me and my spouse didn't need to necessitate the need for other relationships to change.

We continue to strive to create an atmosphere of harmoniousness and inclusiveness and even celebrate certain occasions together. The only way to undo old ways of operating is to model the change, not just talk about it. We try to look at it from the perspective of which child's event it is and include who he or she would want to share the day with. Moments before I sat down to write this chapter, I sent an invitation to a party for my youngest daughter's First Holy Communion. We will all be celebrating the occasion together at my house and both sides of our families are invited and welcome to attend. By setting the tone of harmoniousness, we make it easier for others to feel comfortable operating under a new paradigm.

While it is exciting to start with a clean sheet of paper and design something new, it is important to anticipate that from time to time emotions may bubble up, as we are still learning to let go of the past. There are elements of grief and loss associated with that, and we need to remember to honor and validate those emotions as they arise. While we are working to establish new traditions, we are naturally reminded of our old traditions, and it is normal to reminisce. We may feel compelled to dig our heels in and fight for our position and maximize and optimize whatever position we are negotiating. Through my experience, I discovered that the most expeditious way to arrive at a solution that is fair to both sides is to put myself in the other person's position and see the situation from the other parent's vantage point. For example, if the other parent is asking for more time with the kids, avoid the knee-jerk reaction of clamoring for that time by refusing the request. Instead, challenge yourself to consider the other perspective and the potential hidden gems and embedded opportunities. How might the kids benefit from the proposed arrangement? How might I benefit?

Open-mindedness is a critical component of the negotiating and decision-making process. You are not designing this reality alone. Different people bring different perspectives and suggestions to the table, as shaped by their belief systems and life experiences. It is important to remember that there is always more than one way to accomplish the same objective. If you both propose different ideas and neither person is amenable to adopting the other's idea, perhaps compromising by meshing certain aspects of both is the answer. Also, consider that neither may be the answer and you might need to go back to the drawing board and brainstorm alternate solutions.

In addition to creating your new reality, you also need to create your own definitions. Redefine what family is and view the definition as being highly dynamic, flexible and responsive to changing conditions. Society suggests that a complete family needs to have two parents for the kids. I'm telling you that a complete family is defined however you choose to define it. Some families have single dads. Some families have single moms. Understand that families are not defined by their structure, rather they are defined by the love that exists. I will even go so far as to say that even within the scenario of divorce, you can still call yourself a family. You can still preserve certain traditions and memorialize those traditions via whatever photos you decide to take in the moment. Don't get hung up on what things "should" look like as dictated by others or by society. If it feels authentic to who you are and feels right in the moment, do it. The moment when we start to overthink it is the time doubt or regret can start to set in.

When creating your new reality, it is easy to assume that any new situation you enter will be inferior to your past experiences since the measuring stick you are using is based on a unit defined by the old reality. Throw that measuring stick away. You will remain stuck if you are constantly comparing your current reality to what it used to be. Create new experiences and traditions and enjoy them for what they bring to your life. You will be introduced to new people along the way and none of it will be by chance.

Our parenting agreement articulates what we agreed upon and what is legally enforceable, but because we are committed to maintaining a peaceful atmosphere, in actuality it acts like an insurance policy. It sits in my file cabinet and is something I hardly ever reference. Reality often presents us with situations that we couldn't predict or foresee and we are both very flexible with regard to making accommodations that reflect the changing landscape.

We are rock star parents **because** we are divorced. Yes, I did just say that. We are rock star parents **because** we are divorced. We are both living lives that are more authentic to who we are and we are no longer in a place where we need to compromise who we are for the sake of keeping a romantic relationship that has fulfilled its purpose intact. As a result of stepping into our respective truths, we have optimized our ability to be the best parents we are capable of being and know that our children will benefit tremendously from this shift. While the relationship between us has changed, we are still carrying out the mission we have come together to do, and I will always pour my heart and soul into my role as parent. It is even easier to do now because I am aligned with who I am and am truly living authentically.

The kids sleep at my house on Christmas Eve and the kids' dad comes over early Christmas morning so we can all open gifts from Santa together. After opening presents, we were having fun taking selfies and goofing around in front of the Christmas tree, and later in the day, I went back to revisit the pictures. In particular, I noticed on my and his faces something particularly noteworthy. We both looked so relaxed. So happy. You could literally see the lack of tension in our facial muscles in the pictures. Because we were no longer trying to infuse a sense of freshness and vitality into a relationship that was well past its expiration date, we were free to be who we are and enjoy the moment of all of us being together.

Discovering Your Authenticity

- How open-minded do you consider yourself to be, and how can you expand your open-mindedness even further?
- When you are negotiating or problem-solving, how willing are you to give thoughtful consideration to the other person's perspective and ideas?
- In what areas of your life are you stuck in antiquated definitions or rigid thinking, and how can you relax the rigidity of those notions and exercise more creativity?

14

TOUGH MOMENTS

Authenticity is the only way to your truth.

Embedded within the mechanics and practical considerations of designing our new realities came some pretty raw and real moments. In the months after we told people we were divorcing, we were peppered with questions surrounding our decision and the situation as the kids tried to make sense of everything.

Authenticity and the Lack Thereof

After we officially decided that we would, in fact, be moving forward with the divorce, one of the many decisions we needed to make was when we would communicate this decision to the kids. We decided to let them finish out the school year so that their academic performance wouldn't be affected by the many changes that would be taking place over the next several months. We decided that the communication date would be sometime in June.

The time between making the decision to get divorced and starting to communicate our decision to the kids, and subsequently family and friends, was incredibly challenging. Why? Because our current realities, the life we were living on the outside, was not at all authentic. It didn't match up with what was going on in our hearts. It wasn't congruent with the plans we were so meticulously and surreptitiously crafting behind the scenes. We were harboring this secret and the pressure built with each passing day. On the outside, it was life as usual...hockey games, weekend plans, get-togethers and even a birthday party that all of our family and friends attended, during which we had to put on happy faces and pretend like everything was fine. And that's just the day-to-day stuff. Big stuff was happening too. Houses were being purchased. Divorce attorneys were contacted. Meetings were taking place. Decisions about how we would carve up our schedules and share time with the kids were being made, and we could talk about none of it openly.

During this time, I thought a lot about the concept of authenticity and what it means to live an authentic life. I realized that to me it means living a life where you feel free to stand in your truth with confidence and grace. It means aligning your thoughts, actions and beliefs to be congruent with your truth. It means taking off the mask that society makes us feel like we need to wear to feel accepted and loved. It means living without secrets. It means living a life that is free of judgement. It means living a life where you're doing things **your** way. It means a life that embraces your light **and** your dark. It means a life that embodies the essence of who you are at the deepest core of your being. It means living a life that is unstifled by any external factors such as societal conditioning or others' expectations, and free from any internal blocks such as fear or doubt.

Some serious excavating started to happen during these challenging months. I thought a lot about the way I had been living and what factors influenced my reality. I further refined my belief system. I started to think more broadly about all of the situations in which people aren't living according to their own truth. People who choose their careers to please their parents rather than follow their passions. People who are going through the motions of everyday life without putting their heart and soul into it. People who are living with predetermined expiration dates on their marriages. People who seem happy on the outside but are miserable on the inside. People who are stuck in unproductive patterns. People who are living under the society-induced illusion that happiness stems from acquiring material possessions. People who are living in fear of change.

Those three months were unequivocally the most challenging parts of the process, mainly because I was so energetically weighed down as we straddled two totally disparate realities, one that reflected a business-as-usual front, and one that reflected a complete upheaval of virtually every aspect of our lives. It was a total energetic quagmire and to say that it was draining would be a gross understatement. As challenging as those three months were, the one silver lining that I clung on to was that there was a light at the end of this dark tunnel. There was an expiration date on the buildup of this pressure. In three months' time, we would finally be able to take the first step into our authentic realities in a very transparent and public way.

Kids' Intuition

It has always blown my mind how intuitive kids are. We are all born with open hearts and open minds as well as an uncanny ability to read other people's energy. But, before too long, society will imprint its expectations and conditioning on us, and it is easy to doubt our thoughts to the point that we officially silence our inner voice. One evening during the week before we told the kids about the divorce, I was laying down with my daughter at bedtime. After we finished her book, she asked me if a mom and dad can ever break up. I paused for a moment in complete and utter shock that she broached the topic that was on my mind all week, as we prepared to deliver the news to the kids that coming Saturday. I took this opportunity to paint a backdrop and set the stage for not only the conversation but for what to anticipate in the months to come. Very directly, I said "Yes, they can. Sometimes a mom and a dad decide not to stay married, but they still remain friends. When they decide not to stay married, they both still love their kids and care for them just the same. There will still be times that everyone is together and times that are they are not. Some things have to change when that happens but their love for their kids never changes." I was so glad to have the chance to have this discussion with her because it gave me the opportunity to validate the feelings that her intuition stirred.

Telling the Kids

Weeks in advance, we chose a particular Saturday morning to communicate the decision to the kids. Finding a time where all four kids were home at the same time was no small task, and it was important to communicate on a weekend that was relatively free from other obligations so that the kids could process the news in whatever way felt comfortable to them.

We gathered them all in the family room and told them we had something we needed to tell them. Based on the looks of excited anticipation on their little faces, I think they were expecting to hear that we were surprising them with a trip to Disney World. Much the opposite...we were about to tell them that their lives as they knew them were about to change.

All along, I assumed that the kids' dad would be the spokesperson, as, statistically speaking, there was a much greater chance that he was going to be able to deliver the news with much less emotion than I would be able to. We knew we had a very narrow window in which to communicate some extremely powerful messaging before emotions started running high, so we crafted the message carefully in advance. I looked over at him, and it was clear that I needed to be the one to do the talking. So, at the eleventh hour and totally unrehearsed, I took the reigns and was somehow totally emotionally centered as I delivered the following message:

> *"We wanted to tell you that we have decided to get a divorce. Some things will be changing, but the one thing that will always remain the same is that as your parents we will always love you."*

The reactions were about as varied as their ages: one left the room immediately, one was completely silent, one had a steady stream of questions, and one stated that he didn't want divorced parents.

We told them about our respective houses that we had chosen and fielded many questions about logistics, schedules, how often they would see each of us and anything else they threw at us. We constantly reassured them that while some things would be changing, there were plenty of things that would be staying the same. This was their first foray in life with being put in a position to have to deal with change, and a lot of it all at once to boot, and the way in which the message was framed was critical to how they would perceive the news.

While it ranked as one of the least pleasant discussions we had ever hoped to have with the kids, we both felt a tremendous sense of relief since we would now be able to talk about it openly.

Our Daughter Challenges Us

The decision to separate has undoubtedly stirred up many questions in the minds of our children, some of which are internalized while others are vocalized. My firstborn never passes up an opportunity to vocalize her questions, and at one point in the process explicitly called us out on the carpet. While it is challenging to have these discussions in the moment, each discussion propels us to dig deeper so we can explore and articulate our beliefs. One evening, she challenged us with an admittedly valid question regarding our wedding vows. She wanted to know what happened to the "'til death do us part" part of our vows.

Holding ourselves to the "'til death do us part" covenant we agreed to at an earlier time certainly was one option, but wasn't the only option. It can be a viable option in certain circumstances, depending on a number of different factors, including religious beliefs, the happiness quotient of both people, views on divorce and the extent to which each person is committed to growth. With respect to spiritual evolution, I have found that there's no going back. Once the ship leaves the dock, there's no turning it around. At times, truth be bold, I tried. I tried to ignore some of the catalytic experiences, through people, events, songs, etc. that caused me to embark on this journey. In some respects, it's easier to drift along in your unconscious reality. I've also found that lack of growth only delivers a very superficial, unfulfilling journey. It's a surfacy existence of going through the motions and checking boxes. There is no depth. There is no self-discovery. There is no transformation.

Romantic relationships can be complicated, the love is often conditional, and can change over time. It is based on man-made agreements, and our knowledge is limited at the time we enter into these contracts. We always come together to fulfill a soul-purpose, and articulate terms and conditions we force and expect ourselves to live by. In the process, it is easy to lose sight of the fact that behind the scenes there is an agenda orchestrated by the Universe. The fact that we are trying to superimpose a man-made agenda over a soul-based contract is what makes things complicated and confusing. That's why we often struggle to make sense of situations when they don't go according to our plan. We forget that the Universe, complete in its wisdom and foresight, has a grander plan at work.

Regardless of the question asked, I always tried to anchor on the unconditional nature of love that exists between a parent and a child. No matter what our kids do, no matter where they go, no matter who they love, no matter what they decide to dedicate their lives to, my love for them cannot and will not change.

Attending a Birthday Party

Early in the divorce process, the emotions that went along with processing the divorce often came on fast and furious and always without warning. One Saturday afternoon, I took my youngest daughter to a friend's birthday party at a gymnastics facility. I was watching her frolic around on the mats with her friends. I had been looking forward to this small sliver of time when I could simply sit and enjoy watching her have fun with her friends, but before too long I found myself reflecting on our situation. It hit me like a ton of bricks that out of a group of about ten kids, she was the only one who had parents who were going through a divorce. She looked so tiny and innocent. It made me sad to think about her regularly asking whose house she would be at the following weekend, as she struggled to find a rhythm in a new life that involved splitting her time between two parents' houses. At the party she was fully immersed in the fun, but this was one of those moments I had to coach myself through by reframing it and reminding myself to just live in the moment. In this moment, she was having fun with her friends and that's all I needed to be concerned with.

A Family Get-Together

Shortly after we separated, the kids and I got together with my brother, his wife and kids for dinner. The get-together went well as usual, as the adults conversed and the kids were off playing all evening with their cousins. That night when I was tucking my daughter into bed, she started crying, so I asked her what was wrong. She said that her cousin kept asking where the kids' dad was and why he wasn't there. My daughter said being asked made her feel sad because it reminded her that we weren't all together and she wanted him to be there. There were many times in the past where all six of us were not always present for every family dinner, because of activities, his work travel schedule or other unavoidable factors. But, this time was different. This time a feeling of finality hovered over all of us, even the little ones. It was a reminder to me that the profound reverberations of this situation were felt not only within our nuclear family but beyond it as well. We are all learning how to navigate our new normal, and we are all grieving the loss of the way things used to be. Grief is such a strange animal. It always comes with varying intensities, and never with warning. I was so appreciative that she shared this information with me, as it gave us the opportunity to take a deeper dive into what family life used to look like and what it looks like now. I validated that it was completely normal to be sad, and assured her that there would be occasions in the future where we would all be together.

Every End is Really a Beginning

All of the kids have always loved artwork and writing and have grown up spending hours at the kitchen table drawing, painting and writing their own stories. One day as I was going through a stack of papers trying to decide what to keep, I came across a story one of my kids wrote. It described the kids' dad's life story, through her own eyes. It read:

> *I learned how to walk. When I was 13 I met Pam. Then, I was a pizza maker. And I got married to Pam. Pam had four kids. We moved into a house for 10 years. We moved into a ginormous house. And we got divorced. Then moved to different homes. "The End"*

My knee-jerk reaction was to throw it away and pretend I never read it. Of all the things she could have included, she included that we got divorced. Of course she did. How could I expect that she wouldn't? Silently wishing that she hadn't included it was like denying that one of the most pivotal events in her life, and our lives, didn't happen. That would have been total avoidance and denial. It has impacted her, and in a big way. It is part of the way in which she describes his story, and will always be part of the way she describes her story. I had to sit with the realization that as she gets older, she will probably never remember us all living together under one roof. As much as I wanted to throw away the paper and erase from my memory that I read it, that wasn't possible, and it wouldn't at all be authentic and honor what really happened. I needed to sit with the emotions, and mentally write the rest in my mind. It's not "The End", it's actually the beginning, the beginning of a new chapter of our lives where Mom and Dad live in two separate houses and step into their individual respective realities, and are in the best possible position to be their happiest.

A Reason, a Season or a Lifetime

One evening, we were in the middle of making dinner and doing homework and my eight-year old walked up to me and told me that she was sad that we got divorced. She said she was sad that she didn't have more time with us being together like the other kids did. It caught me slightly off guard because while she was smiley and happy on the outside, I was swiftly reminded that on the inside she was still processing her pain.

I think it is a normal reaction for all kids to never stop desiring for their parents to be together. It is, after all, how they remember their prior reality, and it is totally normal for them to want the two people who were responsible for bringing them into this world to remain together in the same space. Even as adults, we often pine for days gone by or for the way things used to be. We may find ourselves wishing that the people who were part of our lives years ago were still a part of them now. The reality is that everyone in your life is there for a reason, a season or a lifetime. Not all relationships as they are today are meant to last forever.

I took this opportunity to explain it to her from a spiritual perspective. I said, "You have lots and lots of friends, and I know that you probably hope that you will have this group of friends, all together exactly as they are today, for the rest of your life. As you move through life, you will go to different schools, some will move to a different state, some will have different interests and be pulled in different directions. As much as you wish to remain friends with everyone you know today throughout your whole life, the truth is that you won't know all of them forever. That happens to adults too. We meet different people and may lose contact with others. The relationships that we have in our life today may look very different at some point in the future. Your dad and I spent time in a marriage together to fulfill a very important mission. Our purpose together was to give the world four really amazing gifts, and those gifts are you and your siblings. Once that mission was fulfilled, there was nothing more that our spirits needed to accomplish and the relationship no longer satisfied what our souls yearned for. There was nothing left between us and we were not in a position to model for you and your siblings what a marriage is. We don't have to be married to continue to love you and care for you in the best way we know how. That has not and will not ever change."

Having it All

When we announced that we were getting divorced, many people were surprised. From the outside, we seemed to "have it all." Between us, we seemed to have the whole package, including the high-powered career, the full-time mom, the kids, the gorgeous house and everything else anyone could ask for. The dizzying pace of everyday life and everything it entails can lull you into autopilot mode and mask deeper issues. We were a classic case of two people drifting apart, and never took the time to stop and ask the important questions along the way.

"Having it all" is defined by you and is a matter of the heart. It is determined by the answers to questions that only you can answer, such as "Are you happy?" "Are you fulfilled?" "Are you living a life that is authentic to your inner being and who you really are?" Those answers can only be found after doing some deep excavating and exploring ourselves in the depths. They can only be found after taking a close look at yourself in the mirror and doing some serious self-discovery work. Living life on autopilot will ensure that everything gets done, but it won't ensure that you get in touch with who you really are. It will only allow you to keep skimming the surface and will never facilitate deep-sea diving.

Discovering Your Authenticity

- Examine some of the important relationships in your life. Do you think each of those people crossed your path for a reason, a season or lifetime?
- Think back to some of your toughest moments. How might you be able to reframe them from a growth-based perspective?
- What spiritual significance did these challenging moments have?
- How did these challenging moments change the way in which you navigate life?
- Sit quietly with yourself and listen to the whispers of your soul. Go ahead, ask your heart, "Do you have it all?"

15

REFRAMING THE NEW REALITY

Life unfolds with ease when we learn to flow ***with*** *the current rather than against it.*

As much as we may have welcomed the change and attempted to meticulously craft our new realities with as much due consideration as possible, we couldn't possibly anticipate all future scenarios and we would inevitably be presented with situations we couldn't foresee. We have a choice in how we respond to these situations. We can either flow with the current or against it. Life is so much easier when we flow with the current. It's normal to cling on to what **we** want or fixate on **our own** idea of a particular outcome, but with that comes a desire to control, which only creates resistance.

Adjusting to New Schedules

Throughout all of my parenting years up to that point, I had never had regular and extended chunks of time away from the family. I remember struggling to find a three-hour window in which to get my roots touched up at the hair salon, and even late-night Target runs were met with an embarrassingly high level of excitement because it was one of the few times I'd be able to get away without any kids in tow. Between my husband's jet-setting travel schedule and the kids' activities and other obligations, our family calendar already resembled a strategic game of "Risk", and I used to feel guilty about scheduling any time away from the kids.

I remember in exquisite detail the first night the kids were at their dad's house. I packed up their belongings and organized them by the door so that everything would be ready by our transition time of 6:30 p.m. They have duplicates of basic necessities at their dad's house, but of course always want to bring along some of their favorite possessions. It felt extremely surreal as I stood and stared at the heap of bags, blankets and stuffed animals waiting to be loaded and transported to their dad's house. Packing them up was always something I thought we weren't going to have to do until they went away to college. He came to pick them up, the door closed and the house was eerily quiet. For the first time in years, I had a golden opportunity to hear myself think, and I didn't even want it. I shuddered at the thought of staying home in an eerily quiet house with no one to tuck into bed, so I would often make plans to go out. In those early days, I spent much time and energy trying to figure out my new normal, and now I have fallen into a groove that I absolutely love.

With a new schedule comes abundant opportunities to make more mindful decisions about how time is spent. Things we took for granted in our prior reality such as time that was unlimited and unstructured, is now viewed and treated as a cherished treasure because we now each have less time with them than we used to. Our new realities prompt us to make more conscious and mindful decisions about how the time is filled. Fortunately for us, because our situation is amicable, we have settled into a groove in which everyone is comfortable being in the same space and sharing certain experiences together, and there is more overlap in the time that we have with the kids as compared to what is articulated in our official documents.

Witnessing Growth

Any life situation where there is a significant amount of change or one that causes us to re-think, re-examine and re-define ourselves inevitably presents a golden opportunity for significant personal growth. Human relationships are our greatest teacher and play a vital role in making the unconscious parts of ourselves conscious, as each interaction sheds light on unhealed parts of ourselves and prompts us to heal them. As we take self-inventory and redefine what is important to us, we reprioritize what we give our attention and energy to. As we transform and evolve into higher levels of consciousness, those around us can't help but notice the change.

We have both grown tremendously as individuals as a result of this process, and in the spirit of true authenticity, sometimes it feels a little bittersweet to witness growth in the other. It may sting a bit to see a former spouse march into the future as a refined version of himself or herself, complete with tools and skills that have been honed as a result of this relationship, and bring that to future interactions and relationships. It's normal to wonder how the outcome might have been different if other behavior patterns were in effect. Part of me thought, "Wouldn't it have been nice to benefit from more open communication during our marriage?" And he could easily think that it would have been nice if I had been more carefree during our marriage and had stressed less about things that really weren't that important. But then I remind myself that this is precisely how it's supposed to work. Human relationships are meant to help us bring the unhealed, unconscious parts of ourselves into the spotlight, and we use that new-found awareness to craft the new and improved version of ourselves. Our time together and time spent restructuring our family allowed us to bring certain aspects of ourselves under the spotlight, and such growth and transformation would not have been possible in the context of our marriage. We are both bringing the best version of ourselves into the next chapter of our lives, and I am truly grateful for the opportunity for growth and transformation that this relationship has bestowed upon me.

Recently we were exchanging texts on a topic that we saw from two different vantage points. It was a respectful, open exchange and afterward I asked him what he thought of my response. He replied that he could tell I wrote it in coach-mode. I laughed, and said that, in the spirit of full disclosure, the first draft of my text consisted of three paragraphs that defended my position eloquently and tried to convince him of my point of view. But, I deleted them and simply responded that I wanted to sit with it, and thanked him for his perspective. That is growth. Growth is being able to put your own agenda on hold and suspend your opinions as you attempt to step into the other person's shoes for a moment and try to understand from that perspective. I was immensely grateful for this interaction, as it allowed me to sharpen my sword even more as I get more and more comfortable with practicing the skills of empathy and compassion.

We are all coaches of each other. We are all students and teachers. We all play a part in helping each other heighten our own self-awareness so that we may continue to grow and evolve. It doesn't matter where we are on our own journey; we can all learn from one another. The evolved are teachers of the less-evolved, and the less-evolved are teachers of the evolved. Every human interaction is an opportunity to heighten one's own self-awareness. The key is to totally abandon any superiority complex that may be hovering, as that is a sure-fire way to get back into your ego, which will not allow you to come at everything with love.

Truth be told, it took some getting used to sharing our parenting responsibilities in a way that we hadn't shared them before. During the process, it was suggested that we have a weekly call to go over logistics, plan for future events and discuss any pending issues regarding the kids. It was sort of a business call. Early in the process, I was not amenable to this idea because I was feeling somewhat possessive and protective of my role as Mama Bear. I had been owning and orchestrating all things kid-related over the years, and I think it was an attempt to continue to operate as we had been. I was somewhat resistant to the idea of the kids' dad taking a much more active role in parenting and also embedded in this was probably a little resentment. After a couple of months, I realized that in my resistance, I was actually making it more difficult than it needed to be and that if I just flowed with the way things were in the new reality then things would be that much easier. Now, we have regular calls and the heightened communication really does make everything much easier.

Seeing the kid's dad step up his game and take on a role and responsibilities that were formerly solely mine took some adjusting for me. He had always been an active and present dad for the kids, but I was not accustomed to involving him in every minute detail of the kids lives, mainly because it simply wasn't necessary and wasn't part of his role. I was witnessing him stepping into his parenting role more than he ever had before, and I remember thinking that had he been doing this throughout our marriage,

I wouldn't have felt spread so thin and we might not be in this position. The reality was that he probably felt spread thin, too, just in other ways. He was burning the wick at both ends too, with work and travel, and it just wasn't part of his role to be involved in every single detail. We were both stepping into a new reality and the way in which we operated in the past notwithstanding, it was and still is in everyone's best interest that we all be as involved and informed as possible.

The Grieving Process

I wouldn't be honest with myself if I said that I don't miss being in our original, intact family unit from time to time. I don't dwell on it and I don't stay there long, but from time to time my thoughts are there. It's a normal part of the process. Even in the absence of stress and change, who doesn't look back on a former period of their lives and miss it on occasion? When in college, it's normal to miss certain aspects of high school, such as seeing all of our close friends on a daily basis, now that everyone is scattered across the country at various universities. When we are engrossed in the work world, it's normal to pine for the care-free college days, where the work-to-play ratio was a lot lower than it is when you have to juggle a full-time job and other responsibilities.

Early on in the process when I least expected it, the harsh reality of no longer living in an intact family unit would rear its ugly head. Stepping out into public for the first few times under our new status was challenging. I felt like everywhere I turned I saw intact families that included a mom and dad with kids in tow. The experience reminded me of how I felt going out of the house after my pregnancy losses. It seemed that everywhere I looked there were pregnant women, and not only had I just lost a baby but had to wait several months before we tried for another. It takes a while to get used to your new normal, so remember to be patient with yourself during the period of adjustment.

Hidden Gems

I'm a firm believer that there's a silver lining in every situation. Sometimes we have to look harder than others, but it's always there, waiting to be discovered. Not all post-divorce realities are challenges or losses, and there are plenty of small victories and hidden surprises if we choose to recognize them.

One of the benefits of our newly restructured reality is that I have the emotional freedom and logistical flexibility to invest in and cultivate relationships with people who are important to me. Because of our parenting plan, I have regularly-scheduled time when the kids are at their dad's house. Prior to our restructuring, I always had this cloud of guilt that would hover over me any time I was out doing something for myself, which was not often.

One of the most challenging parts of being a full-time mom over the years was keeping my life in balance. The vast majority of my time was spent with our family or on the house, and while I feel grateful to have had all of these opportunities to spend so much time with my kids, my life was totally out of balance. In fact, it was so out of balance that even my three-year-old son called it into question and wanted to know why I was so dressed up on a weekday. I wasn't really dressed up, it's just that he wasn't used to seeing me wearing something other than a hoodie and yoga pants during the week. I replied, "I'm going out with my friends," and his reply suggested that he didn't realize I had friends.

Having built-in time to myself on a regularly-scheduled basis gives me the opportunity to restore balance in my life and invest in relationships and activities that are important to me as an individual. It has forced me to look beyond the scope of my formerly all-consuming mom-role duties, and expand into areas of my life that I hadn't previously explored. I have found my purpose and am pouring my heart and soul into an endeavor that is tremendously fulfilling and serves the greater good. There really is something to be said for having time to celebrate my individuality and recharge on a frequent basis, and when the kids return to me, I find that I am more refreshed and energized and ready to re-immerse myself in my mom role.

Additionally, I am fortunate that, because our situation is amicable, we give each other the opportunity to see the kids on our off weekends when we want to build in extra quality time with each of the kids by doing a one-on-one outing.

Kids - Are They Safe? Are They Cared For? Are They Happy? Are They Loved?

The reality of your newly restructured life is that both parents will no longer be sharing all of the kids' experiences in the same way that they used to when everybody was part of your intact family unit. As much as we might want to keep our protective Mama Bear or Papa Bear hat on at all times, we must dutifully recognize that just as we are having our own individual life experiences, our kids are on their own individual journeys as well. As they get older and move through their human experience, they will be carving out their own individual paths. It is normal to experience a sense of sadness because we feel like we are "missing out" on certain parts of their lives. It's an element of the grieving process and it's important to take the time to validate your emotions and understand that they are normal and justified.

As I write this section, the kids are on a ski vacation with their dad, and I'm experiencing some of the sentiments described above. I'm not sharing in the experience, much like he was not sharing in the experience when I took them on our beach vacation. But it's all okay. It's yet another reminder that as much as we all crave togetherness and are accustomed to operating in groups, whether it is in a family context, a work group or a group of friends from childhood, we are all on our own individual journeys and will have different experiences.

One of the tools I used to help me process this fact, not only in a healthy way, but in a way that allows me to actually celebrate their experiences even though I may not be physically present to partake in them, is to reframe my thoughts and run the experience through a filter by asking the questions: "Are they safe?", "Are they cared for?", "Are they happy?", "Are they loved?" If I can unequivocally answer "Yes" to those questions, everybody wins. Remember it's the ego that prompts us to think about **us**...**our** desires, **our** wants, **our** need for control. Coming at it from the soul will make it easier to shift into selflessness and naturally want the same joyful and exciting experiences for others in addition to wanting these experiences for ourselves.

Discovering Your Authenticity

- In what areas of your life are things playing out differently than expected, and how can you reframe your current reality in a healthier way?
- In a situation that is particularly challenging, what are some of the hidden gems? What are the growth opportunities?
- Where in your life are you resisting rather than flowing with the current? What is preventing you from letting go and accepting the way things are?

PART IV

TAKING FLIGHT

Making the commitment to invest in yourself is the ticket to allowing the Universe to lift you to new heights.

16

ENERGY

The game changes when we view the world through the lens of energy.

To be able to apply the ideas and concepts in this book, you need to maintain an open mind and be willing to entertain the idea of seeing the world through different lenses. This chapter contains an overview of the basic behind-the-scenes concepts at work in the spiritual framework.

Energy and the Law of Attraction

Everything changed for me when I started to view the world through the lens of energy. The way in which I viewed the world changed. They way in which I lived on a daily basis changed. My thought process and belief system started to change and I began to approach life in a completely new way.

I was having a conversation with someone and I distinctly remember him saying that everything is energy, even inanimate objects like paper or a pen. My initial thought was that his comment was way out there. There's no energy associated with inanimate objects, I thought to myself. There are really just two categories of things in this world, living things such as people and animals and everything else.

Despite my doubt-filled thoughts, I was intrigued nonetheless and started to research the topic of energy almost immediately. I've always had a curious mind, and whenever I would hear of an intriguing topic or concept that I hadn't heard of before, I would research it until it quelled my curiosity. Unbeknownst to me at the time, this was just the first domino to fall on an entirely new trajectory.

What I discovered was eye-opening, game-changing and energizing. There was a small part of me that was somewhat disheartened when I thought about having lived for nearly four decades and was just then starting to discover how the Universe really works. I had always thought there had to be a better, more empowered way to play this game of life, but just never knew what it was. All I knew was that the old-paradigm way of letting life direct my sails and doing my best to slalom around obstacles was not at all fulfilling or enjoyable and not at all how I wanted to continue living.

I started to research energy and vibration, and as I got further into my research, I wondered why no one talks about this stuff. I mean, this is, in fact, how the Universe works. I felt like someone had just handed me the keys that unlock a door that had long been deadbolted. What I learned was not subjective. What I learned was not somebody's opinion. It had scientific underpinnings and I was determined to understand the underlying mechanics so I could learn how to use them to create my own reality.

So here's quantum physics in a nutshell, as I see it. Think back to elementary school when we all learned about matter and its associated constituents. Atoms are the building blocks for our entire Universe. Subatomically, atoms are composed of tiny whizzing units of energy made up of protons, neutrons and electrons. Most of an atom is empty space. Everything in our world vibrates at a different frequency, and that is what gives rise to the physical separatism.

Everything has an associated vibrational value. People have a vibrational value. Plants have a vibrational value. Animals have a vibrational value. The food you eat has a vibrational value. Thoughts have a vibrational value. Emotions have a vibrational value.

Looking back, it's a little preposterous to think that we are all briefly introduced to this concept early on in our schooling, but the only ones who really take it beyond this point are people who decide to study physics. It forms the foundation of the Universe and the tenets are incredibly powerful in creating our realities. The issue is that most people are not aware of how our own vibration is broadcast into the world and therefore serves as a beacon for what we attract.

The Law of Attraction is based on the premise that "like attracts like." The Universe plays the matching game all day every day, constantly matching things of like vibrations. What we attract into our physical world is a reflection of what we have cast out into the Universe. Life is an echo, and what we send out shall return. Therefore, to attract high vibrations, we must emit high vibrations.

What we consume has a direct impact on our vibration, and what we consume is not only limited to food. It includes the activities we engage in, the people we surround ourselves with, the thoughts we think, the beliefs we embody, and everything else that makes us who we are. This book will explore various ways to raise your vibration.

Your Thoughts Create Your Reality

These concepts are important to understand because embracing them will empower you, totally change the way you live and will prompt you to more consciously choose your thoughts.

Everything in the Universe is energy, and our thoughts are no exception. Thoughts are known to have a quantifiable, measurable frequency. We attract what we think about. That thought alone can be both refreshing **and** sobering. We must choose our thoughts carefully and curate a narrative that reflects what we want to attract.

Human Emotions and Vibration

Every sentient being emits a vibration. If we harbor a low-vibrational emotion we are contracting, where as high-vibrational emotions allow us to be in expansion mode. The best indicator to shed light on the relative human emotions and their associated vibrations is by taking inventory on how you feel when you are harboring various emotions.

When you are feeling guilt, how does your body feel? Do you feel light and energized or do you feel heavy and lethargic?

How about when you are feeling joy? Do you feel vibrant and energetic? Are you smiling? Content? Optimistic?

Each human emotion vibrates at a different frequency. Emotions such as joy, peace, love, and gratitude all vibrate at high frequencies. Low vibrational emotions include fear, guilt, regret, shame, and anger. High-vibrational emotions facilitate our expansion, so it is important to stay anchored on embodying high-vibrational emotions. The spiritual alignment chapter of this book will show you strategies for how to accomplish this.

The concepts introduced in this chapter are introduced purposefully and briefly, but the significance of how these concepts and laws affect our lives on a daily basis cannot be overemphasized. There is much research out there backing up these concepts, and I invite you to explore these topics in greater depth if you are interested. This is not intended to be a scholarly and technical textbook, rather I am providing the basics of what you need to know to put the concepts presented throughout this book into practice.

To effectuate the concepts in this book, put on your "Everything is Energy" corrective eye-wear and watch the world reveal itself to you in new and refreshing ways. Start to cultivate your self-awareness by paying close attention to how you feel as you encounter various situations in your everyday life. Start paying attention to how you feel when you eat certain foods and when you are around different people.

Discovering Your Authenticity

- In what ways has your current mindset played a role in creating your current reality?
- Start a daily journal. Document your feelings and emotions as well as what you have consumed, including food, how you spend your time and the people you spent time with.
- What are some experiences that allowed you to see a direct correlation between the vibration you were casting into the Universe and what was echoed back to you?

For a special bonus on the foundational laws of the universe, visit https://liveauthentically.today/soar-resources to download the guide.

17

SELF-LOVE: NOURISHING YOUR MIND, BODY AND SPIRIT

Become so addicted to feeling amazing that you refuse to feel any other way.

Self-love is about taking care of all aspects of **you**, including physically, mentally, spiritually and emotionally. It's about making sure you are honoring your personal needs and desires and feeling balanced and whole **first**, before taking care of others. Self-love is not selfish, it's necessary.

Self-care and self-love are not one and the same, and it's important to make the distinction between the two so that you can fully explore both. Self-care is a subset of self-love and incorporates activities that involve nurturing your mind, body and spirit. Examples of self-care include exercising, eating healthily, sleeping, meditation and journaling. Self-love is more expansive and requires us to embrace much deeper concepts so that we may illuminate all aspects of ourselves, both the light and the dark. It calls us to take a close look at the current version of ourselves through the lens of acceptance, forgiveness, grace and compassion. It is not until we do this that we will be positioned to bring the best version of ourselves into the world and unleash our full potential.

Self-love is the key that unlocks the doorway to personal growth and transformation and its importance cannot be overemphasized. It is my belief that self-love is unequivocally the most important practice to embrace.

Self-Care

The analogy I use for the concept of self-care is "keeping your pitcher full." We often try to fill up others' cups without realizing that our own pitcher is empty. Are you making commitments to nourish your mind, body and spirit? How can we expect ourselves to be able to keep filling up others' cups if our own pitcher is empty?

This is another area where society conditions us to behave in a certain way. It conditions us to **always** put others first and guilts us into thinking we've fallen short if we put ourselves first. Putting others first 100 percent of the time eventually costs us the expense of our own health and happiness. We should never compromise our own well-being for the sake of others because that model has an expiration date and at some point your pitcher will be bone-dry and you'll have nothing left to give.

As a product of societal conditioning and prior generations' beliefs, for years I tried to take care of others before I took care of myself. I was tired most days, and looked to caffeine or some form of sugar for energy. I didn't know any better. I didn't realize there was a better way to nourish my mind, body and spirit...a way that would deliver the energy I needed at the moment as well as provide long-term benefits in the years to come.

Holisticism is a multi-faceted endeavor that takes a mind/body/spirit approach to self-care. It's very much a proactive and preventative way of living and focuses on keeping all aspects of your being in optimal operating condition. Remember, it's about making mindful decisions about what you consume, which not only includes food, but also encompasses thoughts, people you spend time with and activities.

I view the holistic approach as being similar to a car and the necessary maintenance required to keep it running smoothly. We need to have things like regular maintenance checks, oil changes, getting fluids topped off and rotating the tires to keep our cars in optimal condition. If we don't make these efforts along the way, one day the car will end up broken down and stranded on the side of the road.

Our own health should be maintained and optimized in much the same way that we care for other things in our lives. Rather than waiting until we have symptoms of an illness and reacting, there are things we can do to stave off illness and ensure that our bodies and minds and souls are nourished properly.

How different my life may have been if I would have incorporated these practices much earlier. I consider myself to be a "late-bloomer" in this world of holisticism, and it is mind-boggling for me to think that just five short years ago, I did not follow a holistic regimen. Not because I didn't want to, but because I wasn't aware of what it truly meant to live a healthy lifestyle. I am grateful for the health-conscious individuals who were placed in my path and am grateful to have been open-minded enough to incorporate new practices into my routine. Wherever you are along your path, it is never too late to start.

In prior generations, people needed to rely on the exclusive expertise of a select few who happened to study such material professionally. Now we are fortunate to live in a world where information is readily available to us. It's a commodity. The vast majority of what I have learned over the last five years is self-taught. I'm not a dietician, a doctor, a nurse, a weight-loss specialist or a personal trainer. I am, however, someone who has discovered the secrets of living a healthy lifestyle and enjoy the benefits of said lifestyle every single day. The good news is that you don't need to be any of these things either to learn how to follow a healthy lifestyle. It's something that's readily available to all of us, and with a healthy dose of curiosity blended with an unwavering desire and commitment to consciously make healthy lifestyle choices, you can radically change the way you live, and most importantly, change the way you **feel**.

If I hadn't embarked on the mission of incorporating several holistic modalities into my repertoire, I'm certain I wouldn't have had the physical strength, mental wherewithal or emotional energy to withstand the stress of the divorce process and come out of it the way that I did. The divorce process, of course, is only one of many stressors life can place before us, and the benefits of following a holistic approach can be enjoyed and will serve us well under any conditions, stressful or not.

Not only will the incorporation of healthy lifestyle practices position you to handle the stressors during the process, but doing so will have a direct impact on what you attract into your life going forward. Remember the Law of Attraction states that we attract what we **are**. Not what we hope to be tomorrow, not what we hope to be in 10 years. But what we are **today**. Everything comes to us **through us**. By adopting healthy lifestyle practices, your vibration will heighten, and as a result, you will attract more high-vibrational experiences and people into your life. The Universe won't let it happen any other way.

There is no "one-size-fits-all" approach to this lifestyle. Within each of the arenas there are several choices, and the fun part is that you get to develop your own "recipe." You have a menu of options available to you and you get to choose what works for you. The fun part is "trying on" different options and seeing how you feel.

It is my belief that self-love is the most important concept within spirituality. I view self-love as a lifestyle that involves making conscious choices that raise your vibration on a daily basis so that you can attract from the highest point of attraction. We are so conditioned to chase what we want and often become so focused on "the prize" that we lose sight of ourselves in the process. If you remember only one thing from this book, it is my hope that you will come away with the understanding of the importance of self-love and how to apply it to your life.

Everything Stems From Self-Love

One of my life-coaching clients came to me during her first session and told me that her life was a mess. I asked her to define "mess." She said that she was exhausted and frustrated and felt like she was never doing enough in any area of her life. She had been working long hours at her job, not getting the results she wanted and felt under-appreciated. She said she had no time to work out or do anything that she loved to do.

Her pitcher was totally empty. Bone-dry. She had nothing to give to others because she was totally physically, emotionally and mentally depleted. She kept trying to give more to others but didn't realize she had nothing more to give. I knew exactly what was going on, but I helped her come to that realization on her own. I said "There are 168 hours in the week. How many of those are you spending on **you**?" She admitted that she spent no time on herself because she felt like she had no time to. I challenged her with the idea that time is a choice and that she needed to make time for the things that are important to her.

I asked her to make a list of all the things that "fill her up," including things she enjoys doing and make her feel happy and energized. Much to her surprise, we filled up an entire page of activities, ranging from baking to going on walks to getting massages. I could visually see and feel the energy shift as she revisited activities that she had lost touch with in her attempts to take care of everything and everyone else. She selected a few of those activities that she wanted to commit to making time for before our session the following week, and was excited to rearrange her week so that these activities were prioritized.

Everything starts with self-love. It doesn't matter whether you are going through a divorce, experiencing financial distress, taking care of a family member who is ill, dealing with a challenging work project or simply wanting to feel better in your own skin. Filling yourself up with love is the most important thing you can do each day so that you can respond to the events of life with kindness, joy, forgiveness and grace. Consider this familiar proverbial situation and its moral:

> If someone bumps into you while you are holding a cup of coffee and it spills everywhere, your first inclination may be to to think that you spilled the coffee because someone bumped into you.
>
> **Wrong answer.**

> You spilled the coffee because there was coffee in your cup. Had there been tea in the cup, you would have spilled tea.
>
> **Whatever is inside the cup is what will spill out.**
>
> When you put this scenario in the context of your life, when something comes along and shakes you at your core (which WILL happen), whatever is inside you will come out. *It's easy to fake it until you get rattled.*
>
> We each have to ask ourselves, **"What's in my cup?"** When life gets tough, what spills over? Is it joy, gratefulness, peace and humility or anger, bitterness, harsh words and negative reactions?
>
> You choose!
> - Author Unknown

The two words that pack the most punch in this passage are... "You choose." You have to be the one to consciously **choose** what you will fill yourself up with. Nobody is going to do that for you. It's just like going to the grocery store and **choosing** what to put in your empty cart. Do you take a trip down the snack food aisle and fill it up with cookies, crackers, chips and sugary drinks or do you head to the produce section and fill your cart up with fresh, nutritious produce that will give you long-lasting energy and nutrients to nourish your body?

By choosing to love yourself by doing things that nurture your mind, body and spirit, you are taking an active measure to not only react to life with love, but you are proactively and directly affecting the people and experiences you attract. Choose to love yourself first, so that you have more love to give to others.

Why it is Especially Important to Practice Self-Love and Self-Care During the Divorce Process and During the Healing Period

The divorce process is densely packed with stressors. No matter how you slice and dice it, regardless of how harmonious you may categorize your divorce situation to be, it is still a stressful time with an inordinate amount of decisions to be made, all while under the weight of emotional stress. It's a normal response of the human condition to feel the effect of these stressors. But, the extent that we allow them to affect us is directly related to how well we have positioned ourselves physically, mentally, emotionally and spiritually to respond to these stressors in a healthy and transformative way. During this time, your mind, body and spirit are under a constant assault from these stressors and you may struggle to perform basic self-care activities that you once took for granted in your pre-divorced life. Additionally, it is easy to get stuck in a constant loop of a self-deprecating internal dialogue that consists of thoughts like "Why did this happen to me?" These are all patterns that keep us tied to the pain and prevent us from moving forward.

We are all at various points in our own evolution, and whether you are just entering the world of growth and transformation or are an enlightened being, we all feel the effect of stressors. No one is exempt from that. The good news is that there are powerful tools you can add to your toolkit so that you can transmute this stress and pain into power and ensure that you are well-equipped to navigate the divorce process with the energy and stamina you need to not only survive the process, but come out on the other side feeling like you are thriving, and there is no better way to feel as you embark on this new and exciting chapter of your life.

Metaphorically speaking, I describe overall wellness as a "three-legged stool." For the stool to remain upright, there must be stability and soundness in the mind, body and spirit. When we talk about the three-legged stool of holisticism, we often hear the terms "mind, body and spirit," in that order. Here, I address the body, or physical piece first with purposeful intent. For me, discovering the importance of investing in my physical self through exercising and eating a clean diet serves as a foundational piece and as a springboard that opened up other realms for me. This section contains ideas for you to explore as you begin to craft your own recipe for self-care and self-love.

Nourishing Your Body

For almost four decades of my life, I viewed food as a vehicle to satisfy hunger. I followed the standard American diet, like most of us are conditioned to follow. I remember when I was pregnant, I was reviewing the list of foods to avoid, and I found it unfathomable to think that I needed to avoid lunch meat for nine months, as that was typically my go-to lunch every day. That's a product of conditioning. I was conditioned to think that I should eat cereal for breakfast, sandwiches for lunch and some type of meat and a starchy side dish for dinner.

I used to view weight management as a simple math equation: calories in versus calories out. I rarely paid attention to the source of the calories. I ate without regard to nutritional value and ate until I was full, without regard to portion control. I ate pasta and breads and other refined carbs without limitation because they contained minimal fat, and I thought minimizing fat was the name of the game. I used to avoid eating any type of fat, even the healthy ones such as avocados, nuts, seeds and oils, because I thought they would cause me to gain body fat. I only bought vegetables when I needed them for a particular recipe or was asked to bring a veggie platter to a party. I used to look to sugar for energy. During my attempts to lose weight, I would increase my exercise and decrease my food intake, and found that I was gradually moving further and further away from my goal.

I had no idea that keeping your physical body healthy was a multi-dimensional endeavor that involves an interplay between diet and exercise. It started to become impossible to ignore the fact that the choices I was making for my body over the prior several years were in large part responsible for the way I felt. While I wasn't dealing with a chronic illness, I did get sick frequently and always felt tired. The more I learned about food and the importance of nourishing our bodies with healthy foods, it became quite apparent to me that I had significant room for improvement.

In a relatively short period of time, I have made a radical shift in the way I eat, and most importantly, the way I view food. I now have a healthy relationship with food and experience the positive effects of eating a healthy diet on a daily basis. Furthermore, I have created an ecosystem within my body that makes it difficult for disease to flourish by following a plant-based diet. The diet I follow also has favorable implications on longevity.

I had some serious deprogramming and reprogramming work to do to completely overhaul my relationship with food. Through shifting my mindset about food and getting really clear on what underlying motivating factors were driving my food choices, I have found that my cravings have naturally and organically shifted. I now crave healthy foods that I used to avoid, and foods that used to satisfy my sweet tooth years ago now taste sickeningly sweet to me.

Now I think of food as fuel and as nourishment. Just as there are different grades of gasoline with which to fuel our cars, there are also different grades of food with which to fuel our bodies. Just as we have a choice about what type of gasoline we choose at the pump, we also have a choice about what we will fuel our bodies with.

When I overhauled my diet, I quickly noticed that I started to feel differently. I had more energy. More mental clarity. I slept sounder. I didn't get sick as often. My skin started to glow. I had a spring in my step and a sense of vitality that I had never experienced before.

For me, feeling good physically is the gateway that opens up all of the other portals for self-care. I'm more receptive to expanding my mind when I feel good physically, and it has served as the foundational piece and a springboard to catapult me in other areas of my life. I'm more open to incorporating spiritual practices when I feel good physically and I bring my best self to relationships when I feel good physically. I exude a totally different aura when I feel good physically, which attracts even more positivity.

Back to the Basics

The healthcare industry is a multi-billion dollar industry. The pharmaceutical industry is a multi-billion dollar industry. The weight loss industry is a multi-billion dollar industry. We often look to these systems for our answers, but it is my belief that the answers to the vast majority of our health and wellness issues can be found in the produce section of the grocery store.

Like anything else in life worth having, maintaining your physical health takes commitment and consistency and a ton of hard work. The issue is that we have created a society that over-complicates this health stuff. We overthink it, and we want results fast. We jump from one diet trend to the next, picking up this exercise gadget or that weight-loss gizmo along the way. We have become inundated with options for weight loss programs and we barely even know where to start. People really just need to step away and go "back to the basics." The awareness and application of just a few fundamentals is all that's really necessary.

We live in a society where instant gratification is the expectation. Every direction we turn, we are faced with things that fuel this mentality. It permeates every area of our lives, including communication, technology, food and service to name a few. Weight loss programs guarantee you'll lose "x" pounds in "y" weeks or your money back.

I'm no stranger to that way of thinking. In my younger days, I was always looking for that quick-fix, no effort, maximum-results magic bullet-type approach. I've long been consumed with (and at times obsessed with) controlling my weight, even dating back to my high school years. I had a totally unhealthy relationship with food and with working out. I always had healthy home-cooked options available during those years, but when left to my own devices, I wasn't making good choices. I hated working out, and I enjoyed eating, and I wasn't willing to put in the hard work to achieve the results that I wanted. I thought people who were fit just had a favorable gene pool. I was so anxious to get results that I even tried SlimFast in high school.

More often than not, fitness efforts are event-driven or season-based. How many times have you heard someone say "I need to lose 10 lbs before my daughter's wedding"? or "I better start working out - swimsuit season will be here soon." Embedded in both of these thoughts is an implication of impermanence. Both have a transitory nature because of their short-term focus. What happens after the wedding, or after summer is over? The same cycle ensues. How about permanently changing your **lifestyle**?

I employ a "back-to-the-basics" approach in most areas of my life. I remember when I was newly married and we purchased our first home, I was excited to accumulate just about every kitchen gadget known to man. The more specific the use, the more likely that I owned it. Apple peeler/corer/slicer. Egg separator. You name it, I had it. Over the years, I have decluttered and simplified to the point where just my wooden cutting board and my favorite chef's knife are now the mainstays in my kitchen. My approach to keeping my body healthy is much the same. I have gone to a back-to-basics ideology that involves simple, clean eating coupled with regular exercise.

Barring any major health concerns that require special considerations or modifications, here's my coveted secret recipe that has worked quite well for me:

- Go to the grocery store and hang out in the produce section. Toss in some proteins and healthy grains and good fats.
- Full-body strength training and cardio a few times per week.

Note that this description is an extremely simplified explanation of the approach and each area can and should be colored in with more detail and tailored to the specific needs, goals and desires of each individual, and sometimes the guidance of a professional is warranted.

When people see someone who's fit and wonder what the "secret" is, realize that there is no secret. No magic bullet. Don't assume fit people live at the gym, it's not true. Don't assume those people barely eat anything, that's not true either. It's simply the cumulative effect of incremental changes from living a healthy lifestyle over a long period of time. The two most important ingredients are consistency and patience. We have to wait for some of the best things in life, and this is no exception.

In the spirit of being totally authentic, I will say that I mindfully set aside 5-10 percent of my diet to eat certain foods that I enjoy. While these are always still within the realm of plant-based eating, they may include foods that contain a little extra sugar, for example. It isn't practical or sustainable to follow a perfectly clean diet 100 percent of the time, and expecting yourself to do so will not be setting yourself up for success.

The key is to keep a positive narrative around these indulgences. Life is meant to be enjoyed. We aren't supposed to walk around with limitations 100 percent of the time and with a cloud of guilt hovering over us any time we have the slightest deviation from a healthy diet. I don't like calling them "cheat" meals because that creates a negative association in my mind and suggests that I am doing something I am not supposed to be doing. Instead, I reframe it by creating a positive narrative and call them "mindful indulgences." I consciously choose what I will enjoy in advance within my 5-10 percent and find the best food that I can. For example, if I'm going to eat chocolate, I don't pick it from the Halloween candy bowl. I seek out and find the best chocolate I can. I don't feel guilty about it because I know that I have allotted some of my calories for this purpose.

As much as we may try to stay within the 5-10 percent rule, we all are subject to experiencing those days where stress gets the best of us and we eat for emotional reasons, or are on vacation and don't have access to our usual food choices. Don't beat yourself up over it. You may feel like you have fallen off the wagon after having a piece of cheesecake and may feel inclined to eat without regard to nutrition for the rest of the day, but don't let that be your excuse to have even more. The most important thing to remember is that this is all cumulative and you'll be that much further from your goal. The best thing you can do is stop and get back on track by making good choices again.

Food is Our Fuel AND Our Medicine

Prior to my mid-thirties, I had no idea that the food we eat plays such a powerful role in fueling the human body appropriately and keeping us free from disease. I didn't make the connection between what I was eating and how I was feeling. I was often tired, but didn't realize that it was because I wasn't fueling my body appropriately.

It is my personal belief that there isn't enough dialogue around the connection between food and its power in preventing and treating disease. We're accustomed to operating within the construct of a self-feeding system that is focused on industries feeding other industries, rather than what we are feeding our bodies, and it's all so simple. All you have to do is buy the majority of your foods in the produce section and ensure that you consume adequate fats, proteins and carbohydrates from healthy sources. That's really all there is to it.

As with any change, the first step is awareness, and I'm excited to share my personal journey through this with you in the hopes that it will give you a new perspective and help you to make more empowered and conscious decisions for your own life. It's never too late to expand your mind and consider adopting a new way of living.

The process of transitioning from the standard American diet to officially following a plant-based diet has been a process of rich self-discovery. In transitioning from an omnivorous diet to plant-based eating, I initially went from one end of the spectrum to the other. I was totally vegan for about seven months, but at that point in my evolution found it to be a bit too extreme and not sustainable long-term.

I periodically stepped away from plant-based eating and lapsed back into my prior omnivorous diet. In the interim, I educated myself and explored the topic in greater depth and detail, and spent time discerning whether or not this was the right approach for me to follow. I noticed that each time I stepped away, I was able to re-immerse myself with more knowledge, clarity, energy and a commitment to this new way of eating. While these deviations felt like setbacks at the time, now I am able to look back and understand how they were a crucial part of the process. There were people trying to convince me that a plant-based diet was the healthiest way to eat, but I needed to discover the truth for myself and follow my own process. I resisted and even met them with counter-arguments that had no empirical basis or scientific evidence whatsoever, in an attempt to justify staying in the rhythm of the only way of eating I had ever known. I've finally reached a point where I am currently a plant-based eater and am very close to being a vegan.

Why I Choose to Follow a Plant-Based Diet

Adhering to a plant-based diet is a big piece of who I am, so it wouldn't be authentic if I didn't include some commentary around it. Transitioning to a plant-based diet has played an instrumental role in my personal transformation and spiritual awakening, and I'm excited to share a little bit of the knowledge others imparted on me over the last five years. Everything in our Universe has a vibration, and the reality is that the foods we eat directly impact the vibration we embody.

Know that there are no judgements whatsoever about the eating regimen you choose for yourself. Remember that you are the designer of your reality and you make your choices, right down to whether or not you choose to read this section. If you're not in a place to entertain the idea of plant-based eating, go ahead and skip it. I totally respect your choice. If at a point down the road you want to come back to this section, it will always be here for you to reference.

It blows me away that five short years ago I was standing toe-to-toe with plant-based eating advocates defending my position as an omnivore. Quite frankly, I thought vegetarianism was a bit extreme and exited many discussions around the topic. After following a long and winding journey of self-discovery in this arena, I am now a passionate plant-based diet advocate, and have fully embraced a sustainable lifestyle rooted in plant-based eating. I am totally energized as I impart my knowledge on others so that they may be educated and empowered and make the choice for themselves.

I'm super-excited to see collective awareness starting to shift in this area. We are starting to see plant-based food options populate restaurant menus and are starting to see more veggie burgers in the freezer next to traditional hamburgers. It's so exciting to see awareness heightened at so many levels.

Plant-Based Eating is Better for Me

Plant-based diets are rich in nutrients, vitamins and minerals, low in saturated fat and high in fiber and antioxidants, and as a result, offer numerous health benefits. During my journey to becoming a plant-based eater, I read "The China Study" and watched documentaries that defended the assertion that following a plant-based diet is without question the most powerful and influential factor in optimizing your health.

The food we eat plays a huge role in creating an ecosystem within our bodies that either fights or fuels disease. The goal is to maximize your body's alkalinity to create an environment that will make it difficult for diseases to flourish. Examples of highly alkaline foods include spinach, broccoli, kale, cucumbers and avocados. At the other end of the spectrum are acidic foods that bolster a biochemical environment that encourages the proliferation of various diseases. Examples of acidic foods are dairy, meat, poultry, certain beverages such as alcohol or drinks with artificial sweeteners, refined sugars, processed foods and fried foods.

The benefits of eating a plant-based diet are numerous and include, but are not limited to, the following favorable health-related implications:

- Reduces the risk of certain types of cancer
- Reduces the risk of diabetes
- Reduces the risk of obesity
- Reduces the risk of autoimmune diseases
- Reduces the risk of hypertension

Plant-Based Eating is Better for the Animals

From my perspective, I see a lot of contradictions in how we treat animals. Humans tend to practice kindness and compassion toward some animals but not others. We regularly enjoy the company of our house pets, yet support the slaughtering of pigs, cows and other animals. We interact with cows at a petting zoo but then don't think twice about stopping to eat a cheeseburger on the way home. In the same way, it can seem perfectly natural to enjoy eating a fish that was pulled out of the ocean but would never think of plucking a pet fish out of the tank at home and tossing it into the frying pan.

In short, people tend to view some animals as superior to others while some are deemed not worthy of life on this planet. The issue as I see it is patterning. Many people simply don't stop to think about the origin of the food they eat. We simply aren't conditioned to make the association between the animal and what is on our dinner plate. There is a greater focus on the macronutrient split (carbs/protein/fats) rather than the source of the food. For example, from the time we are children, we are told to eat chicken so we get enough protein.

I'm often challenged by omnivores with the question of where I get my protein. The answer is the same place meat eaters' protein gets their protein. From plants! Cows don't dine on pigs for lunch and pigs don't snack on chickens. We justify eating animals by allowing ourselves to subscribe to the general public belief that protein must come from animals. We are so fixated on meeting our daily protein quota and look to fish, chicken, pork and beef to accomplish that without even realizing that we often consume significantly more than our bodies need and overtax our organs in the process. There are, of course, different schools of thought with regard to protein sources, so if you are interested, I encourage you to research this to further educate and empower yourself.

Plant-Based Eating is Better for the Planet

Plant-based eating affords many benefits to the environment, such as reducing our carbon footprint, slowing the rate of global warming by reducing carbon dioxide emissions, conserving water, freeing up more land and other benefits.

Learning to Speak My Truth

Early in my transition from the standard American diet to a plant-based diet, I was worried about being judged for not eating meat. I was worried about what others would think and found it challenging to go against the mainstream diet that seemingly everyone else was following.

Now I've completely shifted, and every time I am asked about my food regimen or challenged about why I follow a plant-based diet, I am excited to educate others and empower them to make the right choices for themselves. Now, when someone asks me why I don't have cow's milk in my fridge, I let them know that cow's milk is a substance produced by mother cows for their babies. We are the only species that consume another animal's milk. What I do have in my fridge are several plant-based milks like almond milk, rice milk and coconut milk. I also take a moment to shed light on the fact that we are led to believe that we need to consume cow's milk for the calcium and Vitamin D and explain that those same nutrients are found in plant-based sources.

People may not decide to shift during our conversation, but we should never underestimate the impact of planting the seed. My journey progressed because several people planted the seeds for me, and I researched the topics until I had enough information to make the right decision for myself. I didn't have to spend much time researching until it was apparent that I needed to make some radical shifts.

I am passionate about plant-based eating because of all the benefits it provides, and it's nearly impossible for me to talk about healthy eating without presenting this idea. It's part of who I am. Even as passionate as I am about it, I'm still not in a position to tell you what you do. It's your body and the food you decide to put into it is your choice. If your curiosity has been heightened about this dietary choice, I invite you to dive in head first and research the topic to educate and empower yourself further. If you decide to try it, remember to meet yourself with compassion and grace and understand that there will be much learning and discovery along the way.

Food Affects Our Vibration

Everything in our world is energy, and the food we eat is no exception. What we consume is absorbed into our bodies and directly impacts the frequency at which our bodies vibrate. To optimize our overall well-being and quality of experiences and people we attract into our lives, our goal should always be to maximize our vibration.

High-Vibrational Foods

Here are some great examples of high-vibrational foods:

- Fresh vegetables
- Fresh fruits (consume minimally-it's still sugar!)
- Nuts
- Nut butters
- Seeds (pumpkin seeds, sunflower seeds, chia seeds, hemp seeds)
- Oils (avocado oil, olive oil, sunflower oil)

Low-Vibrational Foods

These low-vibrational foods should be consumed in moderation or eliminated from the diet:

- Processed foods
- Canned foods
- Refined starches and sugars
- Alcohol
- Artificial sweeteners
- Genetically-modified foods
- Fried foods
- Soda

While the foods we consume are critical for nourishing our bodies, it is not the only form of nourishment. There are several other ways in which we can keep our bodies in optimal condition.

When we think about food in terms of its vibrational value, we develop new cravings.

Exercise

The importance of engaging in some form of physical activity each day cannot be overemphasized. Create a weekly regimen that includes weight training, cardiovascular exercise, stretching and any other activity that keeps you moving. There are so many options and the key is to explore them and adopt a routine that is enjoyable and sustainable for you. I have also found that switching up my repertoire every so often helps to keep me enthusiastic and excited about working out. Mixing in a new activity such as biking, swimming, running or a group fitness class are just a few ways to keep things fresh and exciting.

Participating in a race or competition can help you stay motivated and requires you to hold yourself accountable. I have challenged myself by doing obstacle course races such as "Tough Mudder" and "Spartan" and by entering running races like 5Ks, half-marathons, and marathons.

The important takeaway is to find ways to incorporate movement into your life as you go about your day. You do not even need to be officially exercising or working out to get it done. For instance, you can opt to walk or ride a bike to the store rather than drive.

Rest and Recovery

While exercise is crucial to staying healthy, it also places stress on the body. You must counterbalance this effect by building in adequate time for your body to recharge and rejuvenate. Make sleep a priority and create a space that is conducive to quality rest. Getting adequate sleep is important because it provides the opportunity for the body to rebuild tissues, rebalance hormones, regulate appetite, reduce risk of certain diseases and optimize athletic performance as well as many other advantages. Soft music, candles, oil diffusers and meditation can all play a part in relaxing your mind and body so it can recharge adequately.

Detoxification

Over time, our bodies absorb toxins from various sources such as the foods we consume, the air we breathe and the products we use on a daily basis such as makeup, skin care products, cleaners, detergents and even the water we drink. Toxins have an unfavorable impact on our health and it is important to rid our bodies of them on a regular basis so we can remain in optimal physical condition.

Our bodies have naturally-occurring detoxification processes that involve various systems of the body, and various holistic practices can help our bodies detoxify. These practices include, but are not limited to:

- Exercise
- Drinking plenty of water
- Eating a diet rich in fruits, vegetables, nuts and seeds

- Sweating in a sauna
- Getting sufficient sleep
- Minimizing stress levels
- Taking epsom salt baths
- Exfoliating your skin
- Getting regular massages
- Using essential oils

In addition to incorporating these daily practices, some people invest in more formal detoxification programs for a finite period of time to give their bodies a "hard reset" and boost the body's ability to detoxify. These detoxification programs often come in the form of water cleanses, juice cleanses, and specific products sold by companies to aid in the detoxification process. It is always advisable to consult with your health practitioners before embarking on such programs.

It is extremely important to become acutely aware of how you're feeling in each moment and give your body whatever it is craving. Learning to listen to your body is one of the most important skills you can develop in this area, because your body always knows what it needs. If it's a workout day and you're feeling fatigued, invest time in activities that relax and rejuvenate your body instead. It's okay to deviate from the plan to give your body the nurturing and care it deserves.

This section has given you some food for thought but by no means is an all-inclusive list. There is no one regimen that works for everyone, as the preferences and special conditions of each person must be considered before incorporating a new modality into your regimen. Remember to consult with a professional if you are uncertain as to whether a certain modality is appropriate for you.

Start small by incorporating some basic practices. When they have been incorporated and the foundation is solid and a natural part of your day, then layer on more. This practice is an art not a science. The fun part is to experiment and see what works for you.

Why it is Important to Take Care of Your Body During the Divorce Process

Our bodies are vessels that house our souls during the time we are here on Earth. Much like we maintain the homes in which we live, we must also maintain our bodies and keep them in peak operating condition. Even in amicable divorces, the process can still be emotionally, physically and mentally draining. It is especially important to prioritize self-care by mindfully carving out time in your day to exercise, fueling your body with nutritious foods and by investing in yourself by incorporating other modalities discussed in this section.

Nourishing Your Mind

Getting in the right headspace is a critical component of self-love. The dialogue we have with ourselves can either work for us or against us. It also plays an instrumental role in creating our outlook and our reality. I had a negative mindset for years, as I worried constantly and obsessed about unlikely outcomes. Through my commitment to personal growth and spiritual development, I learned that what I was telling myself had a direct correlation to how my life was playing out in certain areas. If you tell yourself you can, there is a greater possibility that you will. If you tell yourself you can't, there is a greater possibility that you won't.

Our minds are so incredibly powerful in creating our own realities. Our thoughts have a vibration and the laws of the

Universe are at work behind the scenes turning these thoughts into things in our physical world. We must first become aware of our own thoughts and then make strides to reframe them so that they are productive and in line with the realities we are trying to create for ourselves.

The field of psychology is expansive and encompasses so many concepts, and it is outside the scope of this book to take an in-depth look. I find it fascinating to learn about the role the different parts of our minds, including the conscious and subconscious, play. While it isn't practical to explore these topics here, I will share with you a personal belief that was crafted by first-hand experiences as well as observations of and conversations with others. It was a powerful game-changer for me personally and played an instrumental role in my paradigm shift.

I believe that people fall into either a competitive or growth-based mindset. I have experienced both firsthand and understand the benefits and drawbacks of each.

A competitive mindset is externally-focused and ego-driven. It keeps us focused on the environment around us and we keep measuring ourselves up against everyone and everything based on egoic barometers. It is difficult to find happiness while we are in this mindset because we are always coming from a place of lack, limitation, wanting, insufficiency and inferiority. We don't have to look very far to find people who are prettier than we are, wealthier than we are, fitter than we are, more successful than we are and we always walk away feeling discouraged and like we are not enough.

A growth-based mindset is internally-focused and propelled by the soul. People who have growth-based mindsets are happier because they know how to put the blinders on and not worry about what everyone else is doing or what anyone else thinks about what they are doing. They know that working on themselves is the most important thing they can do every day. Their focus is to become a better version of the person they were yesterday, and they aren't derailed by what everyone else has or is achieving because they are focused on their own growth.

The vast majority of this book centers around concepts that involve rewiring our minds to harbor a growth-based mindset by undoing programming that no longer serves us and replacing it with programming that empowers us and aligns us with our own inner being.

Nourishing Your Spirit

Spirituality is about expanding awareness by examining our lives and the choices we make for ourselves and recognizing the interconnectedness of everyone and everything. By looking at our life experiences through the lens of growth, we learn to trust the process and surrender to the infinite wisdom of the Universe.

We are conditioned to think that we are limited by what is available to us in the physical world, but in reality there is another dimension we can access by mindfully incorporating new practices into our lives.

Engaging in spiritual practices allows us to reconnect with our own divine essence. Universal Energy is something we all can access, and the good news is that it's unlimited and it's free. There are several practices that we can incorporate into our daily routines that allow us to connect to this abundant Source Energy, and no two people's regimens need to look the same. There isn't a one-size-fits-all option, and in fact it's best if each individual experiments with different practices and determines which ones resonate the most. The list of options for spiritual modalities is quite extensive, and it isn't practical to cover all of them in this book, so I'm giving you this "starter kit." Once you have incorporated some of these practices into your daily routine in a natural way, you may decide to research additional modalities to incorporate.

Journaling

Writing has long been a go-to modality for processing my thoughts. As a kid, I always had a diary and have always loved the creative process of putting a pen to a piece of paper, either to document day-to-day happenings or to commemorate festive occasions or vacations.

No prerequisites are required for journaling, no creative writing class is necessary and you don't have to have aspirations of being the next Ernest Hemingway to start writing. Spend a few moments each day writing down what you're grateful for, what you want to accomplish that day, values you want to work on or anything else that comes to mind.

Breathe

Breathing sounds like it's simple and assumed. Obviously, we're all breathing. But in this context it's about carving out moments to take deep, intentional breaths to recenter yourself. Pay attention to the depth of your breath when you are rushed or frustrated or stressed. You will notice that the physiological response to your mental state is the taking of very shallow, rapid breaths. Our bodies naturally tense up when we are not at ease and we block the flow of Universal Energy when we are in this state. I find that it is always helpful to consciously carve out a few moments to take a few deep, intentional breaths, particularly when I am starting to feel stressed.

Meditation

The first few times I tried to meditate, I was very frustrated. Sitting still and focusing on one activity is not part of my genetic makeup, as for years I thrived on multi-tasking and being as busy as possible. Like anything else, learning the art of meditation takes practice and must be met with self-compassion as you explore this new territory. Start small, and continually raise the bar over time as you become more comfortable with it. You'll know when the time is right to graduate yourself to the next level. Start off aiming to meditate for 10 seconds, then 20, and keep gradually increasing the time. The idea is to become an observer of your thoughts and to do so without judgement. Don't try to categorize or judge or analyze them. Instead, simply watch them float in and float out. Your entire mind and body will start to relax and you will open yourself up to the flow of Universal Energy as you connect with your Higher Self.

Daily Affirmations

Early in the divorce process, I sat down and wrote out some affirmations. To me, affirmations are qualities that I want to embody. The key to incorporating affirmations into your reality is telling yourself that you already are these things. "I am" are two very powerful words. The Universe doesn't recognize negative words such as "not," so it is important to phrase your affirmations positively. My affirmations looked like this (in no meaningful order):

- I am strong
- I am selfless
- I am happy
- I am positive

- I am loved
- I am kind
- I am patient
- I am vibrant
- I am magnetic

As part of my mantra I regularly recited this reminder as well:

> *"I only hold space for things that are in my highest good... positivity, nurturing and loving relationships, etc."*

There is no template for reciting affirmations, and the opportunity for customization is limitless. Declare it as a current, present day condition. Say it with assuredness and conviction.

Asking for Help From Spirit Guides

Our angels and spirit guides walk with us on our journeys every day. It is easy to forget that they are there just waiting for us to ask for their help and guidance. Requests for guidance need not be anything formal or fancy, and should be articulated in the moment that you recognize you need to summon their help. Trust that after you issue your request, they are all collaborating on a plan that is in your highest good. Requests should always be personal and heartfelt, but for illustrative purposes I have included examples of requests that I have used in the past:

- Help me to release anything that doesn't support my highest good, like negativity, toxic relationships, etc.
- Communicate with me by showing me signs that I am on the right path.
- Put the people and experiences in my path that propel me on my journey.
- Help me to use my experiences to acquire the necessary

skills and wisdom for my evolution.
- Help me remain committed to growth.
- Help me to be a magnet for positivity.

Connecting With Other Like-Minded Individuals
Seeking out and surrounding myself with other individuals who are committed to growth plays a huge role in ensuring that I remain on my own growth trajectory. It's so important to connect with people who speak your language and have similar priorities. Hold space for the ones who share core values and enrich your life in some way — either spiritually, mentally, emotionally, or physically.

I love being surrounded by super-ambitious people who are committed to continually improving themselves in some way and who are willing to play a supporting role in my growth. Sometimes all it takes is a few simple words to shift you into a totally different headspace. I signed up for a half-marathon recently and was telling one of my friends who was running it with me that I hadn't been training for it because the weather had been so hot. He was having none of it, and told me that I just needed to get up super-early before the temperature was too hot and just get it done. The next morning, I got up early and ran nine miles before 9 a.m. In the absence of that game-changing conversation, I probably wouldn't have been able to shift back into training mode. We all have moments where we doubt ourselves or lack the motivation that we need, which is why it is so important to have growth-minded people in your tribe who know how to encourage you.

Yoga
While some may regard yoga as a physical practice, for me the practice has been largely spiritual.

Yoga did not initially feel like a natural fit for me, and incorporating it into my regular routine has been an exercise of tremendous self-exploration, discovery and growth.

The process of embracing yoga and incorporating it into my weekly routine has been more enriching and transformative than I ever could have imagined. Yoga forces practitioners to focus on their breath and stay present in the moment. All that matters is what's happening on **your** mat. There is no judgement, and you learn to accept wherever you are, knowing that's exactly where you're meant to be.

My journey has led me to a place where I now crave it. I look forward to taking a hiatus from the external stimuli in the physical world and immerse myself in the darkness and heat and soul-stirring music in the yoga studio. Not only do I look forward to the time I spend in my yoga sessions, but I enjoy the benefits of yoga during the other 167 hours of the week, through improved sleep, increased mental clarity, stress reduction, enhanced circulation, increased flexibility as well as other benefits.

Spending Time in Nature

Technology has permeated every aspect of our culture and it's often difficult to disconnect from it. Spending time in nature is rejuvenating because it encourages us to be more mindful and soak in the present moment, devoid of any man-made distractions. Spending time in nature forces us to slow the frenetic pace and constant accessibility that ensues in everyday life, as we slow down and enjoy the beauty and the wonderment that nature has to offer. It is truly majestic and there is no shortage of naturally-occurring, awe-inspiring creations to admire. From the individual blades of grass under our feet to a canopy of towering trees filled with birds chirping and squirrels frolicking amidst the branches, we don't have to look very far to find miraculous creations.

Trust the Process

Everything in our lives is unfolding according to a pristine divine plan. You are exactly where you are meant to be. It is by no accident or coincidence that you are in your current situation, and it is ripe with opportunities to fine-tune yourself and use your current reality as a springboard to launch yourself into higher levels of consciousness. Surrender to the infinite wisdom of the Universe and trust that it knows what is in your highest good. It is a natural part of our human condition to want to engineer the outcome by controlling the process, but in doing that, we limit the possibilities and stifle the Universe's ability to surprise us with something that is far superior to what we could have envisioned for ourselves. In the manifestation chapter, we will explore ways you can partner with the Universe to co-create your reality.

Summary

In this chapter, you were given a variety of ideas for nurturing your mind, body and spirit. Taking care of yourself and loving yourself is unequivocally the most important initiative you undertake because everything starts with you. Remember that before you can take care of others, you first need to make sure your pitcher is full, and if you do that you will have even more to give to others. Energetically, you will attract better vibrational matches and experiences into your life because you are operating from a higher point of attraction.

The fun part is that you get to "try-on" various ideas that have been discussed in this section and see how they work for you. Focus on how you feel. Your body is acutely aware of what resonates with you energetically and what doesn't, so focus on what your body is telling you. View the list of ideas as a menu of choices from which you can choose.

It wasn't feasible for me to incorporate every health and wellness-related practice within the scope of this book. I've given you a lot to get started with, and hope that the knowledge I have imparted will ignite the spark in you to continue along this spectrum as you continue on your own path.

The divorce process contains so many demands that are beyond the scope of normal activities associated with daily living. There is so much change concentrated within a relatively short period of time, including potential moves, finances and adjusting to new parenting schedules, not to mention the emotional weight of the situation. Now is not the time to completely overhaul your daily routines and expect that you will be able to sustain the routine during the process and beyond in a healthy way. Start small. Try a few things and if they are working for you, layer on a few more. Rome wasn't built in a day, and remember your new way of living won't be built in a day either.

Discovering Your Authenticity

- What are your current self-care practices?
- Have you experienced differences in how you feel based on how much time and energy you are dedicating to your own self-love and self-care?
- What are some new modalities you are open to incorporating into your life?
- What changes in your life do you need to make to support these lifestyle changes?
- In what areas of your life have boundaries been blurred? What steps can you take to tighten them up?
- Do you fill up your pitcher first before taking care of others?
- How would you describe your self-talk? How can you be kinder, gentler and more forgiving toward yourself?
- How would you describe the five people with whom you spend the most time? How do they support your growth and how do you support theirs?

For a special bonus on nourishing yourself holistically, through mind, body and spirit modalities, visit https://liveauthentically.today/soar-resources to download the guide.

18

SELF-LOVE: HONORING YOURSELF

The relationship you have with yourself sets the tone for every aspect of your human experience.

Self-love is about **the self**. It's about pulling back the curtain on all aspects of yourself and embracing the light and the dark. A prerequisite to self-love is the willingness to take a close look at yourself in the mirror as you take an introspective journey into the soul.

This section contains various facets of self-love that are crucial to explore as you move through your journey. There are so many potential areas to explore the self in greater depth, but these are the 10 areas that will get you well on your way to loving yourself. In this book, it isn't feasible to explore each in great detail, but I will provide some reflections and considerations and give you ideas for incorporating them into your healing and growth process.

Self-Acceptance

Self-acceptance is the practice of learning to love yourself unconditionally. This includes all parts of you, even the ones that are not so pretty. All of your strengths, all of your weaknesses and everything else in between. It doesn't mean that you aren't willing to grow or improve, but an integral part of the process is accepting your weaknesses and challenges, incorporating them into the image you have of yourself, and learning to love yourself along the way.

It includes accepting and appreciating that where you are on your journey is where you are meant to be. A divorce scenario offers a plethora of avenues for self-critiquing in this area, and with each realization you will have to make the choice to either accept or reject where you are. With marriage comes a series of milestones, some of which will be realized during the course of the marriage while others will not be. As we approach certain milestones, it is easy to get caught up in how things "should have been." When the negative thoughts start seeping in, train yourself to recognize them and quickly reframe them into a more constructive and optimistic rhetoric. For example, replace "I should have been celebrating my 20-year anniversary today" with "Because of my new single status, I have the opportunity to choose to do something exciting today."

Accept that divorce is part of your story. It will have a highly influential role on who you are today and while it doesn't have to define you, it certainly will shape you. It's not a failure or a defeat or anything to be ashamed of or embarrassed by. Wear it proudly as a badge of honor. Let it be another notch in your belt and another challenge you faced and triumphed over. Be proud of who you are and what you embody. In demonstrating your own self-acceptance, you will naturally inspire others to learn to accept themselves.

Self-Awareness

Self-Awareness involves developing an acute perception of all aspects of our own characters and personas. It involves becoming intimately familiar with your personality traits, characteristics, behaviors and patterns and knowing how they contribute to you as a whole. Bringing these aspects into focus will give you the opportunity to observe your patterns relationally, which will provide tremendous insight into how you interact with those around you.

Self-awareness is an incredibly powerful tool to use any time, but is particularly critical during the divorce process because a significant part of our healing begins to occur when we take inventory on ourselves and what we may have contributed to the ending of the marriage. It's easy to play the victim and point a finger and say it was the other person's fault. The reality is that every event has preceding events, and no events occur in isolation. The only thing that playing the victim will do is keep you stuck in anger, resentment, bitterness, regret and fear, and to the extent that you remain stuck, you will never be able to move forward and begin the next chapter of your life as the best version of yourself.

It's not easy to take inventory of your traits and highlight the ones that we may not be most proud of, but the sooner you do it, the sooner you will move through the healing process.

Self-Care

Self-care is the practice of nurturing your mind, body and spirit. What you choose to nourish yourself with, whether it is food, thoughts, hobbies or the people you surround yourself with, plays a vital role in the relationship you have with yourself and are all demonstrations of self-love. Rather than viewing self-care as an obligation, self-care should be viewed as a lifestyle, whereby you make conscious, mindful choices all day every day that nurture your mind, body and spirit.

The importance of self-care must be underscored particularly during the divorce process. The process is fraught with opportunities to erode virtually every aspect of ourselves, leaving us with the potential to feel physically depleted, mentally discouraged and emotionally drained. We must become mindful of our current practices and get honest with ourselves about which ones are truly serving our highest good and which practices are masking the real issues and serving as distractions. The self-care section of this book explores several considerations in much more detail.

Self-Respect

Self-respect involves honoring yourself and living in integrity with who you are. It entails bringing your thoughts, feelings and actions into harmony. Holding others to these standards is a big part of self-respect as well.

The divorce process is a prime opportunity to sharpen your skills on practicing self-respect. It's a perfect time to get crystal clear on what your standards are and hold everyone and everything up against those standards. Defining standards needs to be the first step in the process because it empowers **you** to set the bar where you want it. In the absence of standards, you are more likely to be willing to accept and tolerate anything that comes your way, even if it falls woefully short of what you think you deserve.

When certain parts of the process cause emotional flare-ups, which will undoubtedly happen, it is important to hold others to the standard of self-respect you have set for yourself. Maintaining healthy boundaries is also part of this category, learning when to say no and not feeling guilty about it and learning when to make healthy disconnections is crucial to maintain your desired level of self-respect.

Self-Confidence/Self-Esteem/Self-Worth

In my mind, these concepts are all closely intertwined and it is almost impossible to extricate one from the others. At their core, they all come down to holding one's-self in high regard. Self-confidence is a trait that's hard to miss. We all know people who have self-confidence and when they have it, there's no missing it. They radiate it. They exude this unmistakable, undeniable self-assuredness and it permeates every aspect of their being, from the way they walk and the way they talk to the way they show up unapologetically as they are and stand in their truth. They aren't concerned about who thinks what, because they know they won't please everybody. They're staunchly committed to being who they are and trust the process knowing that who is meant to be in their life will be and the others will simply fall away.

Certain things in life have the potential to strip away one's self-worth, and divorce is most certainly one of them. Divorce can leave you meeting every aspect of your existence with hesitancy and uncertainty and make you wonder if you will ever measure up. It can leave us wondering how we will ever start over and rebuild our lives and create a life that we are excited about. It can make you question if you have the ability to do a job or if an employer will have faith that you can fulfill the responsibilities required of you. It can make you wonder if others will find you attractive when you are ready to start dating again. It can make you wonder how hard it will be to overcome the stigma of divorce.

Every aspect of your life can be eroded with negative self-talk and there is enormous room for self-doubt to creep in. But, rest assured, the value and confidence you have in yourself can be restored through various mechanisms such as positive self-talk, mindset, manifestation and other modalities that are explored in different sections of this book.

Self-Compassion/Self-Forgiveness

We are often our own worst critics. We judge ourselves against everyone and everything and are quick to point out where we fall short. We are constantly comparing ourselves to others or what seems to be the socially-expected norm. This journey has nothing to do with being perfect and everything to do with being present. Making mistakes is part of the process. If we never made mistakes, we would never be learning and growing and evolving into the best version of ourselves. Trust the process, knowing that wherever you are on your journey is where you are meant to be.

A divorce situation requires an inordinate amount of self-compassion and self-forgiveness. Personal chatter can take a turn into negative territory without us even realizing it. As soon as we step out into public, we run the risk of seeing other families that present exactly the way our family used to. It is natural to reflect on your own situation and feel guilty and remorseful that it didn't turn out the way it was supposed to. Remember that in the spiritual world, the only "supposed to" is the way things are in this very moment.

Release the self-judgement and self-criticism and anchor back on self-acceptance. Untether yourself from past regrets, disappointments and grudges. Remind yourself that you were doing the best you could do with the information, knowledge and resources that were readily available to you at the time. Hindsight is always 20/20 because we have the benefit of additional wisdom and experience that we did not have then. Practice holding a sense of gentleness in everything that you do, remaining unwaveringly empathetic and extending the same kindness to yourself that you extend to others.

Pleasure

Pleasure is one of my favorite areas to discuss because it's all about **fun**!! Work hard, play harder is one of my favorite mottos, and in my humble opinion, the socially-accepted ratio of work to play is unnecessarily inflated. We've cultivated a culture where we live to work instead of work to live. Of course, we all have roles and responsibilities in various areas of our lives, and recreation time is where we often short-change ourselves. Admittedly, life can become over-scheduled with various obligations. Few of us have more time than we know what to do with, and more often than not, we must make decisions about what we have to eliminate. But, you need to consciously carve out recreational time because it helps to bring us into better balance and feel more fulfilled.

This category looks different for everyone. For some it's watching a football game and having drinks with friends. For others, it's having quiet-time to read a book and enjoying a cup of tea while curled up in a cozy chair. For others, it's an exhilarating run along the lakefront. The exciting part is that there is no right or wrong answer. Anything that makes you feel good, energized, excited, liberated, happy, joyful, content, peaceful and any other high-vibrational feeling is what you should be pursuing.

What hobbies have you been wanting to try? What's on your "someday" list? It's that list of things we'd eventually like to get to, after some external condition is met, like when your life gets easier or when you're not as busy or when you retire or when the kids are older. Don't wait. There will never be a perfect time and you will probably never feel fully ready, so pick something and just start.

Self-Expression

Self-expression involves any forum or medium you use to represent who you are. It can be in the form of words, as you persuasively share your position on a topic you feel passionate about. It could be in the form of artwork, like painting, sculpting or drawing to help you depict your emotions. It could be in the form of a musical piece, as you play your favorite song on an instrument or sing like nobody's listening. Creative outlets should be part of everyone's lives on some level.

Self-Empowerment

Self-empowerment involves owning your life. It's about taking charge (not to be confused with controlling), but understanding that you're the captain of your ship and you are single-handedly (but not without resources) responsible for your own happiness and for doing your life your way. Regardless of the cards you have been dealt, you can make great strides each day toward the life of your dreams. We hear stories of triumph every single day. People who beat insurmountable odds. People who persevered when the cards were stacked against them. The quality they all have in common is that they were all totally obstinate in their refusal to give up. The Universe loves stubbornness. It quickly recognizes when desires are heart-centered, and conspires to make it happen. The Universe loves when we make an effort to claim our own personal power and will always join us in our endeavors.

This is where you get to dream big. It's where you get to revisit the road not traveled or brainstorm where you might want to pave your own road. No idea is too outlandish. This is where you get to claim the world as your oyster.

View divorce as a gracious invitation from the Universe for a new beginning. You have just been handed a blank canvas and your palette has a variety of brilliant colors. You have a variety of brushes in all shapes and sizes at your disposal. Wield your paint brushes with confidence, dignity and the knowingness that you are guided and supported by Universal forces and begin painting your masterpiece.

Self-Realization/Self-Actualization

An antecedent to the self-empowerment process is self-realization and self-actualization. Both are closely linked and involve shedding what remains of our fear-based egos as we are immersed deeper into our soul journeys. Here is where we develop cravings to ask ourselves deeper questions, like, "What are my passions?" "What is my life purpose?" "What am I meant to accomplish?" "What comes naturally to me?" "What gifts do I bring into this world?" "How can I use these gifts as a service to humanity?" "What sets my soul on fire?"

Practicing self-love on a regular basis requires commitment. This paradigm shift will involve learning to recognize when you are lapsing back into your old ways of operating and will prompt you to replace that programming with new programming that better serves you. Like anything else, the more you practice it, the more natural it will become over time.

Lifestyle Choices

Loving yourself also includes making lifestyle choices that support your overall physical, mental and spiritual well-being.

Engaging in activities like excessively drinking alcohol, smoking, recreational drugs, gambling or other addictive behaviors on an excessive and consistent basis is not congruent with a holistic lifestyle and will make it more difficult for you to achieve the peace, harmony and balance that comes with connecting to your Higher Self.

Establishing Boundaries

Boundaries are crucial because they are a mechanism that encourages us to honor who we are by mindfully making decisions about what we allow into our space. This is where we set guidelines about how we want to operate within relationships, what we will accept and what we deem to be unacceptable.

Make Necessary Simplifications

You may consider making some simplifications to make day-to-day life more manageable. You still have the same number of hours in the week to work with...168...and every hour spent on the divorce process and other necessary activities related to the divorce is one fewer hour you will have to spend on other things. You will have to be the one to decide what areas of your life require simplification. It is important to try to simplify proportionately across the board by making mindful decisions. For example, don't keep certain categories whole at the expense of eliminating all of your recreational time.

Under normal circumstances, I love to cook. I totally geek out on raiding the produce section of the grocery store and coming home, turning on music and chopping fresh veggies on my island. We all have our "thing," and this is one of mine. There were days during the divorce process when I simply did not have the time, and other days I didn't have the energy to cook. So, I took the liberty of picking up dinner on those days. Initially, it felt like a failure to me. The kids would normally ask me what we were having for dinner, and during the divorce process, they started asking me "if" I was making dinner. At first, I felt guilty, as if I was falling short of my motherly duties. They had clearly grown up accustomed to me cooking regularly just as I had experienced growing up, but I had to remind myself that this was temporary and as soon as the process was over I would get back in the kitchen and resume doing what I love doing.

Decluttering

The spaces in which we live and the way in which they are organized have an impact on us energetically. The less cluttered the space, the less cluttered my mind feels. I find that I have more clarity and a sense of calmness when my space is devoid of extraneous items. Less truly is more.

One thing that I discovered about myself during the process is how insignificant material items are. I never considered myself to be materialistic, but throughout the course of my journey, I've had to dissect all facets of my life and really pinpoint where I should be focusing my energy. Intertwined in my decluttering initiative was preponderance on the concepts of happiness and freedom. I found that the more time I spent contemplating those topics, the more detached I became from material items. It was becoming quickly and abundantly clear that for me happiness is tied to freedom...freedom of choice, freedom from judgement, freedom from being tethered to something that I don't feel passionate about. This phase of my journey has catapulted me to a place that is all about the experiences, not at all about the stuff. Energetically, decluttering has helped me to feel free and less tethered and supports the direction in which I am taking my life.

We all need to find our own equilibrium and figure out what our own happy medium is. Like so many other things in life, there is no one right answer, and the joy is in discovering what works for you as you evolve.

Accepting Help From Others

Divorce is not the time to play the hero and cast the image that you're fitting in all things divorce-related in between bites of lunch. Again, the divorce process can be mentally, emotionally and physically taxing. Realize that you don't have to go this alone, and it's okay to ask for help.

We are often hesitant to ask others for help regardless of what is going on in our lives because we don't want to overburden other people and don't want to be perceived as if we are unable to handle everything on our own. It is my belief that the vast majority of people enjoy helping others. I know I love it when I'm asked to help someone. Some people don't want to overstep their bounds, and others don't know what you need. If you need help, simply ask for it. The people in your life who care about you and want the best for you will be honored to be asked. Maybe you need someone to pick up the kids. Maybe you just need someone to listen as you process your thoughts. Maybe you need someone to watch the kids as you take some time to recharge. Asking for help will play a huge part in cultivating the spirit of "we are all in this together," and the same people you ask to help you will most likely feel comfortable reciprocating the request for help in the future, and you'll be happy to help.

Limit Social Media

Social media is great for some things, and not so great for others. While it has its merits and allows us to share in the lives of our friends and family, social media content is filtered and skewed and is not an authentic representation of people's lives. Furthermore, you have limited control over what shows up in your feed, and you're often inundated with pictures of happy, smiling faces, some of whom fit the model of what your family used to look like, and it can be a harsh reminder and catch you off-guard at a time when you're feeling particularly vulnerable.

Social media is often used as a place to vent feelings and frustrations, but in the case of a divorce or any other situation where emotions are high and information is sensitive, it is best to process those feelings and emotions within the context of the appropriate professional setting. Broadcasting on social media may be your first inclination when you're seeking retaliation or revenge or trying to rally troops for your army, but nobody ever regretted taking the high road. Regardless of the other person's actions, you are responsible for yours. Be the first to disengage. Be the first to ignore. Be the first to break the cycle. Be the first to take the high road. Then, watch how your former spouse responds. One of my favorite phrases is "Is it kind? Is it appropriate? Is it true?" This is a great filter to apply not only within the social media context, but in all aspects of our lives.

This chapter has given you several ideas to consider on the journey to loving yourself. Adopting self-love ideals into your everyday life with a sense of gentleness and balance will allow you to weave these new modalities into your life naturally and organically.

Discovering Your Authenticity

- What aspects of yourself need the most work in integrating and accepting them as part of who you are?
- What are examples of interactions with others that have heightened your self-awareness?
- Which of your current lifestyle choices are serving you and which ones are not?
- How can you make adjustments in your lifestyle to fill your time with activities that support your growth and transformation?
- What are some things you need to forgive yourself for?
- How would you rate your self-worth, and what are some adjustments you could make to heighten it?
- What are some creative endeavors that you currently enjoy, and what are some new creative endeavors you would like to explore?
- What are some ways in which you could simplify your life?

For a special bonus on loving yourself, visit https://liveauthentically.today/soar-resources to download the guide.

19

SPIRITUAL ALIGNMENT

Spiritual alignment is the ticket that allows you entry into the arena of unlimited personal power.

What is spiritual alignment anyway, why is it important, and how do you achieve it in your day to day life? This chapter will address one of the most worthwhile initiatives in the world of spirituality.

The most powerful thing you can do every day is to make it your mission to take steps toward getting spiritually aligned. What does being aligned mean? Being aligned means connecting to your Higher Self. It means making decisions that make you feel amazing. It means living your truth. It means honoring **you**. It means doing what resonates with your soul. It means doing what feels right. It means plugging into Universal Energy. The best way to put yourself in a position to receive what is in your highest good is to align yourself with Source Energy. Source Energy... you can call it what you want, be it "Higher Power", "God", "The Universe", "Universal Energy", "Creator", it all goes back to the same place. It's that limitless energy that flows through the Universe and each of us every moment of every day. When we learn how to take steps in our daily lives to become aligned is when the magic really starts. We begin to tap into the never-ending, constantly-flowing energy source that sustains all life and allows us to access our personal power.

There are lots of fancy-schmancy metaphysical definitions of spiritual alignment, but mine is simply feeling amazing physically, mentally, emotionally and spiritually. It requires a healthy dose of self-awareness coupled with a mega-dose of creativity and open-mindedness.

The exciting part is that every moment of every day presents us with the opportunity to choose alignment. Alignment doesn't happen by accident; it's something that we consciously strive for in every moment of every day. Like anything else, the more you practice it, the better you become. Before too long, it becomes second-nature and being aligned will be the underlying motivating factor and you will intrinsically and effortlessly choose thoughts and activities that support your alignment.

I think back to when I first seriously started diving into spirituality a few years ago, and I remember feeling overwhelmed by all these grandiose, lofty-sounding terms referring to metaphysical concepts. I so desperately wanted to dive in and learn as much as possible as quickly as possible but didn't quite know how. Many of them described states of being I wished to attain or described concepts I wanted to master but I didn't know where to start. I knew that being aligned meant honoring myself and while I made efforts to align my thoughts, actions and behaviors with my beliefs, my approach felt haphazard and I wasn't able to sustain it for any respectable length of time. I felt like I sort of stumbled my way into alignment from time to time by way of blind luck and didn't know how to make it last. I remember feeling frustrated because there was no how-to guide or formulaic approach to get from where I was to where I wanted to be, which was, of course, the state of being aligned.

This feeling of frustration and confusion propelled me to relentlessly explore the topic and attempt to incorporate certain strategies into my day-to-day life. I found that the process of teaching myself how to get into alignment has been a fascinating and eye-opening process of self-discovery and has involved much trial and error along the way. Remember that everyone's path to spiritual alignment will look different, and this section will give you ideas to think about on your journey to alignment.

The most important thing you do every day is to align with Source Energy.

Cosmic Flash

We've all experienced those moments in life where things suddenly clicked..."ah-hah" moments, epiphanies, call it what you will. It's those moments of sudden realization when we begin to look at something in a new way.

It clicked for me when I made the association that feeling amazing is the pathway to spiritual alignment. Despite all the fancy-shmancy metaphysical definitions of alignment, at its core, it's simple. All you need to do is take steps toward feeling amazing and you will illuminate the path to Source Energy.

What Does Spiritual Alignment Feel Like?

Alignment can come in the form of a variety of different feelings. Sometimes it's a feeling of pure joy, bliss, childlike wonderment and excitement. Sometimes it's peace. Sometimes it's contentment.

Sometimes it's satisfaction. Whatever it is though, it always feels good. For me, it reminds me of that feeling I would get when I was a kid laying on my back on a blanket on a hot summer night watching fireworks. I remember being so fully immersed in the experience to the point where everything else faded away. It's the feeling that you're practically bursting at the seams with excitement thinking that life doesn't get any better than that moment. That's how I feel the majority of each day because I have learned to live in the present and only allow emotions that feel good.

As we go through life, we become saddled down with limitations placed on us through societal conditioning, as fear and doubt move closer to the front row of our psyche. We gradually begin to lose touch with the essence of who we are in our purest and most authentic form, as multiple layers of external influences are piled on.

The good news is that we can absolutely get back to that place and feeling as adults, but it's not something that happens overnight. We have to be willing to commit to our own personal growth by abandoning any programming that no longer serves us and replace it with new thought patterns that place us on a trajectory that will allow us to reconnect to who we are.

We still can and do have those moments, but they are fleeting and are often crowded out by thoughts of worry, fear, doubt, anxiety and all of our day-to-day responsibilities. We don't even realize that they are fleeting moments of alignment. We often can't put our finger on how the feeling arrived and don't know what to do to make it stay. We need to anchor on that feeling and get really comfortable with what that feels like. When you're there, make a conscious effort to stay there. When anything, whether it is a thought, an external stimulus, another person or something else, attempts to pull you down into a lower vibration, challenge yourself and say, "No, I don't want to feel like **that**; I want to feel like **this**." When those thoughts come back in, push them right out. Tell yourself that you are making the decision that you are not going to give them any attention right now or put any energy there. You will choose where your attention goes and you choose to keep your thoughts happy and joyful and all the places that make you feel amazing.

Staying in Spiritual Alignment

We are all peppered with things that compromise our spiritual alignment every day multiple times a day...it's called life. Life can throw us curveballs, and they come in all sizes and at all speeds. From waking up late to dealing with challenging people to losing a job, opportunities to pull us into a lower state of being abound. The magnitude of the issue will have a direct relationship to the size of the adjustment needed to realign, as well as the duration required to achieve it, but it is important to remember to anchor back on the present moment. It's easy to become overwhelmed, discouraged, frustrated or hopeless, and most of the time it's because our minds are in a place that is lightyears away from our current realities. Anchoring on to the present moment and consciously choosing how you want to feel is the best way to navigate these feelings.

Here's a real-life example of something we all deal with from time to time, and how to not let it pull you out of alignment. If someone wants to suck you into a self-made drama, make the commitment to yourself to **not allow** them to. Understand that for you to be pulled into something, you are effectively giving the person permission to pull you in. You are handing over your power and letting him or her effectively make a decision for you.

Say to yourself "That's not where I want to be right now. I'm feeling amazing and on my high-flying disc and I don't want to be pulled down into low-vibrational feelings that make me not feel good. I'm going to stay where I am. I'm going to stay in that happy place. I'm going to stay in a place where I feel totally invincible. I feel like I'm in a car in the fast lane, going around everyone and everything and nothing is slowing me down." When you achieve that feeling, you don't want to be anywhere else. As you practice this affirmation, it becomes increasingly challenging to tolerate living any other way.

Living in the Moment

The best way to achieve alignment is to live in the moment. When you are truly living in the moment, you allow yourself to experience the depth and richness life has to offer to the greatest extent possible. Being deeply immersed in it leaves no room to ruminate on the past. You recognize that the past is the past, and understand that everything that occurred has played an instrumental part in delivering you to where you currently are. You don't have to worry about the future because you understand that you have a very powerful role in creating it, and what you attract into your existence is driven by how you feel and what is needed for your evolution. The better you feel, the more amazingness you attract, and the more amazingness you attract, the better you feel. Life is nothing but a series of moments and each moment gives us the opportunity to make a choice. Make a choice in each moment to embody high-vibrational emotions and over time your world will begin to reflect that. The Law of Attraction won't let it happen any other way.

Spiritual Alignment Must be Earned Every Moment of Every Day

Alignment is not a permanent condition. It is not akin to earning a degree or certification or title and having it forevermore.

It's more like the process of getting into shape physically and subscribes to the "use it or lose it" ideology. You can achieve peak levels of physical fitness, but to maintain your level of physical fitness, you must continue to work at it. If you discontinue your efforts, you'll end up right back where you started.

It's a practice that you keep at the forefront of your consciousness throughout the day by maintaining a high level of self-awareness and mindfully making choices in each moment about your behaviors, thoughts and emotions. The goal is always to consciously choose thoughts that make you feel good.

You want to get to a place where you can quickly recognize when you are falling out of alignment and consciously choose to replace those thoughts with happier thoughts. Attempt to identify where the thoughts that don't make you feel good are originating and replace them with thoughts that get you back into alignment. It usually stems back to a fear or doubt. I encounter this all the time. In fact, in the spirit of full disclosure, I encountered it while writing this book. One day my ego decided that it would try to infuse a little doubt and I started thinking thoughts along the lines of "I'm going to have a hard time reaching my daily word-count quota today. I'm not sure if enough material will come to me." I quickly tuned into how that made me feel, and it was clear that I didn't like it. I felt deflated. Discouraged. Stifled. Rather than try to push through it and force it when I was in an energetically unfavorable state, I stepped away and took about 15 minutes to regroup. I cleared my mind, and did things that make me happy. I turned on music. Really loud music and sang like nobody was listening. I summoned assistance from my spirit guides and asked them to help me deliver the message I'm supposed to deliver. I completely rewrote my script and coached myself through it by saying "This is why you're here. You're living your purpose. You're meant to share your gifts with the world in this way, so get excited about sharing what you know, and start writing." I subsequently sat down and wrote some of my most powerful content. I was so grateful that my ego decided to assert it's voice because it gave me the extra boost that I needed. Everything serves a purpose.

"You've Changed"

Spiritual alignment feels different from the inside, so it would stand to reason that it looks different from the outside. We all know people who make it their mission to stay aligned. It's pretty obvious when someone is aligned because the way they approach life is radically different than it used to be and the energy they exude is unmistakably radiant and magnetic. It's often hard to describe because feelings and words are different vibrationally. There is significant growth associated with becoming aligned. In the process of becoming aligned, you shed your old programming and adopt new ways of living. In this process, others can't help but notice your growth. It's not uncommon for others to articulate their recognition of how different you are than you used to be, and "you've changed" is a comment that isn't uncommon to hear. That's the point. When someone notices a change in you, it is a sure sign you have experienced growth and transformation.

What You Think of You is the Only Opinion That Matters

One of the more pleasant side-effects of being aligned is that you will no longer be concerned with people's opinions of you. Even if others express disapproval or discontentment with something that you are doing in your own life, you will learn to not let it permeate your energy field and allow it to lower your vibration. Others' reactions and opinions can only affect you negatively if you allow it to. Retain your power. Don't hand it over to anyone else willingly and let them be the creator of your reality. You should be the one to continue to wield the magician's wand to work your magic in your own life.

Sometimes when others' opinions and thought forms are infused in your process, the atmosphere quickly becomes congested. It reminds me of the "too many cooks in the kitchen" analogy. There's only room for one executive chef at your restaurant, and you're it. You don't need others dictating what they think should be on the menu in your restaurant. When this issue becomes pervasive or recurring, it is best to address the issue to make sure others understand that it's important for you that they respect your autonomy and independence when it comes to decision-making for your own life. Certain discussions are easier to have when you are aligned. I believe that most good-hearted people sincerely want to help when they are giving advice but there are some extremely significant oversights being made when advice is given freely and without permission. First and foremost, the recipient may not be in a place where he or she is open to receiving external input. Additionally, the advice that person is giving is coming from his or her vantage point which is not the same as yours, and is filtered through the lens of that person's personal experiences and belief systems as the backdrop.

You'll also find yourself becoming less tolerant of others' behaviors that you may have tolerated in the past. You will become more comfortable with articulating your standards because you are more sure of who you are and more confident that the way you are living is in line with your Highest Self. You'll understand that making healthy disconnections is an important part of the process, as you experience that holding on to toxic relationships or relationships that you have outgrown only hinders your personal growth. Remember that none of this is personal; it is all vibrational. Disconnections and rejections are just two of the mechanisms the Universe uses to help us create space in our lives for what is truly meant for us.

Trusting the Process

When you achieve alignment, you realize that there is no room for fear. Fear doesn't have a remotely supporting role in your play because you realize that no matter what happens, you will be okay. You may be living a different reality than you envisioned yourself living at this point, but you will be okay. Recognize the value of harnessing and optimizing your personal power and understand that you are limitless. You take risks that you didn't take before, and even some of the decisions you make and risks you are comfortable taking now would have been unfathomable at earlier points in your evolution. You understand that everything is unfolding perfectly and place your utmost trust in the Universe.

What Activities Do You Naturally Gravitate Toward?

Consciously and subconsciously, we know that we like to feel good. Joy is our natural state and the totality of our being. The mind, body and spirit naturally gravitate toward activities that make us reconnect with feelings of joy and bliss. We like how we feel when we are embodying high-vibrational feelings. When we become aware of how addictive feeling good really is, we start to crave activities that promote these feelings.

How do I know what makes me feel good? There are some obvious answers to this question as we can consciously choose what we do, but there is an operational element actively at work at a subconscious level too, and we might not even be aware that it's taking place unless we pull back the curtain further and really dissect our choices. One of the best barometers for this is by looking at how you spend your discretionary time. I started to pay attention to the activities that I naturally gravitated toward, and as a result of observing my own patterns and evaluating where I spent my time, certain aspects of myself were revealed. I found myself gravitating toward activities that I know will flow because they were natural and easy and creative and fun.

Activities that I would subconsciously avoid were activities that were challenging or those that would exploit internal blocks. For example, I usually have a master to-do list handy. It's what helps me keep track of things across all areas of my life and helps to minimize the chance that something will fall between the cracks. Sometimes a week will go by, or sometimes two, and I'll notice that I carried over activities from day to day or from week to week and hadn't started them. My initial reaction was to find justification for the inaction like I was too busy or didn't have time. Some of these tasks would have only taken 10 or 15 minutes, and I had to get really honest with myself and remind myself that there are 168 hours in a week, so the reason for not getting it done was likely not that I didn't have enough time. When I looked at this situation in more depth, I realized that the common thread is that there was an element of avoidance or resistance. For instance, I may have subconsciously embodied the belief that the task wouldn't have gone smoothly or wouldn't "flow" the way my other activities did. Another possibility could have been that the task involved a conversation that may have had the potential for being uncomfortable or an activity that involved a length of time over which I had no control, like getting a driver's license or passport updated. Often, it stemmed back to some type of underlying fear or doubt. Energetically, I find that situations like these weigh on me more heavily than I realized and I find that it helps to identify the block and decide how to handle it. I address it and push through it, and after I clear it from my space it never ceases to amaze me how much lighter I feel energetically.

The process of evaluating our "feel good" activities can get a little sticky because certain activities that we perceive as entertainment to make us feel good in the moment might actually be masking underlying issues or acting as self-medicating tactics to avoid dealing with our own current reality. For example, people may say activities like gambling or drinking alcohol make them feel good. But, it's important to maintain balance and be mindful when one has crossed the line that separates fun and entertainment from avoidance and self-medicating behaviors. A licensed professional can always help you make the determination and help you discern that your time is being spent in healthy and productive ways that nurture your mind, body and spirit.

The Universe fully supports situations that foster connectivity among people and it loves situations that cultivate relationships. After all, human interactions and relationships give us the forum to bring aspects of ourselves into our awareness and give us the opportunity to evolve. Connecting with other people is what gives us the opportunity to be vulnerable and transparent, which are portals for accessing and expressing unconditional love. Sometimes it's necessary to spend time recharging in solitude, but when we spend time with others, we choose to spend time with people who make us feel good. People who energize us. People who are fun.

The Energy of Creation

Creativity fuels spiritual alignment and spiritual alignment fuels creativity. The Universe loves it when our energy is poured into creative endeavors because we are expressing our own individuality and sharing our uniqueness with the world, which can come in a multitude of different forms, like art, playing a musical instrument, writing, singing, dancing, sharing your sense of humor, cooking or baking. When we are plugged into Universal Energy, we draw directly from that same creative energy from which the Universe originated. Pay attention to how your creative endeavors are unfolding. If it's flowing and feels organic and natural, you can be assured the Universe is working with you as you imprint your unique energy signature on the world.

In the many years I spent living prior to becoming conscious, I thrived on high-productivity activities and crossing things off my to-do list because self-worth was almost entirely dictated by being busy and by "doing." I've arrived at a point where first and foremost I am acutely aware of how I feel, and everything else is secondary and fills in around that. Now I know that self-worth is measured by the feeling and the being, not by what I'm doing. Everything that I used to work so hard to achieve flows naturally as a result of being aligned. Creativity soars, productivity is a natural by-product, and happiness and fulfillment abound.

Creativity fuels spiritual alignment and spiritual alignment fuels creativity.

Transmuting Pain Into Power

Early on in my divorce process, professionals expressed concerns that I wasn't exhibiting the normal behaviors commonly displayed by people in my situation. The concern was that I was suppressing my anger and if I didn't release it somehow, I would only be deferring it. There was no way to totally avoid it and it would eventually show up somewhere. I could totally see where they were coming from. I just decided that we were getting divorced and the life that we had so meticulously curated over 20 years of married life was imploding. I don't think I could have conjured up any new and unprecedented expression of anger, either in the form of words or actions, that hadn't been witnessed before. Where are the outward expressions of anger? Shouldn't I be kicking him out of the house? Shouldn't I be making it my mission to make his life as miserable as possible? I think everyone was just waiting and wondering when I would finally react like most people. But I am not "most people." I do things that are in accordance with who I am and what resonates with me at a deep level. I don't follow conventional norms. I don't break rules out of defiance, but I am willing to test and bend them out of a deep desire to find a new and improved way of doing things. I've gotten comfortable with making waves because that's where people have the opportunity to learn to surf.

I'd be dishonest if I said I didn't experience some degree of anger and sadness and a variety of other unpleasant emotions at various points during the process. That's normal, and regardless of where a person is on his or her journey, we all have the potential to experience the full range of human emotions. My secret sauce was staying acutely aware of how I felt in each moment and making conscious, mindful choices that were in my highest good. I honored and validated the emotions as they arose, particularly the unwanted ones, and subsequently redirected my energy into a more productive purpose. I had conversations with myself and my self-talk sounded much like this, "How is wallowing in this anger and perpetuating any feelings of self-pity helping me or anybody else in this situation?" "How would bringing more negativity into the situation serve my highest good?" "I am responsible and accountable for my actions and they are not justified or admissible on the basis of anyone else's choices or actions." Knowing that my kids were my audience twenty-four hours a day, seven days a week and that I had eight tiny eyes watching my every move helped to motivate me to conduct myself with grace and dignity, knowing that this would serve all of us now and in the future. I coached myself all day every day by constantly challenging myself with questions centered around "What would love do?" and "What is the highest pathway through this?"

I did and still do experience the same range of human emotions that everyone else is subject to, across a wide range of different situations. Regardless of one's level of spiritual evolution, none of us are exempt from that. We will all feel anger, sadness, guilt, regret and various other emotions that do not make us feel good. Being spiritual doesn't make one exempt from getting dealt some pretty crummy cards and doesn't prevent us from feeling the painful emotions commonly experienced during those situations. But what spirituality **does** do is affords us the opportunity to transmute our pain and use these experiences as springboards for our personal growth and transformation.

It would not always become readily apparent into what exactly I could transmute my emotions. Sometimes I channeled my energy into short-term expressions of creativity such as music or art. Other times, I simply planted the seeds and surrendered to the infinite intelligence and wisdom of the Universe that the garden I was planting would eventually yield an abundant crop. I had no idea what would bloom, but I flowed with the Universe and signed on to be a co-creator in my reality as I agreed to tend to my garden and water it every day. I cultivated my garden and sprinkled it with frequent doses of self-love, self-compassion, empathy, and many other forms of self-care. There was a huge element of trusting the process that entailed frequently reminding myself that I was precisely where I was meant to be at every moment in time. It felt like a huge leap of faith but knowing that the Universe always has my highest good in mind is all I need to know.

This won't be the last time I have to deal with a challenging situation in this lifetime; that's for certain. I'll watch people I love gradually transition out of human form. I'll unexpectedly receive a phone call one day that will feel like it's straight out of a nightmare and I'll want nothing more than to wake up and wish it would go away. I'll encounter roadblocks and unexpected detours on my path. Our true power is harnessed when we mindfully and consciously choose our response to a situation rather than letting our emotions lead the way, and learn how to transmute our pain into power.

We all must deal with situations we wouldn't necessarily choose for ourselves at various points in our lives, but we always have a choice in how we deal with them. Sometimes life dishes out a lemon. Sometimes it dishes out two. Sometimes five. Sometimes a bag, at which point it is natural to wonder how much more you can possibly be expected to handle. Remember that there is always divine orchestration behind everything. What appears to be chaos on the surface always has a foundation of underlying perfect divine order. The Universe always knows what it will take to shake up our current reality and shift us out of stagnant paradigms. It knows us so well that every aspect of the catalyst it sends us, right down to form and magnitude and every other conceivable element, is specifically chosen for us and is meant to propel us further into our personal growth and unleash our true power. The bag of lemons very well may be a nudge from the Universe to open up a lemonade stand as you share your secret recipe that only your energy signature can share.

Discovering Your Authenticity

- Have you experienced what it feels like to be plugged in to Universal Energy?
- What changes do you notice about yourself?
- What changes do others notice in you?
- What creative endeavors do you currently enjoy?
- What new creative endeavors are you interested in exploring?
- Have you experienced how your feelings are the best barometer for how aligned you are?

For a special bonus on connecting to the essence of who you are, visit https://liveauthentically.today/soar-resources to download the guide.

20

GETTING REAL WITH YOURSELF

Transparency and vulnerability are the keys to unlocking the doorway to the world of spiritual growth and transformation.

What Can I Learn From This?

When life isn't playing out as you once planned, it is easy to fall down the rabbit hole of negative self-talk and wallow in thoughts of self-pity, like "Why me?" "Everyone else has it easier." "Woe is me." "It's all her fault." Phrases centered around self-pity are endless, and when you repeat them like a mantra, before you know it, you'll be on a runaway train of hopelessness.

The breakdown of a committed relationship is a golden opportunity to take a personal inventory on what you may have contributed to the breakdown. This exercise has nothing to do with proving who was right and who was wrong and everything to do with your growth and transformation.

Every relationship, regardless of the outcome, is a tremendous gift. It's a landscape that offers lush vegetation and ripe fruit that all bear the potential to be incredibly nutritious, delicious and sweet if you cultivate it in the right way. It's an opportunity to go deep within yourself and do the healing work necessary so that you can emerge as a stronger, more authentic version of you.

Every human interaction and interpersonal relationship holds up a mirror to us and gives us the opportunity to take a more introspective look at ourselves. Sometimes we like what we see and other times we notice things that may not be pleasurable to see and the natural reflex is to quickly put the mirror down. It may work for you in the moment because you choose to redirect your attention to something that is more pleasing to the eye, but at the end of the day, the "flaws" and other characteristics you didn't like to look at are still there and unchanged.

It's easy to bask in the ambiance of the parts of yourself that you like. It's not so easy, however, to own up to the parts you aren't so proud of and keep your walls up so that others will think you are smart, pretty or strong. We are human, and we have the potential to embody a wide range of elements in our own personas, and some of them leave us feeling unworthy, undesirable, unlovable and a variety of other self-deprecating feelings.

The opportunity to heal yourself comes in many shapes and sizes. Therapists are particularly instrumental in escorting you through the healing process and there are several methods available. Regardless of the method or methods chosen, the objective is to fully heal yourself and emerge from the process as your authentic self so that you will be in a position to move forward feeling whole and empowered.

I'm going to take this opportunity to do a brief commercial for therapy. I think everyone, regardless of what phase of life he or she is in, could benefit from seeing a therapist at regular intervals. Life can be complicated. It can present challenges. It's a steady stream of changes. It is prudent to proactively arm yourself with the tools and skills necessary so that you are in the best possible position to thrive, rather than just survive, or worse yet — get beaten down by life. During periods of transition or high-stress situations, it is a good idea to make visits more frequently, and when you are coasting comfortably all you may need is a simple wellness check, just as you would schedule an annual physical with your general practitioner. We invest in our physical well-being through lifestyle, diet and exercise and do so proudly and publicly. Why is it that we are not making investments in our mental and emotional well-being on a regular basis? There has long been a stigma associated with working with mental health professionals, in part because people often associate them with conditions that nobody wants to talk about like anxiety and depression. I think it's time that society at large start to talk about this more openly as people embrace the idea that it is a necessary part of our overall wellness.

Shadow Work

Think about yourself like an ornately-adorned treasure chest that is hand-painted with metallics and sprinkled with radiant eye-catching jewels. Inside the treasure chest are thousands of brightly colored, vibrant, sparkling, glistening gemstones. Scattered amongst the gemstones are some rocks and pebbles, in dark colors, rough textures and matte finishes. You keep those meticulously disguised at the bottom of the heap so that nobody will ever notice them. Your treasure chest is locked. The keys to unlock the treasure chest are not given out freely and are only attainable to those who are willing to work for them. The "work" to be done is growth-based and transformation-oriented, and involves vulnerability, transparency and authenticity. One of the ways you can earn your key is by doing "shadow work."

The goal is to arrive at a place of wholeness, and it is this state that will support our expansion. It is not until you earn the key and open your treasure chest that your jewels will spill out into the world for everyone to admire and enjoy.

I used the process of shadow work to unlock my treasure chest, based on the work of psychologist Carl Jung. It refers to the process of integrating all parts of ourselves, both the light and the dark, so that we may come from a place of light and love.

The shadow part of ourselves is the place where we relegate all the facets of us that we want to disown. We all walk around with masks on trying to uphold a certain image to others. We all want to feel accepted and minimize the chance that people will judge or reject us, so we cast an image to the world based on what we think people want to see, rather than striving to project a real, raw, unadulterated, authentic representation of ourselves.

To fully heal and emerge as an authentic version of yourself, you must acknowledge all parts of your being and fully integrate them. Shadow work can induce fear because in this place there is nowhere to hide. There is no running from yourself anymore. It's you, looking at yourself in the mirror with no mask on and all your flaws exposed.

It is an incredibly deep process and it is important to go through this process at a comfortable pace. This is a long-distance run, not a sprint. There are no medals for the person who finishes first. The most important thing is that you finish the race at your own pace and feel whole and energized as you cross the finish line.

A comprehensive overview of shadow work is beyond the scope of this book, but here's a small excerpt from my personal experience.

After I enumerated everything that lived within my dark side, I began the process of dissecting each aspect, one by one. I had to come to a place of acceptance for each characteristic within my shadow self and then began pulling back the curtain and inviting all parts of the shadow onto center stage under the spotlight for their own solo performance.

I have been a procrastinator for as long as I can remember. It's a trait that I've grown accustomed to keeping tucked away because I was fearful that people would view me as being disorganized or unreliable, and I think I did a pretty good job of keeping it under wraps because if you would ask people who know me well, they would most likely guess that I am not a procrastinator.

After years of becoming really frustrated and super-stressed because I was resisting how I naturally operated and tried to force a different way, I've finally learned to accept that it's just part and parcel of how I operate. I had to let go of the idea of how I thought I should be operating, and flow with how I am operating. I've finally learned how to embrace it and flow with it rather than resisting. I found that resisting takes so much effort and doesn't translate into anything productive or enjoyable.

I've come to accept that most of my best ideas come at the eleventh hour. I will notice a sharp spike in creativity as deadlines approach and ideas come with ease. I work efficiently when I feel crunched for time. I have fun with it. So, now in the interim rather than stress about any lack of productivity, I pour my energy into other things on my plate and trust the process and know that it will get done, and I will be extremely satisfied with the outcome. Now, I finally have the confidence and the trust-filled knowingness that the ideas will come but just on their own time.

Life is so much easier when we stop trying to swim upstream. We're not salmon. Release and swim **with** the current. Let go of the totally self-deprecating thought of how you **should** be doing things, and embrace how you **are** doing things. All parts of us work together to make us the perfectly imperfect individuals that we are, and all parts of us should be welcomed and celebrated.

Discovering Your Authenticity

- What are some parts of you that reside within your dark side? How might they be reframed and used as your greatest assets?
- Think back to various situations where you blamed someone else for something. Challenge yourself to assess how you contributed to the issue or outcome.
- When have you played the role of the victim, and how can you use that experience for growth and transformation?

21

FORGIVENESS AND RELEASING JUDGEMENT

Karma is an invitation from the Universe to expand your awareness.

Let Go of the Past

Regardless of the situation you are in, learning to let go of the past is one of the most freeing things we can do for ourselves. Often, people stay fixated and remain stuck on an event that occurred in the past. Sometimes the events are as significant as past traumas. Sometimes people are pining for days in the past when life was simpler. Regardless of the origin, we must recognize that the past is gone and there is no way to undo, redo or recreate it, and ruminating on it simply doesn't serve us well. Your past has played a huge role in shaping who you are today, and while you must recognize and honor the impact prior events have played in creating today's version of you, you must be careful not to let it limit or stifle you from moving forward in a healthy and productive way.

How to Not Judge

If you are anchored to a belief system that ties people and their behaviors to man-made agreements and right versus wrong, it will be very challenging to learn how to release judgement. Judgement will keep you stuck in a place of bitterness, resentment and anything else that prevents us from moving forward. To truly free ourselves, we must abandon the inclination to judge. Getting to a judgement-free place of acceptance and forgiveness is a process of self-discovery and will launch you to unprecedented levels of consciousness, as you learn how to step into the human experiences of others and master compassion, empathy and forgiveness. Learning to release judgement requires a sustained effort over a prolonged period of time, but my hope is that this section gives you a few insights for starting down that path.

In the weeks immediately following the discovery of my husband's affair, I found myself lapsing into thoughts of judgement. It's a natural reaction of the human condition to go there. It was in these moments that I forced myself to dig deeper. I started to have feelings of anger. Anger is an extremely low-vibrational emotion, and I have grown acutely aware of how I feel physically when I harbor emotions of low vibration. I simply don't like how I feel. So, over and over again, I would try to figure out a way to climb out of that deep, dark hole that I had fallen into. The only way out was to allow myself to feel the more vulnerable feelings and get really honest with myself about why we shouldn't be judging others' actions.

I found myself measuring his actions up against the definition of "integrity," which involves doing the "right thing" even when nobody's looking. I had always taken that expression at face value, but in the depths of my despair and deep-seated desire to heal and move through the process as efficaciously as possible,

I had no choice but to dissect the definition further. What did "right thing" mean anyway? Who defines that? Is that the ego-based definition or the soul-based definition? Why is it that I should be the one to judge his "right thing?"

If I had the right to judge him, then wouldn't it stand to reason that he would have the right to judge me? Had I been totally open and honest with him and shared my doubts and concerns about the long-term viability of our marriage, from my vantage point? Had I been totally open and honest about the fact that I had been in fear mode for a while and was totally overwhelmed by the idea of making changes to our family structure? Was the life that I was living congruent with what was going on in my heart?

Judgement presumes a "superiority complex," the idea that certain people are superior to others and are more experienced, all-knowing or evolved than others. There is no place for ranking in the world of spirituality. We are all equals and hierarchies don't exist. We are all students and teachers and we are all exactly where we are meant to be, and we all are doing our best from our own particular level of consciousness. Every soul comes here with a predetermined set of lessons to master and each soul calls in the experiences with predetermined agreements with other souls.

We enter these man-made agreements and make promises that entail "forever" based on what our conscious minds know and perceive at that particular moment in time, but fail to recognize that our souls have other agendas.

Karma

The word "karma" often conjures up thoughts of a punitive,

retaliatory ideology. The comments about it are common — "Karma bus," "What goes around comes around." These statements suggest a spirit of retaliation and revenge, precisely what the ego would want us to seek.

When we step out of our egos and into our own spirits, we can more productively view karma as an invitation from the Universe that graciously summons our willingness to learn from our experiences all day, every day. Every experience we have is a karmic lesson. When we accept the invitation, the lesson becomes an exciting opportunity to learn and grow. I view it as a brilliant mechanism the Universe has put into place to help us bring the unconscious parts of ourselves into the spotlight as it gives us the opportunity to make them conscious.

Every human relationship and every interaction we experience is meant to intensify and magnify human emotions and is meant to help each of us evolve. Anything that continues to elicit an emotional charge is a part of you that you have not yet healed. Every time you are triggered, a part of your unconscious is called onto the carpet and you have the opportunity to make it conscious. Pay attention to the lessons that keep recurring. The lessons repeat until they are mastered. Are you continually attracting the same experiences over and over and over again? Do you find that the situations that trigger you fall within a certain pattern? If so, ask yourself what the common thread is and how you might be able to react to the situation differently.

Be the First

Life is an echo. What you put out comes back. Regardless of someone else's behavior, meet it with love and kindness. Be the first to be kind. Be the first to forgive. Be the first to include. Try it. It's normal to have your guard up and not want to let anyone in, particularly at a time when you feel hurt and are trying to heal. It is natural to want to appear brave and strong on the outside, while on the inside you are feeling empty and hurt. There's no better time to take a risk. We all have soft cores with hearts wanting to be cracked open.

Becoming Unstuck

The process of becoming unstuck begins with the realization that clinging on to anything that doesn't serve you only holds **you** back. In so many situations in life, another person has already moved past the situation but one person is still perseverating and stuck on it.

Learning to let go of the past is not a talent that some people have and some people don't. Sure, we all have behavioral predispositions in this regard. Some people have a tendency to hold grudges while for others the events of life roll right off their backs like water off of a duck's feathers. Letting go is a choice. While it may be harder for some of us than others to make this choice, it is something that is available to all of us. Sometimes we don't let go until we have become so completely dissatisfied and frustrated with where we are and how we feel.

One thing that makes the choice easier to make is to anchor on your feelings in those moments and choose to be joyful. Feelings of anger, resentment and guilt are low-vibrational emotions. Choose a high-vibrational emotion and find a way to get on that high-flying disc. The chapter on alignment addresses how to make this choice in greater detail.

When you hold onto anger, this energy is totally misdirected because these feelings only serve to weigh **you** down and don't have an impact on the person or situation you are dealing with.

Harboring these feelings prevent you from moving forward with a healthy mindset. The best thing you can do for yourself is to work through releasing the anger and direct your energy into more productive initiatives.

In many cases without even realizing it, people can be so wrapped up in a past event that their own identity becomes infused with prior pains or traumas to the point that their entire existence is built around it. They harbor the "victim" mentality and don't even realize it. Understand that you are not what has happened to you. You are not your past. Some people get really cozy in their pain and they can't envision a life that doesn't revolve around their traumas. Unless you are making serious efforts to break free from the hostage position you are allowing your pain to hold you in, you will remain stuck in that pain. When you find that the majority of your thoughts are those of self-pity, like "Why me?" "Why did this happen to me?" "Life is unfair." "It's all his fault." or "I'll never get out of this.", the most powerful questions you can ask yourself instead are, "How bad do I want it? How hard am I willing to work to become unstuck?"

I recently saw a sign that had a picture of a super-fit girl with a perfectly-sculpted body lifting weights. It read "Want it? Work for it." That statement really resonated with me. While I always aspire to have a perfectly-sculpted body, my effort doesn't always match up with my desired outcome. I'm like anyone else. I have periods of time when I'm super-motivated and periods of time when I feel like powering down. I love to operate at intense levels, but there are plenty of times where I'm not always feeling like I'm operating with high octane. Sometimes I show up at the gym and find myself just going through the motions. My body will be on auto-pilot and my head isn't in the game. I can be on the treadmill, but not really making progress toward my goals. I can find myself curled up in a cozy place on the intensity spectrum but not truly be pushing myself. I was kinda-sort-of showing up but not bringing my A-game. I had to get really honest with myself and ask myself, "How bad do I really want it?" I had to revisit the reasons why I was doing this in the first place and bring my deep-seated "whys" into focus. Reacquainting myself with the underlying motivating factors is usually all it takes to give myself the boost I need.

Remember that your past doesn't define you. How you respond to life defines you. Choosing to let go and move forward is one of the responses you can choose that will serve you well for years to come.

Life is a Series of Lessons

Understanding that life is a series of lessons is one of the main pathways to forgiveness and non-judgement.

Human relationships come in many different forms, including romantic relationships, parent/child relationships, sibling relationships, friendships and coworkers to name just a few, and each is rich in its opportunities to teach us something about ourselves. Within every human interaction lies the potential to expose and subsequently heal a part of ourselves so that we may become more conscious and take the depth and richness of our personal human experience to unprecedented levels.

Rather than ask, "Why did this happen to me?", ask yourself, "What is this trying to teach me? What can I learn from this?" Discovering our answers to these questions and experiencing the growth along the way is the fun part of life.

It is never your job to "teach somebody a lesson." All of us have the responsibility to learn our own lessons on our own timeline. The best thing you can do is become a silent observer of others' human experiences and let them do their individual soul work. If someone does ask for guidance, tread lightly and understand that the guidance you are giving is based on your perspective and your belief system as the backdrop. Just as your human experience is uniquely yours and a masterpiece that only you can curate, other people's own human experiences are uniquely theirs.

Everybody evolves at his or her own pace. Trying to accelerate someone else's growth process is akin to prying the petals of a rose open before it is ready to bloom. All flowers bloom on their own time and in their own season. They absorb what they need from the environment around them. Sunshine, water, nutrients from the soil and nature miraculously and beautifully produce the final product and all we need to do is sit back and observe.

Often, when people have been hurt by others, they feel the need to seek revenge and retaliate on the individuals that inflicted pain on them in order to teach them their lesson. Remember that's not your job and nothing good comes from it. Negativity breeds more negativity, and the same cycle ensues. Be the first to stop the cycle of negativity. Vibrate higher. Be an example. Be the change.

I never advocate for seeking revenge by inflicting pain. Some people feel that they have to do something. They have so much pent-up energy and feel the need to channel it somewhere, and I respect that, as it is challenging to sit and do nothing. In these situations, the best thing you can do is pour that energy into taking care of yourself.

As the old adage goes, "Living well is the best revenge." If seeking revenge is an itch that you just have to scratch, the best way to do it is to "live well." It all goes back to self-love. Invest in you. Invest in your physical, mental and spiritual well-being. Remember that spirituality is an individual journey. You have pre-selected your lessons, and through free will you are able to call in the experiences that give you the opportunity to master these lessons. Focus on **your** journey in a productive and healthy manner and let others focus on theirs. The best thing you can do to support others in their own Earthly journey is to become a silent observer of their reality. Jumping in and trying to be their fixer disempowers them and prevents them from mastering their lessons.

Everybody is doing their best from his or her own respective level of consciousness. No one's human experience is identical to anyone else's, nor are they expected to be. Everything they do and say, including their reactions, behaviors and responses are all filtered through their own unique life experiences. We are all fighting our own battles and most of the time no one else even knows what they are.

The depth of emotion that people are able to bring to any experience is dictated by the depth at which they are able to meet themselves, in other words, the extent to which they can feel their own emotions. It isn't reasonable to expect that others will be able to feel the same depth of empathy, compassion and other emotions that you might be able to because they may be at a different point in their own evolution. The best thing we can do is remain firmly committed to our own personal growth and trust that other people's lessons will be learned on a separate timetable and via different forums. Your only job is to stay committed to your own growth.

Life is such a patient and tireless teacher that it will repeatedly send us similar experiences until we master a lesson. Have you ever noticed that you keep attracting the same types of people or find yourself back in the same situation over and over again? The Universe is trying to show you something and give you another opportunity to learn.

Your emotions can be an excellent barometer of what parts of you still need healing. Any time you find that an experience is triggering low-vibrational emotions, such as anger, shame, hate or fear, the Universe is revealing another part of you that still needs to heal. It is an invitation from the Universe to look within and do the soul work necessary to heal that part of yourself.

I am constantly trying to reframe experiences as lessons, and each time I do this, I take my consciousness to new heights. I maintain the overarching mindset that life is always trying to teach me a lesson, and I think about the following reminder:

> Anything that annoys you is teaching you patience.
> Anyone who abandons you is teaching you how to stand on your own two feet.
> Anything that angers you is teaching you forgiveness and compassion.
> Anything that has power over you is teaching you how to take your power back.
> Anything you hate is teaching you unconditional love.
> Anything you fear is teaching you the courage to overcome your fear.
> Anything you can't control is teaching you how to let go.
> —Jackson Kiddard

Forgiveness

Forgiveness is one of the best gifts you can give yourself when you are dealing with a situation where someone hurt you. We have all been there and have experienced pain in one form or another. Forgiving a person for the pain he or she caused benefits you, as it lessens the burden that you carry on your shoulders. It releases the anchor that's been holding your ship at fixed coordinates and allows you to begin to explore the seas freely and without restraint.

Forgiving someone does not mean that there's an implicit message that you are in some way excusing the action or potentially deeming the actions as justifiable. Forgiveness does not dictate that you have any obligation to communicate your forgiveness to the offending person. This is for you, not the offender. This is something you can do solemnly and privately in the sanctity of your own space and in the privacy of your own mind. Forgiveness does not mean that you condone the other person's actions, and it doesn't mean that you forget. It doesn't mean that you weren't hurt or that you are denying that a particular event played a significant role in shaping who you are.

What forgiveness does mean, however, is that you are releasing any strong, negative thoughts and emotions, like animosity, revenge or blame and that you are untethering yourself and no longer allowing those thoughts and emotions from preventing you from moving forward with your life in a healthy and productive way.

Once you get to a point where you are acutely in tune with how certain emotions affect your body, you will notice a remarkable difference energetically after you forgive someone. You have been dragging around a wagon full of rocks and it will feel like someone just emptied it. Sometimes we don't even realize how much dead weight we drag around with us until our load is lessened. That is the point where we begin to truly experience feeling lighter, freer and happier.

Discovering Your Authenticity

- What from the past are you holding onto that is weighing you down?
- Why do you think you aren't able to let some things from the past go?
- What do you need to forgive yourself for?
- What do you want to forgive others for?
- Think of a situation in your life where there is negativity or unproductive behaviors perpetuating. How can you break the cycle? How can you be the first to take the high road?
- Do you keep experiencing things in your life that have a common theme? Why do you think the Universe keeps sending similar situations? What lesson or lessons do you think it is calling you to master?
- What judgements of others are you currently making and how can you recenter and redirect your energy on your journey and let them focus on theirs?

22

CLOSURE, GRATITUDE AND LESSONS ON LOVE

If we are truly a walking embodiment of love, we must want the same things for other people that we want for ourselves – happiness, joy, freedom, peace. We cannot cherry-pick where and when we do this in our lives.

Wrapping up each significant chapter of my life has always been an important part of the process. I've found that before I can truly move forward and approach the next chapter in any arena of my life with boundless energy and anticipation, I must first package up the last chapter and wrap it up with a giant bow and view it as a gift.

I've always turned to writing to help me process my thoughts and emotions. Sometimes I send a letter to someone. Sometimes I send an email. Sometimes it's a quick text. Sometimes I simply journal but don't actually send anything, and hold my sentiments close to my heart, knowing that I've processed the experience in a way that allowed me to achieve the closure that I needed.

Regardless of how painful the experience, there are always tiny glistening jewels just waiting to be found. Sometimes they're easy to spot, and sometimes it takes some sifting to discover them. Regardless of the time it takes to find them, they are always there waiting to be discovered. It's so important to encapsulate the time and memorialize it with positivity and gratitude.

Gratitude

Several years ago, I heard someone say that there is always something to be grateful for. It is a relatively common thing to say, but I thought to myself, "Really?!? Even when you're struggling to make sense of a situation? Even when you're in the midst of pain?" Believe it or not, the old adage is correct. Times like that are, in fact, **the best** times to articulate what you are grateful for. The exercise forces you to reframe the situation. It forces you out of a mindset of "lacking" into a mindset of abundance. It raises your vibration instantly. Tying back into how the Law of Attraction works, it is precisely the pathway through which we will attract more positivity and bring things to be grateful for into our existence.

One blisteringly-hot summer weekend in July when the kids were at their dad's house, I decided to hole-up in the coziness of my air-conditioned house to dedicate some time to closure. We were just weeks away from finalizing the divorce and I was really feeling the need to encapsulate the recently-closed chapter of my life by reflecting on all of the blessings and amazingness in my life that had been bestowed upon me. Despite the fact that my life was taking a turn I did not foresee twenty years ago when we were preparing to say our wedding vows, I still had much to celebrate, and truly felt blessed beyond my quota.

I was also feeling a huge sense of relief that a great deal of my time and emotional energy would no longer be consumed with this process and that I was reaching a point where I would be able to pour my energy into initiatives that truly resonated with my soul. I wanted to convey my gratitude for all of the countless hours invested by the professionals who helped us reach an agreement that balanced both of our needs and desires. I sat down with pen and paper in hand, and crafted this letter:

> *As this process comes to a close, I would like to take this opportunity to express my gratitude for the role you each have played in ushering me through this profoundly transformative time. Regardless of your allegiance, you each found ways to cut across any internal dividing lines and help us reach an outcome that contemporaneously balances everyone's needs and desires. While your professional expertise was a critical component of this process, you know me well enough by now to know that what resonates with me most is one's ability to demonstrate qualities that appeal to the human spirit. Seeing this process through those lenses, you have each blown me away with your words that embody compassion, empathy and kindness.*
>
> *I truly feel empowered, energized and untethered as I step out of a stagnant reality into my new authentic reality that allows me to explore my passions as this new chapter organically unfolds. This process has been a significant catalyst for my personal growth and has catapulted me to unprecedented levels of consciousness, and as a result I am standing squarely in my truth. There is no place I would rather be.*
>
> *Business is behind us, but I'm confident that our paths will cross again in a different context. Wishing you all the best*

in your professional and personal lives, and I look forward to staying in touch.
- Pam

The professional tone of the preceding email satisfied my inner businessperson, but it didn't satisfy my spirit. It was craving more. My spirit wanted me to plumb the depths of my heart and soul and take this opportunity to reflect on my marriage, our family and communicate my sentiments in such a way that would serve as a springboard for the next phase of our journey by locking in a tone of harmoniousness. The only way to quell this unsettled, unfinished feeling was to craft the following email that I would send to my soon-to-be former husband:

Looking at these last 20 years in retrospect, I don't think this part of our journeys was ever really about us, and without a doubt, it had everything to do with bringing these four amazing kids into the world. This being said and all things considered, I still deem this period of time to be a smashing success, and will always treasure the memories I have that we all spent in an intact family unit.

I have no doubt that we are all perfectly positioned, kids included, to effectuate a reality that honors who we are as individuals now that we have stepped into our respective authentic realities.

I do not want you to feel bad about not sharing your sentiments earlier in the marriage. Truth be told, I think we both knew the writing was on the wall years ago, but subconsciously blocked it out, and with good reason. Spending time in a vulnerable place and stepping into the unknown are not comfortable places for anyone to go. We both had different coping mechanisms, and I think we were both doing what we needed to do to cause the least disruption for the kids. At some point, I think we both realized that we weren't doing them any favors by giving them this template from which they would formulate their mental image of what marriage is.

I am truly grateful for all your unwavering dedication to this family over the years and for giving me a lifestyle that allowed me to maximize and optimize my time spent in my mom role. I do highly value this condition of financial security that you have worked so hard to bestow upon this regime, and am particularly grateful for your cooperation during the process we just completed and for your willingness to continue to provide the resources for me and the kids going forward. I also have a deep sense of gratitude for you giving me the logistical freedom to pursue efforts that are in alignment with who I am and the direction in which I plan to take my future.

I am enjoying sitting back as an observer and watching you embrace your role as Dad. I think you are doing an amazing job being present and involved in their lives and I know they recognize this as well.

I am confident that we will continue to be an effective co-parenting team and am excited to see what they all have in store for this world as they discover their passions and contribute to society in a meaningful way. I know that before too long this transitional time will be a distant memory and that the six of us and anyone else who is important to us will be able to coexist harmoniously. The scenario I envision smashes antiquated paradigms as new templating is occurring, congruent with the current shift in collective consciousness (you know I just ***had*** *to!) insert eyeroll...I know, I know.*

And, lastly one universal truth that ***always*** *holds for each and every person every single day...* ***The best is yet to come!***
- Pam

It isn't always easy to muster up the strength to come at things with a grateful heart when your heart may be shattered in a million pieces, but remember that anything worth having doesn't come easy. Push through it. Do it anyway.

I remain steadfast in my belief that there are no mistakes. There is no such thing as a waste of time. Our time together was undoubtedly still very much a success and every single moment of our journey together served a purpose. The time we spent together gave rise to experiences that allowed me to learn about love. Experiences that allowed me to learn about loss. Experiences that allowed me to learn to embrace change. Experiences that allowed me to overcome fear, and above all, experiences that allowed me to dig deep and do the soul work I needed to do to discover my soul purpose. Because of the richness and diversity of my experiences, I have embarked on this new chapter of my life with an indescribable sense of excitement and anticipation about what the Universe has in store.

Lessons on Love

Throughout this phase of my journey, I've learned that to receive love, you have to give it out first. There are many different types of love, and the type of relationship, whether it is a friendship, a romantic relationship, a parent/child relationship or any other type of relationship, will command different expressions of love. We all speak the language of love in our own dialects and it is important to remember that every individual has his or her own personal expressions of love.

About eight months after our divorce was final, I decided to add an adjunct topic to one of our weekly co-parenting calls. We had been living in our new realities, free from the pressures and obligations associated with the divorce process for a substantial enough period of time, and I thought now was a good time for a check-in on a deeper level. I knew where my happiness quotient was and I wanted to get a read on his.

He didn't know that I had been spending the last several months in pure spiritual growth mode, refining my belief system further and had been giving much consideration to the concepts of happiness, forgiveness and authenticity. I had been doing some deep soul-searching and had arrived at a place where I was truly happy. I can say without a doubt, I would have not been able to achieve this happiness quotient in our marriage. My hope was that he could also deem himself "happy," or at least well on his way there, and the only way I would find out was if I asked, so I did. He said that he is happy in his new reality and we both agreed that we are all in a better place.

Because we both made the decision to step in to our respective authentic realities, we each now have the logistical latitude and emotional freedom to move through our own human experience in a way that is authentic to who we are. It feels incredibly freeing to no longer be in a position to try to force something that was no longer meant to be. We are both in a position to be better parents because we are honoring ourselves first. We had some deep conversations during the last few months of our marriage and had to come to grips with the fact that, based on the individuals we each had become, we were no longer in a position to give each other what we needed on all levels. I believe that the highest expression of love comes from wanting the best for someone, even if it means letting that person go.

The ultimate expression of love is to give someone the freedom to live a life that is congruent and authentic to who he or she is. If we are truly a walking embodiment of love, we must want the same things for other people that we want for ourselves. There are certain things I want for myself, like happiness, love, joy, freedom and fulfillment to name a few. The things I want for myself I wish for everyone else universally, regardless of who they are or what my past history is with them. We cannot cherry-pick where and when we do this in our lives, and it's not my place to deem who is deserving and who isn't. The only way to truly step into authenticity is to make a wholesale shift toward love and apply it in our lives across the board. The highest path through this shift is to selflessly give out love freely and unconditionally. There is no place for conditions, limitations or discrimination when you are making such determinations. No one can say he or she wants someone else to be happy as long as what that person is doing works for me. Instead, you need to approach it with the attitude that you want someone to be happy because that's what everyone deserves. In relation to my former husband, that puts him in the best possible position to be a fulfilled individual and a great dad, and that's exactly what I want for my kids. Why do I do this? Because I like how that makes me feel. I like how I feel when I scatter joy and give out love freely and wish happiness upon everyone.

Discovering Your Authenticity

- Is closure something you practice on a regular basis?
- In what ways do you express gratitude in your life, and how can you express gratitude more freely and openly?
- Why do you think it is important to thoughtfully reflect on significant events in your life?
- Why do you think it is important to express gratitude?
- How can you formalize expressions of closure and gratitude and make them a natural part of your lifestyle?
- What do you believe about love?
- Do you give out love freely and unconditionally?
- Do you expect others to reciprocate?

PART V

SOARING

By partnering with the Universe and honoring your soul's purpose, soaring is the only possibility.

23

THE ART OF MANIFESTATION

The art of manifestation requires a partnership between you and the Universe, and the Universe is wanting and expecting you to participate in the creation of your own reality.

Manifestation, simply put, is the art of co-creating your reality with the Universe. While there is science behind it, I view the process as more of an art because there is plenty of room for creativity and individual customization.

Everything in the world, from everyday items to momentous movements, started small. It started with one thought. **One** thought in one person's mind. I've always found this concept to be fascinating. Think about it for a moment...one thought in one person's mind became equal rights for all. One thought in one person's mind is the reason iPhones are ubiquitous. One thought in one person's mind produced the piece of furniture you're sitting on. You get the idea. At first, many of these ideas were viewed as preposterous and met with opposition, but the relentless passion fueling the idea is precisely what brought the idea to fruition. The belief. The tenacity. The drive. The refusal to be discouraged. The dismissal from naysayers. The consistency. The abandonment of doubt. The relegation of fear. The elbow grease. The grit. The grind. The faith in the idea. All of these ingredients were blended together into the quintessential cocktail that eventually helped to bring the idea into our everyday lives, and over time, one generation's radical ideas became commonplace for the next. These ideas ultimately changed the world.

You may be wondering if manifestation is just a fancy word for goal-setting, but it is not. The concepts share the same spirit of reaching for something more, but the process and the mindset used for both are fundamentally different. The process of goal-setting is very rigid and only happens when someone establishes a very specific goal and aspires to achieve it within a predetermined time frame. It's purely driven by the conscious mind and focuses on the physical world resources that are available. It is purely outcome or destination-based. With goal-setting, the end result is binary, either you achieved your goal or you didn't.

The process of manifestation is much more fluid and dynamic, requires a sense of open-mindedness and involves surrendering to the infinite wisdom and knowledge of the Universe and its divine timing. Manifestation involves focusing on the journey rather than the destination. With manifestation, the Universe ensures that you always get the outcome that is in your highest good rather than the one that you have chosen for yourself.

The manifestation process has an underlying spiritual component whereby we learn to use the laws of the Universe and the currency of the Universe (energy) as tools in our toolkit to create our own realities. It is a fascinating process that involves a partnership with the Universe and requires a delicate balance of holding on loosely and then letting go. It involves blending your heart's desires with the infinite wisdom of the Universe, all while you surrender, let go and trust the process.

The mantra commonly associated with the art of manifestation is "Ask, Believe, Receive." I like it because it's concise, easy to remember, and establishes the general framework. To really understand how to make manifestation work for you in your life, we need to break this concept down into smaller, more actionable steps.

Note that this is not a linear, sequential process. The flow follows the general framework of "Ask, Believe, Receive", but note that there is circularity and overlap in some of the steps and they will be going on concurrently. Like anything else in life that you want to master, the more you practice it, the more natural it becomes.

When I started dabbling in the field of manifestation, I started small. I started with simple requests such as "Universe, please give me a parking spot close to the door at the mall." I escalated my requests gradually over time as I became more comfortable with it, and now I've reached a point where I dream big.

We are often so immersed in our own physical realities that we forget to utilize our fifth-dimensional energies. Our spirit guides are always available and anxious to help fulfill our requests, but we first need to ask.

Manifestation is a very powerful tool that will serve you not only during this time of transition, but for years to come. It's something that can be taught and shared with your family and friends, and no age is too young to start empowering children to take an active part in co-creating their realities with the Universe. I have started to incorporate manifestation techniques into my children's lives, and enjoy watching them as they witness their thoughts come to fruition after we execute the steps of this process. I always start with something **they** are passionate about; if I were to ask any of them to try to manifest something that they're not emotionally invested in, the results would be dramatically different.

One of my favorite examples comes from the time I coached my younger son before one of his hockey games by using manifestation techniques. He was in the midst of a dry-spell in the goal-scoring department, and I knew he really wanted to score. Before his games, my last words to him are always "Have fun." That's it. It's not about who wins or who loses in my mind; it's about sportsmanship, teamwork, playing hard and having fun. In my mind, the outcome is irrelevant.

I knew he was getting pretty down about not scoring for a while and his mindset was keeping him from scoring with each passing game because he was losing confidence. Goals aren't exactly easy to come by in this league and each goal scored is well-earned; it's a highly-competitive league, and you don't make the team unless you're really good.

I decided to try my hand at a little behind-the-scenes manifestation by having a conversation with him before his game. I asked him what he wanted out of the game, and he told me that he really wanted to score. When I asked him what that looks like, he said that he liked breakaways that start with a scramble in front of the net that resulted in a teammate getting the puck and then passing it to him. He would then speed up the ice. I took that opportunity to ask him how he feels when he envisions someone passing him the puck and he responded that he gets excited, especially when he feels like he is going to score. I pressed on and asked him how he envisions he would score and he explained how he was coming at the goalie on the right, deked out his opponent, came around the left side side of the goal and jammed the puck past the goalie. I then asked him to describe how he envisioned his physical surroundings. He explained that he was out of breath and exhausted from skating so fast but also excited because he scored. I kept probing and asked about what he heard. He told me that he heard people screaming and cheering and that his teammates came up to give him high fives. I continued my inquiry and asked what he did next. He told me that he skated over to the bench and high-fived his teammates who were there. Lastly, I asked if he felt excited when he scored, and he told me he did.

In his next game, my little hockey player broke out of his slump and scored!

By now I'm sure you're wondering how this story relates to divorce, but there's a reason I walked you through it in exquisite detail. That's exactly how manifestation works. Manifestation is all in the details. It involves living out the experience in your mind before it can come to fruition it in a physical sense. It's not enough to say you want something. It's not enough to think you're going to get it. You must embody the desire. You must feel the emotion. You must experience all of the sights and sounds of the environment. You must believe that it's already yours and walk, talk, act and think like it has already happened.

When you go through any period of significant transition, it is a perfect time to start incorporating manifestation as part of your regular routine, as it marks the beginning of a new chapter, and it is a golden opportunity to design your new life your way. This is your time to dream big, and no idea is too outlandish or too extreme.

Steps of Manifestation

There are several steps in the manifestation process, and while there is a general framework or template in place, there is room for individual customization as you explore what works for you and as you imprint your unique energy signature on the process. While there is a general sequentiality to the manifestation process, understand that certain points can have a circuitous nature because our life experiences may call us to revisit and refine earlier points in the process. As you move through these general steps, remain flexible and open-minded and keep reminding yourself that this is a dynamic endeavor and there is always opportunity to make refinements.

Rather than moving through these steps sequentially, keep the general framework of "Ask, Believe, Receive" as a backdrop, but realize that many of the components will be overlapping and going on concurrently. For example, you will be maintaining spiritual truths and practices such as "trusting the process" and "letting go" and "self-love" as a permanent state of being throughout the entire process. I view this ideology much like a symphony. All parts of the orchestra are playing throughout the symphony. Sometimes the brass instruments are a little louder. At other times the percussions are louder. Sometimes it's the woodwinds and other times the stringed instruments. All sections of the orchestra are always playing throughout and certain sections are prominent at different times.

Get Crystal Clear on What You Want and Ask for It

The manifestation process requires a partnership between you and the Universe, and the Universe wants and expects you to participate in the creation of your own reality. It can't do all the work alone. The Universe is always listening and is always anxious to honor heart-centered requests.

The first step is getting crystal clear on what you want. If you don't, the Universe will deliver something that kind of matches what you want, but not really, and you'll end up with a steady stream of things that are not quite right.

It's possible that you might not even be sure what you want, but this is the step in the process where you challenge yourself to sift through all of your life experiences and determine which aspects you want to pull from each one and include in your request. Abraham-Hicks, the entity that disseminates knowledge and wisdom from universal consciousness, calls this "data gathering," which is the process of sifting through your "data points" and discerning which ones you will incorporate into your physical reality.

Your experiences give you the benefit of contrast. Every dimension has a range of data points, and those data points will illustrate the variance in possible options. Let's look at data gathering for relationships, since that's something all of us can relate to on some level. For each aspect of someone's persona, there is a wide variety of possible attributes. For example, with regard to personality, some people are extremely quiet and others are gregarious and there is everything in between. Some people are more serious and others are hilariously funny and there is everything in between. Some are super-analytical and others are highly-creative and there is everything in between.

Our interactions with others show us what's out there. For

each dimension, you will have as many data points as you have had life experiences of any kind, big or small. View all of your interactions and relationships as opportunities to add more data points, thus giving you more options from which to choose as you manifest.

I've found that writing it down the old-fashioned way, with a pen and piece of paper, makes it really come alive. There's something about writing it down that really solidifies it in your mind and makes it more real.

Heart-felt, intention-filled requests resonate with the Universe at a very deep level. The Universe can tell if something comes from your heart or your head, and it responds accordingly. It can tell if your request is driven by vanity, or if it is your heart's deepest desire. The Universe will only honor heart-centered requests.

Mind Experience

Some people call this stage "visualization"; I call it "Mind Experience." This step involves a sensory experience as you incorporate all of the senses. It calls you to make the experience real in your mind before you can experience it in your physical reality. View it as a dress rehearsal of sorts, where everyone is playing a part, in full costume and all props are in the right place on stage.

Athletes use this performance-enhancing technique all the time. Arnold Palmer used to rehearse all of his shots in his mind before he actually took them on the golf course. Olympic athletes use this technique as well. Studies have shown a link between enhanced performance and the use of visualization techniques.

A critical component of this part of the process is feeling the emotions. It isn't enough to just see it; you must focus on the feeling. Feel how you expect to feel when you achieve what you are trying to manifest.

Believe

You must believe that you are worthy of receiving that which you are trying to manifest. There is no room for doubt and there is no room for ambivalence. Manifestation and the components of the process vibrate at a different frequency than doubt. As we learned earlier, doubt vibrates at a low frequency. Just as we cannot physically be in two different cities at any given point in time, we also cannot entertain the vibration of two totally disparate concepts at the same time. It needs to be one or the other. If you're harboring doubt, then you aren't in a position to manifest. If you're manifesting, then there is no room for doubt. Do not give any attention to the absence of it; that just creates resistance. Believe that it will be yours, and it will be.

Know in advance that doubt will try to pull up a chair at your feast of manifestation. That's your ego trying to assert its presence in this process. Rather than letting it deter or discourage you, transmute the doubt into fuel for your mission. Doubt will also come in the form of external influences. As you aspire and achieve lofty aspirations and rise to new levels, others who may not want to see you succeed may try to pull you down. Don't let that get in the way either. Set out to dazzle them by modeling how you co-create your new reality with the Universe, and do it with utmost confidence. At some point in the future when they are ready, these same naysayers will probably be the ones asking you how you did it. At that point, share your wisdom and teach them what you have learned about manifesting your new reality.

Work on Yourself

This is the fun part. We are so conditioned to relentlessly pursue what we want. We grow up with a "goal-setting" mindset. We establish our goal, keep our eye on the prize and sprint for the finish line. While that approach may have its merits and applications in certain circumstances, manifestation calls us to keep the focus on ourselves while the Universe is strategizing and formulating a plan to deliver what is in your highest good.

"Working on you" includes any activity that enhances your well-being either physically, mentally, emotionally or spiritually. Every time you engage in an activity that improves your overall well-being, you are raising your vibration.

The "Self-Love" section in this book discusses activities that raise or lower vibration, but as a refresher, I have listed some ideas here for reference. Note that this list is not all-inclusive, but will get you well on your way to making some drastic shifts in your vibration:

Vibration Raisers (Add or Increase)

- Exercising
- Eating healthy foods (fruits, veggies, nuts, seeds)
- Listening to, playing or creating music
- Engaging in creative endeavors (art, sculpting, drawing, photography, dancing, singing, cooking)
- Sleeping
- Meditating
- Yoga
- Using essential oils as part of self-care regimen
- Laughing
- Learning new things
- Practicing self-love

Vibration Lowerers (Reduce or Eliminate)

- Eating processed foods
- Eating junk food
- Consuming artificial sweeteners
- Consuming alcohol
- Doing recreational drugs
- Using products that contain toxic chemicals
- Using technology excessively
- Gambling
- Stress
- Anxiety
- Negative self-talk
- Gossipping

Choose to embody high-vibrational emotions, such as joy, bliss, contentment, peace and love. Pay attention to how you feel when you experience these emotions. Get in the business of making it your mission to embody these emotions, regardless of what is going on around you. Remember that you can only control you. We are constantly bombarded with external stimuli and various other things we cannot control, such as other people's reactions. You are only charged with the task of remaining in control of **your** emotions. Depending on the circumstances, this may not always be easy. Of course joy comes naturally when we are at a celebration or there are no major stressors in our lives. The true test comes when we are facing adversity or significant stress. We always have the choice. We may naturally be "wired" to respond a certain way because of patterning inherited in childhood or other factors, but we always have the power to overcome it. It's not easy. It's really hard, in fact, and that's why they call it work. Soul work. Don't meet anybody where they are in low-vibrational emotions; don't give them that much power. When you are able to stay calm in the midst of chaos, that is an indicator that you have really started to hook into your personal power and have accessed life force energy.

Life force energy is unequivocally the most important tool you can have in your toolbox. Everything comes to you through you, and the path to achieving what is in your highest good comes through getting into spiritual alignment. The higher we ascend, it becomes more and more natural for us to access it on a continual basis. It is important because it's what connects us to the energy of creation and allows us to experience life from a deep soul-based perspective, experience the heights of joy, and realize our life purpose. Life force energy has several different names, such as Universal Energy, prana and Chi, but they all refer to the same concept, and learning to access it is the ticket to unleashing ourselves and catapulting ourselves into higher realms of consciousness. Soul-based living is where we begin to fully understand and live by the truth that we are all limitless. We all originated from this energy and can find our way back to it, but we must first undo and strip away all of the ego-based limitations that we have inherited, such as fear, doubt, limiting beliefs, societal conditioning, etc. When these stifling factors have been eliminated, there are no limitations on what can be achieved.

People often ask me how they will know when they are tapped into Universal Energy. I have found that it's particularly noticeable when I am involved in a creative endeavor and am so immersed in the process that I lose track of time. The Universe totally supports creative endeavors particularly when they are intended for the betterment of society or the greater good. When you are partaking in something creative, pay attention to how it is unfolding. If there is ease and it is unfolding effortlessly, and feels like it's flowing, it's meant to happen. It's called "flow" for a good reason. By contrast, if it feels forced and choppy and isn't going smoothly, you're experiencing "resistance." Resistance is the Universe's way of telling you it isn't meant to be. When I'm feeling it, I usually step away, clear my mind, engage in a different activity and ask that the guidance I need be given to me when I am in a place to receive it.

We often think about achieving an outcome in terms of elapsed time and often ask ourselves "How much time will it take to achieve my goal?" In the world of spirituality, remember that our currency is energy, not time. Vibration, not time. Regardless of the circumstances or the desired goal, the answer to that question is always the same: "It will take you as long as it takes for you to become a vibrational match to what you desire." Answering the question in this manner facilitates shifting your focus from the outcome back to you.

Express Gratitude

Under the old paradigm, we are accustomed to receiving something and then subsequently expressing gratitude for it. Expressing gratitude on a regular basis is a foundational element of spirituality and is one of the cornerstones of the manifestation process. Here we express gratitude for things already in our lives as well as that which we are trying to manifest. It may seem counterintuitive because it goes against the normal sequence of events that we are used to (receiving first, expressing gratitude second), but here we must reprogram our minds to adopt a new way of thinking. Act as if you already have it. Think as if you already have it. Talk as if you already have it and give thanks for already having it.

Release and Relax

While all steps of the process require a true partnership with the

Universe, the steps up to this point have required a significant amount of conscious thought and action as you work to craft your new reality. You have reached the point where you get to recline, put your feet up, recognize that you've done the work and turn it over to the Universe to work its magic to execute a plan that is in your highest good. Remember that it is all-knowing, and doesn't have the blind spots we do. It can see every twist and turn in advance, can see around every corner and knows what it needs to do to deliver what is in your best interest. Allow the Universe to show you what is best and remember that with uncertainty or limited knowingness comes the Universe's opportunity to surprise you with something far grander than you could have conjured up for yourself.

Don't worry about the how or the when. The Universe will figure that out. Don't take on more than you need to by trying to control the situation. The Universe is highly skilled at arranging the pieces so that we all receive what is in our own highest good.

Don't worry about the how or the when. The Universe will figure that out.

Receiving Mode

This is the point in the process where things start to feel magical. You've already done the hard work and now you get to sit back and enjoy the fruits of your labor as you watch the Universe deliver to you what is in your highest good. You have co-created your reality with the Universe and now you get to watch it all flow right into your existence.

Surrender and Trust the Process

Everything we've discussed in the manifestation process so far has had a degree of activity associated with it. This step requires a more passive approach, as we simply slide over to the passenger seat and let the Universe do the driving. Life is so much sweeter when we're in the passenger seat. Rather than doing all the driving, navigating, watching for street signs, pedestrians and other cars and everything else from the driver's seat, we get to look out the window from the passenger seat and take in all the views along the way.

We must learn to have faith and trust the process. The Universe always knows what is in our highest good and we must keep that at the forefront of our thoughts. Doubt will creep in, as well as the need to control, and this is our ego that loves to remind us from time to time that it's still there. Learn to recognize when this is happening, and anchor back on the phrase "Trust the process." Everything serves a purpose. Having faith makes it much easier for me to take a more hands-off approach and let things unfold for me the way they are meant to unfold. I spent so many years trying to occupy the "driver's seat" — planning this, forcing that, controlling something else, but I've found that it just doesn't work. Faith affords us the opportunity to sit in the passenger seat and let the Universe do the driving. You may not take the route you initially planned, and there will be detours along the way, but you will ultimately reach a destination that is in your highest good, as determined by the Universe. Furthermore, you will always be where you are supposed to be at any given point along the way, even if it's not where you envisioned yourself at that particular moment in time. Sometimes you will be cruising on the expressway and at other times you will be stopped at a red light or stuck in traffic. From each experience we are meant to learn something — patience, compassion, kindness, gratitude, to name a few. Everything comes to us at the right time, and no timing is more perfect than divine timing.

Detach From the Outcome

Think back to a time when you didn't get what you wanted, but instead got something better. I think we all have a tale to tell along these lines, and what might have seemed like blind luck at the time was actually the Universe working it's magic. It was the Universe's infinite wisdom surmounting our conscious mind-constrained knowledge, by knowing what was in our highest good and formulating a plan to deliver it to us. We are often disappointed when we do not get what we ask for, but we must always trust the process and keep reminding ourselves that everything is always in perfect divine order. There's a reason you're not getting what you want right now. Maybe it's the Universe's way of protecting you from something you can't foresee. Maybe it would be a distraction and keep you from focusing on what it is you're supposed to be accomplishing right now. Not knowing isn't easy. It's normal for us to seek answers and obtain closure. But the Universe doesn't care about answers and it doesn't care about closure. What it does care about is matching you with that which is in your highest good in accordance with divine timing.

It's very important to learn to recognize when something has run its course. Learning to walk away from things that don't serve you is one of the most liberating and empowering skills you can teach yourself. You have to be willing to clear the space so that the Universe can replace it with something that is in your highest good.

Detaching from the outcome is a key step in the process. It may sound counterintuitive to detach, but detaching doesn't mean disregarding; it simply means you are keeping yourself open to a variety of outcomes. It is one thing to acknowledge the existence of your desired outcome in the company of several other possible outcomes and being open to any of them, and it's a completely different thing to stay fixated on your desired outcome and try to force it.

Detaching from the outcome is challenging particularly when you want something badly. This is where faith in a higher power comes in. You aren't doing this alone. Remember that you're the observer in your reality. You're **not** single-handedly steering your ship. You are in a partnership with the Universe and are co-creating your reality.

Your goal here is to take the path of least resistance. How do you do that? By not forcing an outcome to satisfy your personal agenda. It's by learning to flow with it. Forcing things causes resistance. Trying to control causes resistance. Giving something too much attention causes resistance. Set your intention from the heart and trust the process.

Pay Attention to Signs Along the Way

There is no such thing as a coincidence in the spiritual world. They are called "synchronicities" and are signs and signals sent to us by the Universe with intentionality and purpose.

Keep your eyes open for synchronicities, or "cosmic winks." That's the Universe's way of communicating with us. I have always marveled at what a great conversationalist the Universe is. It loves to give us feedback and reassurance that we are on the right track, but we have to heighten our own awareness and raise our antennae so we can receive these communications. Start paying attention to everyone and everything. Observe every aspect of your surroundings, and take note of anything that seems to have relevance or meaning.

The Universe communicates to us in a variety of ways, including songs, numeric codes and other modalities. Have you ever gotten in the car, turned on the radio, and felt like the song lyrics were speaking directly to you and what you might have been thinking about at that moment? When you start paying attention to these little communications around you, you'll start experiencing these synchronicities.

Manifestation is a fascinating process that allows you to partner with the Universe to receive what is in your highest good. Like anything else, the more you practice it the better you become. There is no better time than right now to start co-creating your new reality.

Discovering Your Authenticity

- What aspects of prior experiences have given you clarity about what you desire?
- What high-vibrational activities are you looking forward to incorporating into your lifestyle?
- How can you rewire your mindset and modify your self-talk to optimize your manifestation?
- Think of a scenario you would like to manifest, practice the "mind experience" technique, and practice verbally expressing gratitude as if were already yours.
- Have you noticed any synchronicities that have given you reassurance that you are on the right path?

For a special bonus on partnering with the universe to create your reality, visit https://liveauthentically.today/soar-resources to download the guide.

24

BECOMING THE BEST VERSION OF YOURSELF

When we gain the courage to step out of our own comfort zone into our authentic reality, we open ourselves up the infinite number of possibilities the Universe has in store for us.

You have a blank canvas in front of you, and with every new chapter you get the opportunity to reinvent yourself. Get in the mindset of setting your standard and the bar at "mind-blowing," not mediocre. This is where the fun really begins.

Remember that life is an echo and the Law of Attraction ensures that you always attract what you currently **are**, not what you want and not what you hope to be someday. It is what you are **today**. So, it stands to reason that you would want your point of attraction to be the highest point possible, which means attracting from the most refined version of yourself.

Any highly transformative event presents a golden opportunity to work on yourself and become the best version of **you**. The aftermath of the breakdown of a committed relationship or any other life-changing experience offers fertile ground for taking inventory on yourself and your life and doing your work, physically, mentally, emotionally and spiritually. It's all about putting the growth hat on, and keeping it on. Just as no two people are alike, no two landscapes on the avenue through personal growth and transformation are alike. Everyone's scenery looks different.

The commitment to become the best version of yourself begins with the realization and the acceptance that the old ways of operating won't translate into better results. You must be willing to adopt new practices. It's important to remember to go easy on yourself and not expect radical change overnight, as any large-scale, transformative endeavor takes a lot of work and patience over an extended period of time. Keep reminding yourself that Rome wasn't built in a day, and you can't expect that you will be either.

Designing your new world requires a sampling of the various lifestyle choices, growth-based initiatives and other concepts we have explored in this book. You will blend your reflections on where you've come from, take inventory on where you currently are and start to formulate your new trajectory as you set sail on a new path. This section contains some important concepts for you to consider incorporating into your life as you work to establish the new you.

There is no secret recipe for becoming the best version of you. But, there are limitless options to choose from, and herein lies the opportunity to be creative. Infinitely creative. You get to name yourself Executive Chef of Personal Growth and Development and create your own recipes. You get to add a little of this and a little of that. You get to try out different ingredients. You get to use a variety of different kitchen tools. You get to try out some new spices. You get to call in sous chefs from various areas of your life to join you on your journey. You get to share your recipes with others as they share theirs with you. So put your chef's hat on and let's get started.

If it's not mind-blowing, body-strengthening or soul-stirring, it's not worth your time.

Levels of Consciousness

Before you can roll up your sleeves and get to work, it's always a good idea to take a bird's-eye look at where you are and start to idealize where you want to be. Where do you think you fall on the consciousness spectrum? How would you describe your level of awareness? Remember to make this observation without judgement because you're right where you're supposed to be.

Awareness is like a large chandelier. What does it take to get your attention? Do you notice when one bulb burns out, and do you take the time to change it, or are you satisfied that there is always at least some light in the room, and let it go unnoticed until the last bulb burns out? Where do you fall in that spectrum, and are you satisfied with where you are? How many bulbs burn out before your attention is captured? The good news is that there is no wrong answer to this question! All answers are correct. Everyone is here to partake in the human experience from a different plane. Not everyone is supposed to pack up and go meditate in Machu Picchu for eons. The world needs people at various levels of consciousness, and we must welcome and honor all levels, for each plays a vital role in the interconnectedness of everyone and everything, and ultimately serves to elevate universal consciousness on a broad scale. We need teachers **and** students, for without one there would not be the other. Herein lies the perfect exemplification of the concept of duality.

Living Authentically

What does it mean to live authentically? To me, it means living a life that embraces your light **and** your dark...yes that's right... your dark side too! It's resolving to take the mask off, leaving it off and letting others see that you are perfectly imperfect, just like the rest of us. The idea is **not** to please everyone, or anyone for that matter. The idea is to do you. It's about living a life that embodies the essence of who you are to the deepest core of your being. It's about celebrating and sharing your positive attributes while simultaneously exposing your flaws and doing the work necessary to become a better version of the person you were yesterday. It involves a willingness to go to unprecedented levels of transparency and vulnerability so that you can heal and let your light shine.

You'll know when you're there. It's that feeling of "yes this is who I am and I'm not compromising my beliefs to appease anyone or to fall within societal norms or expectations." Yes, I will go toe-to-toe with you defending my beliefs and I encourage you to do the same. Let's have a healthy debate and both remain open-minded so that we may both consider each other's perspectives yet resolute enough that we may be loyal to our own respective belief systems we've each so meticulously crafted. My belief system, as it is today, is a cumulative amalgamation of beliefs that have been developed from experiences that I've had on my journey thus far. My journey isn't over, otherwise I wouldn't still be here. There will be new experiences tomorrow, the next day, the day after that and so on, and with each new experience comes the opportunity to further refine our own belief systems. We are best served if we maintain the mindset that our own belief system is a fluid and dynamic concept rather than a rigid and stagnant construct.

While our journeys are individual in nature, we can be stewards of each other and each person's respective place on his or her journey by meeting each person with compassion, empathy, and kindness and by being a silent observer of everyone's personal journey.

Practice Acceptance

It is crucial to simply become aware of your current level of awareness with no judgement. Simply be the observer. Practice full acceptance. You are precisely where you're supposed to be at this point in your journey. Accept yourself and get comfortable with being perfectly imperfect. That is something we all share. We are all works in progress and if any of us had already mastered all of our lessons, we wouldn't still be in this Earthly Classroom, still trying to master our lessons.

Understand that all of your experiences have delivered you to this very moment, and this is where you are supposed to be.

On my journey, I had to do a lot of work with accepting certain things about myself, some of which I struggled with for years. For example, I'm a recovering perfectionist. I've had a life-long love affair with perfectionism and it's still an area where I have to work really hard at maintaining balance. After years of beating myself up for it and creating more self-inflicted stress than necessary, I've finally learned to accept that it's just part and parcel of who I am, and have found ways to keep my inner perfectionist from taking over as I make more mindful decisions about what is really deserving of my time and energy.

As you reflect on your life, think about where you are and release judgement about where you are and how you think you **should** be operating. Accept where you are and flow with how you **are** operating. I've finally learned how to embrace where I am and what I embody and flow **with** it rather than resisting it. Resistance takes so much effort and doesn't translate into anything productive or enjoyable, ever. Life is so much easier when we learn to accept certain things for what they are and flow in the direction in which life is trying to take us.

Reclaiming Your Identity

Divorce can leave you feeling like you've been dropped smack-dab in the middle of an identity crisis, particularly for moms whose identity has been wrapped up in all things kids and family-related for years. I hardly even had an identity outside of our kids. Everything I did was either with them or for them, and while I had embraced my role as full-time mom and was grateful for the opportunity to fully-immerse myself in all of the experiences that came with this role, I always envisioned myself doing something when the kids got older. The challenge was going to be figuring out what that was.

I went away for a weekend with a friend while I was in the midst of the divorce process in an attempt to carve out a tiny slice of time where I would be able to escape from all the meetings, conference calls, decisions, emotional weight and everything else that came with the process.

We were sitting poolside and started chatting with some people next to us. After a little small talk that included a game of "guess your zodiac sign" they asked what she and I did for work. It was a given that my friend would reply first, as she's had a successful career for decades and responded that she was a real estate agent. As she was answering, I was thinking about what my response would be. As grateful as I was to be a full-time mom, saying that suddenly felt incomplete to me, and my soul was craving more.

I had always felt the pull to channel my passions and gifts into a grander calling and fulfill my life purpose, but had yet to discern exactly what it would be. It was precisely this moment that I felt the pull to accelerate my soul-searching and really dig deep and figure out what I wanted to do.

As I was contemplating what my response would be, I thought "What do I say? I bake some really amazing brownies!" My friend clearly recognized the hesitation and covertly whispered under her breath that I am a writer. She was right. I **am** a writer. I didn't have a blog and I wasn't a published author, but that didn't disallow me from claiming the title. I had been documenting, chronicling, processing and journaling on and off for many years, and writing has long been my go-to creative outlet for processing my thoughts. I had been saving all of my content waiting for when I felt the time was right to start publishing, and I felt like I was getting closer and closer each day.

Another thing I wanted to do to reclaim my identity was change my legal last name back to my maiden name. Because there were kids involved, this wasn't a consideration I took lightly and I examined it from a number of different angles. When I considered the potential impact on my kids, I decided that, ultimately, a last name is just that…a name. A string of letters that bears no impact on the relationship I have with my kids. I could still take the liberty of using our family last name in certain arenas such as the school environment, but would now have the autonomony to carve out an individual reality as I pursue my purpose professionally. After all, nobody was going to be there to police that I signed our family name instead of my legal name on the field trip permission form for school.

Changing my last name back to my maiden name came with

an incredible sense of empowerment. It was yet another thing I could do that made me feel like I was carving out my own personal niche, and it was refreshing to have an individual identity in addition to the role I play for our family, and it reinforced the "fresh start" feeling with which I wanted to step into my future.

Your Only Competition is Yesterday's Version of You

The game of life is about you versus the person you were yesterday. That's it. It's a natural inclination of the human condition to want to compare ourselves to others, but the reality is that your only competition is yesterday's version of you. You're not in competition with your peers. You're not in competition with your siblings. You're not in competition with the idealistic image your parents may have set forth for you on your behalf.

It's so easy to get mired down in negative thought patterns when we compare ourselves to others. This world is a vast place, and I guarantee you that you won't have to look very far to find someone who you think is prettier, wealthier or fitter than you are. That's an extremely dangerous place to go because of the self-defeating, self-deprecating nature of these thoughts. Negative thoughts breed more negative thoughts, and before you know it you're in a downward spiral feeling fearful, doubtful, defeated and mentally and emotionally exhausted.

I've found that the most effective way to circumvent this pattern is to put on the blinders. Ignore what everyone else has or is doing, and **do you**. Making the conscious decision to abandon the "comparison mindset" takes some "rewiring," but it is a total game-changer.

The comparison mindset is one of many exemplifications of societal conditioning, and stems back as far as I can remember.

For example, I remember being at playgroups when my kids were babies and toddlers and there was always so much chatter about the kids' milestone percentiles. I was the mom who **never** knew the answers to those questions because it didn't matter to me. All I was ever concerned about was that my kids were happy and healthy.

Focus on what you have right in front of you and resist the temptation to size yourself up to everyone else. It's an extremely slippery slope, and I've found that when I go there, I never come out feeling better about myself. Comparing really is highly illusory anyway. What we perceive to be is, in actuality, nothing more than fragmented pieces of someone else's reality that we somehow weave together into a tapestry that we perceive to be more beautiful than our own. I mean, do we ever really know what is going on in someone else's life? Do we really ever know the whole story? Are they showing us **all** parts of them or just the parts they want to reveal? Understand that the way we view their world from our vantage point is likely extensively filtered as well as wildly different from how they view their world.

Standards

The idea of having standards is such a sexy concept. During the self-inventory process, I discovered the sobering truth that my standards weren't up to par in certain areas, and I had quite a lot of work to do in the way of bringing them into focus. Truth be told, I couldn't remember the last time I was honest with myself about what my standards were or whether or not they were being met across the spectrum.

We all can and should have standards in every category and should challenge every experience and interaction to meet those standards. It's the best way to come into alignment with who we are and the most expeditious way for the Universe to deliver a perfect vibrational match. This process of leveling up is as fascinating as it is necessary.

It's a natural element of the human condition to want to be accommodating and flexible, but it's an entirely different ball game when you find yourself compromising, justifying, explaining, accommodating and bending more often than you are standing in your truth and holding your ground.

The leveling-up process is an effective modality for reclaiming your personal power and aligning yourself. Get extremely clear on what your standards are. When I started to contemplate the idea of standards, I realized that I didn't even know what mine were in a number of different areas because I had never officially articulated them. I was stuck in a loop of accepting whatever happened to come my way, and trying to twist and turn and bend and mold to fit that. That's the complete antithesis of what I should have been doing.

Articulate what your standards are **first**, and then see how everything fits into that framework. You've got to get really really clear about defining your standards. Maybe you don't even know what they are, and that's ok. There is no "one size fits all" for this, and the cool part is that you have creative license to design this any way you want it to look. Everyone's list looks different.

However you decide to define your standards, don't settle. Don't compromise. Claim your power. Honor yourself. Know your value. Own your self-worth. You deserve the best of the best, and nothing short of that should be accepted.

Define your standards based on what **you** want for **you**; not based on what you think others are willing or able to give. Set your bar where you want it first, and let others figure out how they measure up to your standards second. Don't give away your power and let others write your standards; you are the architect. It won't work any other way.

This is not the place to short-change yourself. It's not the place to doubt that you might not be able to get what you want. Remember we live in a world where anything is possible. Aim high. Nobody should go through this life settling on a mediocre existence.
One day, I decided to take a pen to a piece of paper and write down my standards in various categories. What are my standards for a friendship? What are my standards for a romantic relationship? What are my standards for communication? What are my standards for confidentiality? What are my standards for respect? What are my standards for sharing responsibilities? What are my standards for others behaviors?

I mentally signed a pact with myself that I was going to model and display the same standards that I expected of others. Embodying these attributes **first** was assuredly the only way I could ensure that the Universe could deliver what I was seeking.

After you define your standards, you need to get cozy with communicating them. Some examples of getting this done include, "I'm not comfortable with that and here's why." "That isn't congruent with who I am." "I'm not going to play that role anymore." "Here's my framework so I can work something in within that."

Sending this message indicates that you are giving the other person a choice. He or she can either meet you where you are, or choose to redirect energy elsewhere. If the person can't meet you where you are, it means that he or she is either unable or unwilling or not ready yet. Regardless, either outcome is fine. In fact, **detaching** from any outcome is key.

There's no better indicator of who is really supposed to be in your tribe than by watching what people do when you speak your truth. Again, don't compromise your standards by meeting others where they are if their truth is not in integrity with who you are. Stand firmly affixed to your standards and stand squarely in **your** truth, and see if they can rise up and meet you. Some people will be able to rise up and meet you, and others will fall away. Not only is it okay if someone falls away, it's an essential part of the process. Understand that none of this is personal; it's totally vibrational. There are 7.6 billion people in the world and rest assured there are lots and lots of choices (vibrational matches) for who we share our human experience with at various points in time.

Healthy Disconnections

Sometimes we don't realize how energetically weighed down we are when we are carrying around weight that isn't in our own highest good. It's not only incredibly cumbersome to carry, but it totally impedes the process of becoming aligned.

A natural part of the process of defining your new standards is that certain things will naturally fall away. Walking away from people and experiences that no longer serve you can be challenging, but getting comfortable with making healthy disconnections is a crucial part of the process. This makes it easier for those who are meant to be in your tribe to effortlessly and organically waltz right into your space.

It can be challenging to decide when to walk away from a relationship that isn't serving you. This includes friendships, romantic relationships, business relationships and every other type of relationship. It's natural for us to not want to hurt anyone's feelings and I believe that the vast majority of people try to take others' feelings into account to the greatest extent that they are able. But, walking away doesn't mean that you aren't kind, or that you aren't compassionate. It means that you're being true to you. It means that you're doing what you need to do to stay aligned with you are.

I've found that one of the most useful barometers to help make the determination as to whether or not you should keep investing your energy in a certain person is by looking at patterns. Be mindful of the tipping point, which is the point at which these one-off accommodations become a regular occurrence. Anchor on how it makes you feel and the emotions you are experiencing. Decide if you are experiencing peace, harmony and compassion or dissonance, uneasiness and unrest.

It usually doesn't take too long for someone to show you who he or she is. When someone shows you, believe what you see. It's one thing to give someone the benefit of the doubt occasionally, but it's a whole different ball game when you need to give someone the benefit of the doubt habitually. When you find yourself making excuses for someone, justifying toxic behaviors or having to repeatedly analyze and interpret actions, it's time to stop and ask yourself why you are tolerating the behavior and if it is serving you. Understand that there's a fine line between being flexible and compromising your self worth, and it's important to become acutely aware of when you're approaching this line and come up with a plan to realign with your standards.

A sure-fire way to come out of alignment with who you are is to be a people-pleaser. The Universe hardly even knows what to deliver because you're willing to accept a patchwork quilt of things. Another tendency that will assuredly keep you out of alignment and out of touch with who you are and your core values, and keep you from truly aligning with Source Energy, is to try to strong-arm people to stay in your space. I am no longer in the business of convincing anyone to stay in my space. On a human level, it can be hard at the time. After all, goodbyes have never been my favorite part of life. In grade school, I was always the kid crying at the end of the year because I was sad to say goodbye to my teacher. But as I've moved through my evolution, I now fully understand that on a spiritual level it means that we are both coming into closer alignment with who we are and with Source Energy, which is exactly where we all want to be.

Admittedly there will undoubtedly be uncomfortableness along the way as you craft your standards and make the necessary adjustments. But, just because it's uncomfortable doesn't mean you shouldn't do it. In fact, in this case you should. There's no growth in comfort. I wouldn't categorize lifting weights as "comfortable" either, but we do it because we know it will make us stronger.

The process of bringing standards into focus and articulating what you desire in interpersonal relationships is exciting and eye-opening. From time to time you will take a historical glance at where you've come from, and the growth will be readily apparent. When what you used to tolerate is no longer acceptable to you, you have grown, and that is the ultimate goal.

Try it this week. Pick an area of your life and speak your truth. You already know what it is. It feels bold at first, but before too long it will just be a natural part of how you operate. You've gotta walk away from mediocre before the mind-blowing can find you. Just stay firmly affixed to your standards and watch awesomeness flow right into your existence.

So go ahead, name yourself Creative Director of your Standards and start designing away. Then make everything conform to that. Keep doing your thing with standards and with love and the rest will fall into place.

Boundaries

Define your boundaries first, and then see how everything measures up against them. Define outer limitations, deal-breakers, no-go zones, etc. If you don't have pre-established boundaries, it is too easy for you to lose touch with what you need in order to honor who you are, and without even realizing it, you will find yourself running in circles. By defining boundaries, you will learn to make more conscious decisions about what you are comfortable with.

An example of a boundary is learning to say "no," completely free from guilt. I spent years saying yes to things I didn't want to or didn't have to do and became totally stressed out and physically and mentally exhausted in the process. I have finally learned that saying no some of the time is not only okay, but it is necessary to truly honor ourselves. Often the decisions we make for ourselves are run through the filter of how it will be perceived or the fear of what **they** will think. Here's the skinny: that's irrelevant. Instead, rewire your mind to ask, "How does this make **me** feel?" When you anchor on the feeling, it becomes very apparent what your tolerance is.

My oldest child, who is extremely observant and perceptive and evolved, never hesitates to point out that I am so different now. There has been significant growth across the entire spectrum as a result of the lessons I've learned during the divorce process, and what I believe is most apparent is that I've learned how to define and honor boundaries. I've learned how to manage my inner-fixer. Without even realizing it, for years I was the self-proclaimed "first responder" on everybody's issues. Someone forgot homework — No problem, I'll drive it to school. Someone left lunch on the kitchen counter — No problem, I'll bring it to school. Just remembered that you need graph paper by tomorrow — No problem, I'll run to Target after you're in bed. I promoted a culture and a mentality of "Mom's the safety net." Allowing anything to fall through the cracks, even the slightest things, used to feel like the world had been jolted off its axis. I hardly even knew how to prioritize anymore. Day-to-day life felt like one big fire drill and the bitter pill I finally had to swallow was that it was because I allowed it. Without even realizing it, I was my own enabler. I was the one perpetuating a culture of not enough structure and boundaries, and since I was the one who created it, it was my job to establish a new framework.

One thing I also needed to do is learn to let go of the idea or the expectation that everything needed to be perfect. There is room for error. We aren't perfect, we are human. Now I've realized that the sun will still come up the next day if someone forgets something. Everyday life has afforded me the opportunity to fine-tune compassion, understanding, flexibility and empathy across the board.

Releasing Expectations

We often create excessive amounts of stress because we romanticize an ideal outcome in our minds only to find ourselves disappointed when the outcome isn't realized as we had envisioned it.

Over the years, I've learned to embrace uncertainty and now have come to view it as an opportunity for the Universe to surprise me. Life is so much more fun this way. I spent so many years trying to force things to work a certain way, planning out every detail in advance, and in doing so, found myself constantly frustrated and disappointed when things didn't unfold exactly as planned. Life is so much sweeter when you let go and let the Universe run the show. Expectation breeds control, and control breeds resistance. The tighter you cling on to a particular outcome, the more resistance you will create because you are more focused on the absence of it. We lose sight of the fact that there are always a multitude of desirable outcomes, and some may be better suited for us than the outcome we are fixated on. It is important to surrender to the Universe and keep reminding yourself that we are making our decision and setting expectations with our limited, conscious minds. It is only the Universe that truly knows the big picture and what is in our highest good.

When you embrace uncertainty, you allow the Universe to surprise you.

We must also learn to release our expectations of others. This should not be confused with lowering our standards, as they are fundamentally different ideas. It's important to set boundaries and ensure that others are treating us with the dignity and respect we deserve, but we must give them the space to move freely and act in congruence with their perception of reality and their belief system. Everything that someone does or says is filtered through the lens of that person's prior life experiences as well as what is ensuing in his or her current reality. In many cases, you do not have complete information and therefore may not fully understand someone else's actions, as well as any limitations such as fear, doubt, distractions, limiting beliefs, or addictions. This is an area where we all can have a tendency to be self-critical and ask ourselves if an outcome was the result of something that was caused by our own words or actions. In most cases, it has very little if anything to do with you, and everything to do with what is going on in the other person's world. Unless you did something particularly negative that provoked an unnecessarily caustic reaction, anchor to the tenet that it is nothing personal.

The sooner we can free ourselves from being attached to a particular outcome, the sooner we can truly shift into a place where we are positioned to receive the abundance and the surprises that the Universe has in store for us.

Who's in Your Tribe?

This time of transition affords you the opportunity to take a close look at all areas of your life and redefine what you want it to look like as you move into your new reality.

We spend a significant amount of time interacting with others. This is a perfect time to take a hard look at the relationships you are investing in and make the necessary adjustments.

As you take inventory, reflect on the following questions. Who are the people you spend the most time with and what are their attributes? Do you feel better after you spend time with them than before? What are their belief systems? Do they support you? Do they have the same values? Will they be open-minded and tolerant and supportive of your new life?

As the old adage goes, variety is the spice of life, and I can't say I disagree. How quickly would we get bored if everyone was the same? While we must remain compassionate and understanding and tolerant of other people's unique lifestyles, we must always make sure we are surrounding ourselves with people who enhance our lives, and not those who leave us feeling drained or depleted. Likewise, they should feel like your contribution to their lives leaves them feeling better, happier, more energized, uplifted, supported or some other positive emotion. There are several possibilities here but the spirit is the same: all parties should always walk away feeling better.

As you sculpt your new life and set sail in a new direction, align yourself with people who share your interests, goals and belief system. This will organically adapt to your circumstances and phases of life over time, as relationships are a dynamic construct. Perhaps during the divorce process and healing time you spend more time with people who you met in a support group because your friendship is helping to heal each other. Perhaps right after the divorce process you join a bowling league because you want to start meeting people. You may also want to start thinking longer-term about the direction in which you plan to take your life, and reach out to groups and communities and start making contacts and connections with your future in mind.

When my spiritual journey really started to go into turbo-mode a few years ago, I sought out and surrounded myself with like-minded people. People who spoke my language. People who didn't think it was crazy that every time we talked on the phone during the divorce process we would always cite the phrase "The best is yet to come." I got it. She got it. We both understood what that meant. And we both understand how powerful words are when said with intentionality and from the heart.

As much as we would love to stay in contact with all of the people we enjoy spending time with, the truth is that everyone has a limited amount of discretionary time to work with each week. This necessitates mindfulness when we make decisions in this regard. This is the time to ask yourself some very powerful questions, and I think that you'll find that your answers will cut right to the heart of it. You may find that the people who are the biggest influencers in your life are perfectly aligned with who you are and where you are going. You may find that some relationships are holdovers from earlier times in your life, and you need to make some "updates" in this regard. Note that it doesn't always result in a disconnection; sometimes we just need to make some adjustments to recalibrate to where we need to be.

It's exciting to infuse your life with new people. New energy. New ideas. New opportunities. New connections. We live in a world with choices, and the decision about who we spend our time with is no exception. We have several choices and we should feel free to choose, with no fear and no judgement. Accept invitations out of excitement and out of desire, not out of obligation. We always want to be living from the heart, with our thoughts, behaviors and actions in alignment. Why do something if your heart's not in it? Why accept an invitation to an event when you'd rather be spending the time somewhere else?

Remember to stay anchored to making conscious choices and be selective about who you invite into your tribe.

Be selective about who you invite into your tribe.

Self-Love

This is such an important concept that it deserves to be brought up again at this phase, particularly as you are making conscious choices about how you will invest in yourself moving forward.

Remember, self-love and self-care are two of the most valuable gifts you could ever give yourself, as well as the people around you. This is a great time to re-read or reference that section of this book as you craft the new version of you.

Discovering Your Authenticity

- What shapes your identity?
- What are some changes you could make to live a life that is more authentic to who you are?
- What are your standards?
- What healthy disconnections need to be made?
- In what areas of your life could you benefit from clearer boundaries?
- In what ways are you holding others to expectations that more closely reflect who you are rather than who they are?
- Who is in your tribe? Are they conducive and supportive of the direction in which you plan to take your life?

25

SHARING YOUR GIFTS WITH THE WORLD

The intersection of your passion, purpose, and profession is precisely the point where work starts to feel like play.

How Did I Find My Purpose?

At the time of our divorce, I had been mulling over what I might like to do professionally as the kids got older, but nothing really resonated with me. I thought about going back to school to pursue a new career and figured that someday I might want to write a book. I wanted to have something to fill my time as the kids got older and eventually moved out, but didn't really have a specific plan.

Well, the Universe has a magical way of making sure we turn our "somedays" into "todays." The Universe's wisdom is infinite and it always knows the magnitude of the catalyst that is necessary for each of us to make a change and launch us into our own authentic realities. I never intended to become a spiritual life coach, and it wasn't until sometime during the divorce process that I started to feel something bubbling up. For the first time in a long time, I was starting to feel energized, empowered, liberated and untethered. I had finally made a decision to step into my authentic self and was in the process of constructing a reality around that, and the Universe was conspiring to help me. At the beginning of the divorce process, I remember feeling somewhat apprehensive about my ability to carry out all my responsibilities because now I would have less time and fewer resources as a single mom. I thought that I would be more overwhelmed and depleted, but what I didn't realize at that time is that when you step into your truth and align with Source Energy, you are limitless. We have a direct lifeline to the same creative, Universal Energy that created us and when we engage in endeavors that are meant for the greater good, they flow effortlessly and unfold organically. Anyone can do this, but first you must be willing to step into your truth and trust that the Universe will partner with you.

Your greatest challenge may, in fact, be an invitation from the Universe to step into your greatness, in disguise.

Stepping into my truth and pursuing my purpose hasn't come without its growing pains. When we were in the midst of the divorce process and were deciding how to delineate our respective parenting roles and responsibilities in our new reality, we decided that the kids' dad would continue in his role of providing financial resources, and I would continue to be a full-time mom. As much as I was grateful to have the logistical and financial freedom to be able to continue in my prior role, my soul craved more. I knew the time to do this was now, so I went after it with relentless and reckless abandon. One of my kids even asked me if I could wait a few more years so that it didn't distract me from my responsibilities as a mom. Without hesitation and with an unwavering sense of resolve and boundless enthusiasm I explained that I couldn't wait. I needed to get started right away for me and for the world. I'm a "strike while the iron's hot" kind of person, and the best time to do what your soul is pulling you to do is now. Don't wait. I followed the same advice that I would give to one of my clients or to one of my own children.

I still have 168 hours a week to work with, and figuring out how to layer on the pursuit of my passion and purpose onto an already full family schedule has been a process of self-discovery and growth as I rebalance my priorities, uphold boundaries and make conscious choices that are supportive of my endeavors and responsibilities.

What are Your Gifts?

We are all sent here with a unique set of gifts and talents that are meant to be shared with the world. Sometimes these gifts are readily apparent and available and sometimes they remain dormant until a significant event in your life happens that causes you to do some serious soul-searching. I'm a firm believer that the real treasures are those that are buried deep within and require the most intense excavating to discover. We all have them, and sometimes our greatest gifts are disguised in the form of our greatest heartbreaks or challenges. Remember that you have a choice about what you do with them, and you already have everything you need to transform your pain into a gift to the world.

What stirs your soul? For me, music has always been my go-to companion, motivator, peace-maker, confidante, teacher and creative director. Music is woven into my soul. It's what can take me from a dark place to a place of comfort and peace. It's what can take a creative spark that resides only in my mind, by the hand, and usher it into the physical world. It's what was playing in the background as I wrote sections of this book. I love to listen to it and I love to play my favorite songs by ear. I started taking piano lessons when I was five years old, and my piano teacher quickly recognized that I have perfect pitch, which is the ability to recognize musical notes and re-create musical pieces by ear. While I never pursued a music career professionally, playing the piano is something that has been a part of my life ever since, and is something that I share with my kids, as we all play various musical instruments and often have jam sessions. I believe that our innate gifts are nurtured by creative endeavors and anything that encourages us to express our individuality counts, and there are no rules or certifications around that. Belting out your favorite song counts. Coloring with a box of crayons counts. Finger painting counts. You don't have to aspire to be the next Mozart or Van Gogh for your creative endeavors to benefit you and humanity.

What gifts do people recognize in you? What are your natural talents? When do you feel most alive and energized? What sets your soul on fire? What comes naturally to you? The things we are meant to do unfold with ease. If you're a natural extrovert and enjoy helping others, sitting at a desk working by yourself probably isn't the best fit for you. If you work best alone and without distractions, placing yourself with a lot of external stimulation and human interaction will most likely leave you feeling distracted and overwhelmed, and probably isn't the best environment for you to optimize your contributions. Place yourself in an environment that facilitates your natural gifts and talents and you will be amazed how natural it feels.

Do what sets your soul on fire and watch the rest fall into place.

Self-Actualization
Within each of us lies the potential to fulfill a much deeper purpose. Are we even aware that a reality other than our unconscious modus operandi of going through the motions of everyday life, feeling accomplished by completing our to-do lists and subscribing to society's proclamations on what makes us happy exists? Are we aware that there are levels **beyond** short-term instant gratification, extending into long-term fulfillment realms?

Once we have attained a certain level of awareness, we must discern if we embody the desire to do the work and take the necessary risks, trading in our alleged comfort and security for a life where every aspect may be subject to change. This is the phase where the rubber meets the road, where the men are separated from the boys, so to speak. That moment of truth where you ask yourself how bad you want something and ultimately decide which way to go at that proverbial fork in the road. It's when you ask yourself if you continue to proceed in your unconscious reality, or if you take a leap and embrace a new beginning, abandoning all that was comfortable and secure and familiar in exchange for a life full of either challenges and hardships **or** adventure, growth, transformation and never-ending fulfillment. You decide. The path that is meant for you is illuminated the moment you decide which mindset to adopt.

Lastly, after you make the decision to follow the "Self-Actualization This Way" arrow, the true test lies in who has the **endurance** to stay the course. This is where it becomes readily apparent who the true spiritual warriors are. How do you respond when, not if, things don't unfold as you planned (or as you thought you planned them in this life) time after time? Do you start looking for the nearest "Exit" sign to disembark this Expressway to your

Highest Self, or do you slide over to the passenger seat, where I'd posit that's where we belong, and let the Universe do the driving, as you surrender to Source Energy and all its divine timing?

You have come here to fulfill a specific purpose and the journey of discovering it is as fulfilling as the discovery itself. My wish for everyone is that they are surrounded by people and experiences that usher them gracefully to that place.

Discovering Your Authenticity

- What do you feel passionate about?
- What sets your soul on fire?
- What comes naturally to you?
- Have you contemplated your purpose?
- What are your gifts and talents?
- How might you turn your life experiences into a gift to humanity?
- In what ways can you shine your light into the world?

26

LET LOVE FIND YOU

*Before you fall in love with someone else, you first need to fall in love with **you** and **your** life.*

This book is not about dating after divorce, and I'm not a dating coach, but I'd be remiss if I didn't address this piece of the puzzle. Many people want to talk about their next steps in the department of romantic relationships after a divorce, which is completely expected and normal.

It's normal to experience some apprehension as you step out into the dating world for the first time in a while. There may be some self-doubt as you wonder how you'll ever meet someone at this stage in your life. So many things may have changed since you were last in the dating world. You may have had fewer real-world responsibilities, and not to mention that the landscape of the dating world has changed dramatically in recent years with people of all ages spending their time swiping left and swiping right trying to sift through the sea of candidates looking for Mr. or Ms. Right.

I hold firm to the belief that the fun and the growth always comes when we discover our own answers. When we develop our own approaches because we are the only ones who are intimately familiar with every aspect of ourselves. I'm going to share my approach and philosophy because it is so counter to what everyone else is doing. Ultimately, how you decide to approach dating is your choice, but I am giving you my thoughts on dating when energy is the currency.

Like everything else I do, my approach is deeply-rooted in spiritual principles, and I create my reality through energy and vibration. By now you're probably not surprised to hear that my philosophy and my ideologies for dating aren't exactly congruent with mainstream culture, but that's why I'm here. I'm here to give you progressive and avant-garde ways of approaching life. I'm excited to share my approach with you with the hope it may help you reframe this process in a more positive and adventurous light and ultimately find the only kind of love that is sustainable and stands the test of time like no other.

You may have several relationships before you find your Forever Guy or Forever Girl. Understand that they all serve a purpose and remember that there is no such thing as a waste of time. This is not a race to the finish line. It's not a competition about who gets remarried faster. Human relationships are meant to help us become more aware and heal us. Every interaction we have is an opportunity to learn more about ourselves and is an opportunity to help us grow and transform. Throughout this journey, keep peppering yourself with transformative, growth-minded questions such as "What did this relationship teach me about myself?" How did it help me refine my standards?"

You may not find the "forever" version of Mr. Right or Ms. Right right away, but it will be Mr. or Ms. Right for Right Now. Maybe you need some light-hearted fun for a while. Maybe you need companionship. Or more profoundly, maybe you need to step up your self-respect and self-worth game and the Universe sends someone to help you fine-tune your standards. Maybe you need someone who tests your boundaries. This is an iterative process and what you learn from each relationship will be interwoven into the new and improved version of you, and that's the point from which you will attract going forward.

It's a natural, knee-jerk response to want to fill the void. Regardless of the length of time you were married, regardless of how disconnected your marriage may have been, you were still operating within a relationship construct and are used to having someone else around, even if your emotional needs were not being met. Even though in your heart, your relationship may have been over for a while, you still had a "placeholder" and certainly weren't casting the available vibes into the Universe, so you really don't have a good barometer for how people will respond when you do "get out there" and start dating and you are casting "available" vibes. You may be anxious to find out by testing the waters.

Do not rush to fill what feels like an empty space. Fill it up with **you**. Fill it up with all the things you love that don't have to do with a romantic relationship. Learn to get comfortable with being single. Go out with friends. Go out by yourself. This is a golden opportunity to reinvent yourself. View it as the making of you. Learn to sit quietly with yourself and enjoy the solitude. No distractions. Just you and the world as your oyster. Spend time dreaming — big. Spend time reading. Spend time writing. Travel domestically. Travel internationally. Volunteer. Take a walk. Take a longer walk. Ponder your purpose.

Before you fall in love with someone else, you first need to fall in love with **you** and **your** life. Just as it is. Fall in love with the world around you. Fall in love with your hobbies. Find your passion and set it ablaze. Learn how to be happy **on your own**. Only then should you begin to entertain the idea of inviting someone into your life.

Work on yourself to the point where you're a complete ice cream sundae: the vanilla ice cream, the hot fudge, the whipped cream **and** the cherry on top. The whole shebang. Then, when someone comes along and knocks your socks off, they'll be the **extra** cherry on top. That extra touch of sweetness that your sundae didn't **need**, but is oh so much sweeter with it. What you do **not** want to do is look for someone to complete your sundae.

If you have to chase it, it's not worth having. If you have to convince it to stay, it's not worth having. If you have to continuously search far and wide, it's not worth having. If you have to compromise who you are, it's not worth having.

I believe that we don't find love when we're looking for it. We find it after we've found ourselves, after we've built a life we love, after we've learned to be happy on our own and with what we have and after we've officially declared ourselves "Actively Not Looking." Pour your heart and soul into doing the things that "fill you up," whether it is your work, your hobbies, your passions or anything else that fits the bill. Whatever it is that sets your soul on fire is what you should be doing. It will happen when you least expect it.

Your objective is to attract from the highest point of attraction, the point that embodies **the best** version of you **after** you've done the deep soul work on yourself. It is natural to wonder,

"But if I'm evolving every day, wouldn't that suggest that I keep waiting with the belief that the more evolved I become the better match I end up with? How do I know it's the one?" My response is that this is where you will follow your inner voice. It always knows.

So many people find the process of looking for a new partner to be daunting. Rather than view this process as a burden, view it as an exciting opportunity. As we covered in the manifestation section, the wording you use is incredibly important. It's an opportunity for the Universe to play the matching game and deliver a person who reflects your new and improved self. Rather than thinking that you don't know how you will ever meet someone, change your mindset. Think about being excited about sifting through all the available people to find a great match.

I'm always interested in trying new and improved ways of doing things, but for certain things I still do anchor to "old-school" approaches. Meeting people is one of them. Dating sites may work for some, but for me, personally, the whole premise is counter to my belief system. Find what works for you. Just because everyone else is doing online dating doesn't mean that you have to. Figure out what feels natural to you and do that. Since my approach to life has metaphysical underpinnings and everything I do is done through the perspective of energy, my approach is radically different from what is being done in mainstream culture. My personal energy-based belief system keeps me rooted in the tenet that by looking for something you are acknowledging the absence of it and trying to fill the void, therefore coming at it from a place of lack which just creates resistance. It prompts us to think about what we need to do and how we might need to fill the space, which pulls us out of alignment from who we really are. If you just show up all day, every day, in full alignment with your inner being, the Universe can't help but match you up with what is best for you at the right time.

I don't look for love; I let it find me. It comes when you least expect it. When you're so immersed in your own amazing life that you've co-created with the Universe. When you can't imagine things getting any better. When you are so consumed with loving your own life. What happens? Love comes walkin' in (Van Halen said it first).

I've always been so amused by the Universe's sense of humor. Right after we declare something, the Universe loves to send us a little sign or "cosmic wink" that it's right there with us and it never misses an opportunity to remind us that it's the one that is orchestrating everything, not us. Along these lines, one cold, snowy December night I was reminded of the Universe's playfulness and sense of humor, which never ceases to amaze me.

One of my close friends asked me if I wanted to meet her out for dinner later that evening. I cherish this friendship dearly because it is based on a foundation of openness and honesty and we give each other feedback on all things big and small. She has been one of my most significant catalysts to date because she challenges me, is highly intuitive and is adept at always bringing another perspective to the situation. We've created a judgement-free atmosphere where we both feel comfortable calling it as we see it (not as what we think the other wants to hear) and we have both experienced tremendous growth as a result.

I agreed to go to dinner, somewhat reluctantly, not because I didn't want to catch up with her, but because in an already overly-scheduled time of year, my day was back to back and I knew I'd be exhausted at the end of the day. I would have zero time to put myself together the way I normally would if I were going out, and was going to show up as I was. I told her that I wasn't going to spend any time getting ready because my intent was to catch up with her and not to meet anyone new. So holding to my promise, I showed up looking and feeling only slightly better than disheveled at best.

I arrived at the restaurant and chose a table in the corner so we would be free from distractions. I texted her to let her know I had arrived. She replied that she was there, too, and that I should meet her at the bar. While we were fully-immersed in our conversation, a guy sitting a few seats down from me broke into our conversation. Within minutes, he and I were laughing hysterically as we share the exact same sense of humor. Fast forward to the end of the night when he asked for my number. We were laughing, but it was really the Universe who had the last laugh...it was orchestrating this all along. Pure amazingness happens when we learn to sit back, relax, and let the Universe do the driving.

Whatever you do, know your worth and hold out for the best. It's really easy to find someone with whom you share common interests. It's really easy to find companionship. It's really easy to find someone who is unhappy and looking for another person to make them happy. It's really easy to find someone to have sex with. It's really easy to gravitate back to a past relationship and recycle old toxicities because they're familiar, and a heck of a lot less work than starting from square one and getting to know someone new. All of these scenarios are just a swipe or a text or a social media search away. There's no real "work" that needs to be done here.

I can assure you that is **not** the way to find unconditional, all-encompassing, soul-bonding, life-altering conscious love. It may work for a month. It may work for a few years. It may work for 10. But ultimately you entered the relationship with some type of need and unless you've done the work on your own to make yourself whole and complete and ridiculously happy before you invite someone new into your life, the same patterns will ensue and the unhealed parts of you will be carried from relationship to relationship and happiness and fulfillment will continue to elude you.

Love lasts only if you love someone for who that person is **now**, not who you expect him or her to become. We should never ask or expect someone to change. Yes, people do change, and external forces, whether it be a person, event, song or something else can trigger the change and serve as a catalyst, but the desire to change and the associated efficacy of one's efforts need to come from within each individual. Everyone is on an individual journey and must do the work independently.

Use Your Manifestation Techniques

The approach for manifesting love follows the same steps for anything else you're trying to manifest in your life. We won't walk through them in exquisite detail here, but I'd like to point out a few key points:

You know the first step by now. If you don't get really clear, what you're going to get will be all over the board. Write out a few of the "must haves" and a few dealbreakers. Remember when you're listing the criteria that the Universe does not recognize "nots," so rather than saying "I don't want someone who smokes" say "I want someone who lives a healthy lifestyle."

Anchor to the feeling you want to embody and don't get too

wrapped up in the "packaging." Keep in mind that we are talking about manifesting a person in your life, not ordering a couch. There's no order form that allows us to check off certain objective criteria and have it delivered to us eight weeks from now. It's really a feeling that you're after. You will meet lots of people who, on paper, meet your criteria but don't deliver the feeling that you're seeking. Only you can determine who truly stirs your soul and it will be so obvious when it arrives. When you resonate with someone on the soul level, it's the connection to Source Energy that you're feeling. Remember that there isn't only one person who can deliver that feeling. It's easy to become narrow-minded and fixate on a particular person, but remember that there are several people who are vibrational matches to you and who can be conduits to Source Energy.

Everything comes to you **through** you. You want to attract from the highest point of attraction after you've done the work to become the best version of yourself. Many people rush to fill the void, but what they don't realize is that if you feel a void of any kind, you have more work to do. Get to a place where you feel whole and complete and aren't lacking anything, and keep investing in you.

Allow the Universe to surprise you. Stay focused on what you think you want, but let the Universe deliver what it feels you need at the time. Be flexible and open-minded in what you're willing to receive. Trust the process and defer to the Universe's infinite wisdom. It knows what is best for us better than we do.

Every relationship we have has the potential to help us grow and evolve, and romantic relationships lead the pack because emotions are intensified, as the connection has a high potency level. This is where the concept of conscious relationships comes in.

Conscious Relationships

The ego says, "I want someone who meets my needs and makes me happy."

Soul says, "I want a conscious relationship."

Conscious relationships are the relationship of the future. The old-relationship paradigm is being shattered, as it is no longer a sustainable model over the long-haul, and this breakdown is making way for the new-age relationship model, conscious relationships.

Conscious relationships, unlike romantic relationships under the old-paradigm, are not formed with need-based conditions. They come about when two people have already committed to their soul work and are committed to the purpose of growth with their romantic partner. Conscious relationships satisfy the following criteria:

1. Growth

Individual growth - Both individuals are fiercely committed to their individual growth and support each other in those initiatives.

Growth as a couple - The couple is continually looking to strengthen the relationship between each other, fortifying their connection, improving their communication, practicing compassion and showing empathy.

Growth for humanity - There are often philanthropic endeavors involved, as the couple feels the pull to partake in initiatives that promote the betterment of humanity. The couple often feels that they have come together to fulfill a certain mission or purpose that would have not been possible to achieve outside of the conscious romantic partnership.

2. Acceptance and Accountability
In addition to the positive attributes each partner brings into the relationship, they also bring with them things from their past. Old wounds that have not been healed, triggers, past traumas and insecurities. We accept each other as we are, knowing that we are both perfectly imperfect. No matter how much we work on ourselves, we are constantly "under construction" and it is never expected that either person is perfect. Each individual understands that he or she is ultimately the one responsible to own their stuff and neither should be projecting their issues on their partner, nor should they be looking to their partner to fix them.

3. Thoughts and Feelings are Shared Openly and Freely
Both individuals feel the freedom and the security to share their thoughts and feelings with each other. Trust is never in question, as these relationships are the "safe place" in which to express all of your deepest desires, fantasies, darkest secrets, fears and anxieties without the fear of being judged or critiqued. Each person helps the other work through those within the structure of the conscious relationship and the willingness to be authentic and show up as he or she is, with no masks or pretenses. This spirit of transparency is precisely how connection is enhanced and maintained.

4. Practicing Love is a Priority
The couple is committed to practicing love all day, every day. Their world centers around it and they are always looking to extend acts of love to everyone in their space as they stretch and

grow. The way in which they express love plays a huge part in setting an example and templating this relationship model.

The Law of Attraction will guide you through your romantic journey in much the same way it orchestrates every other part of your life. Remember that it all happens energetically and matches occur according to vibration. There is divine orchestration behind each and every match and there is always, always a lesson or lessons, if you so choose to recognize them. View the people you encounter as the Universe giving you feedback and express gratitude. Certain aspects of these individuals will give you an indication as to how you are doing vibrationally, and other aspects give you an opportunity to learn more about yourself.

Don't get too caught up in the "packaging" - the other person's packaging and yours. While we all probably have preconceived notions to a certain degree as to which physical attributes our "forever guy" or "forever girl" will have, it's vibration that's the undercurrent and it is infinitely more powerful than any superficial criteria we could put forth. Allow the Universe to surprise you. This is the fun part. Keep the covenant to be open-minded and ready to receive what the Universe wants to deliver. Remember it's the "feeling" you're seeking, and that "feeling" can be delivered via many different messengers.

Don't worry about being too much of this, or too little of that. The right person won't think you're too "anything." That's what unconditional love is. Don't worry about too intense, too cautious or too silly. The right person won't care. The right person won't be afraid to step into your energy, whatever energy signature you embody, and will be drawn to you like a moth to a flame. It won't matter if you have one kid or if you have five kids or if you have 10. It won't matter if you live across the street or if you live across the world. Don't worry if you're not perfectly manicured and facialed; the right person won't care if you have no makeup on and are sporting a messy bun, straight out of the gym. It doesn't matter if you have an extra 10 pounds on you or if you're in Iron Man competition-shape. None of that will deter the right person from stepping into your fire. Don't dim your light or extinguish your flame. The right person will accept you just as you are.

Like anything else, go with your gut. If it's unfolding naturally and organically, that's the Universe's way of telling you it's worth investing in. If the dynamics are forced and unnatural, pay attention to the way it makes you feel and make the necessary adjustments. Again, this all happens on an energetic level. I firmly believe that the feeling you get when introduced to someone's energy even **before** anyone verbally introduces themselves and before any words are spoken, is generally the best barometer for the compatibility of a relationship on a soul level. We are operating from the heart and the heart never fails to make you aware of what resonates with you. Then, the mind kicks in and this is when things become unnecessarily complicated. It's where we start to overthink. Analyze. Doubt. It's the ego interjecting and causing you to weave fear and doubt in the process.

Understand that rejection is part and parcel of the process. I don't know anyone who hasn't experienced it in their path to finding true love, and I don't know anyone who hasn't had a broken heart at least once. It totally stings at the time; I get it. I've been there. Again, how you process it is a choice, and the experience can be reframed and can be used as a steel to further sharpen your sword. It is a normal reaction of our human condition to feel discouraged and take it as a chink in your armor. Everyone wants to feel included and loved, and rejection can at first feel like salt on an open wound. It can be discouraging because while you were trying to take a step closer toward securing that unconditional love you're so desperately seeking, you took two steps backward. The truth, though, is that you didn't. These experiences are like slingshots. They may temporarily pull you back, but have tremendous potential to catapult you to a place that would have been unachievable in the absence of it. You can coach yourself through these moments by asking yourself what aspects of the relationship worked well for you and which ones didn't. Like anything else, you can use it as an opportunity to heighten your self-awareness and illuminate various aspects of yourself. It's yet another opportunity to bring your standards into focus and send them out into the Universe so it can begin the process of orchestrating the delivery.

It's not enough to just hope you'll find love someday. It's not enough to expect that you'll find love someday. You have to believe that it will happen. Really believe it. It will happen when it's meant to happen. Take the pressure off of yourself and ditch the timeline you have in your mind. Remember to have fun. We take life so seriously, but it's so much sweeter when we just relax and remember that we are simply observers in our human reality. Sit back, relax and enjoy the show.

My views on relationships and traditional marriage have changed wildly throughout the course of my ascension. I used to subscribe wholly to the traditional, conventional design of relationships and marriage, as structured under the old paradigm. I used to be focused on what love is supposed to look like rather than how it's supposed to feel. At the end of the day, it's a man-made contract and the pull of our souls always reigns supreme regardless of what words are on the paper. The goal is unconditional love, and there is no room for constraint or limitations in that. Unconditional love is about freedom. The ultimate embodiment of love is loving someone in a way that encourages and supports that person's freedom and expansion.

I think there needs to be a "healthy tension" in all relationships for them to be not only viable over the long-term, but dynamic and fulfilling and leaving both partners in a constant state of wanting to keep coming back for more. I no longer see the need to consummate a relationship in the eyes of the state. While there may be practical, financial or legal implications and considerations for doing so, it should not go unnoticed that with all of that comes conditions and expectations, both of which come with constraints. Nobody wants to feel constrained, and nobody who is committed to loving someone else unconditionally should want them to feel constrained and limited. In my eyes, choosing to stay in a relationship that doesn't have a bloody mess of legalities to unravel is a much more powerful statement than staying in a relationship out of convenience. It encourages both people to bring their best to the relationship by making a conscious effort to practice love every single day. It's a reality that encourages conscious thought by prompting both partners to make a choice day after day after day. Every day the relationship continues, each partner has effectively stated "I choose you again today." It shifts the focus from the "outcome" or "goal" to the journey. Both parties are still making a commitment, but rather than committing their future selves to act in certain ways they can't possibly predict under conditions they can't possibly foresee, they are wholly and completely committing themselves to loving someone exactly as they are, and growing with them as they both immerse themselves in the present moment together.

You have the license to be as creative as you wish to be in any area of your life and a romantic relationship is no exception.

Design your own Spiritual Union the way you want it to look. Choreograph a ceremony the way you want it to be. Call yourselves whatever titles you want to. Define what you want it to embody, and begin the process of manifesting and co-creating with the Universe.

Discovering Your Authenticity

- What are some aspects you discovered about yourself in your last few relationships?
- Do you notice any similarities in the type of people you are attracting?
- Can you identify any correlations between your thought patterns and the results you are getting?
- Have you articulated your standards for romantic relationships?

For a special bonus on attracting conscious love, visit https://liveauthentically.today/soar-resources to download the guide.

27

ASCENSION

Expansion requires a willingness to let go of outdated beliefs and behaviors that no longer serve you.

Sometimes, I stop and think back to the way I was at prior points in my evolution, and I think about how "unevolved" I was. Sometimes it's hard to get my head wrapped around the idea that things that once held great significance no longer resonate with me. When the self-deprecating banter starts, I have to remind myself that I'm judging myself, and recognize that it was my ego peeking out and trying to judge or critique what I was doing. It's the part that tries to infuse doubt and fear and all the other things that impede spiritual progress. I have to recenter and remind myself that where I was is precisely where I was meant to be at that point in time. I quell any lingering disappointment with the reminder that I was acting on the information and drawing from the life experiences I had up to that point in my evolution. Not only is it okay that I was at that point, but it was a necessary stepping stone for the rest of my journey.

That's true for anything. We can always look back and say, "If I knew then what I know now." But, the reality is that you didn't. Years of life experience give you lessons and wisdom and the opportunity to get to know yourself better.

Look at what we know now about health and wellness compared to prior generations. In general, we as a society are more aware of the benefits of living a healthy lifestyle than we were decades ago. There's such a big push on eating organic foods, limiting processed foods and other healthy eating initiatives that it would be easy to question and find fault in the ideas that were being touted decades ago, such as seeking out convenience foods and eating processed foods. Why wasn't there a focus on healthy eating? There are several reasons, but the knowledge that people had then was vastly limited compared to the knowledge that we have available to us now, and people were doing their best with the information they had at the time.

As you progress through your spiritual journey, resist the urge to look back and critique where you were at any prior point. Resist the urge to wish you had done things differently. There's no back arrow in life like there is on a computer. There are no "do-overs." Feelings of regret never lead to anything productive. In fact, it is one of the mechanisms that will only serve to keep you stuck and unable to move forward and enjoy your journey in great depth as you partner with the Universe.

There are also no mistakes and no failures. Relegate those concepts from your mind and reframe them as "learning experiences." All of your experiences have brought you to this moment in a divinely orchestrated manner and you are right where you are meant to be.

As you are awakening, or ascending into higher planes of consciousness, you will start to notice changes across all aspects of your being, physically, mentally, emotionally and spiritually. While achieving enlightenment is the Holy Grail in the spiritual world, we must exercise patience as there is no "Enlightenment" button to push and there's no vehicle to get us there overnight. The process happens gradually and all people must move through it with their own unique signature. No two individuals' paths are alike. Many people want to know how long it will take them to evolve. In the spiritual world, we do not anchor ourselves to time. Instead, we anchor to energy. The answer to that question is always found through vibration. The amount of "time" it takes is always directly related to the individual's willingness and commitment to doing his or her soul work.

Witnessing our own transformation can be scary because we are shedding the old version of ourselves and witnessing a new version emerge. We will see certain aspects of ourselves fall away and new aspects present themselves. With each experience and human interaction we have, our thoughts and emotions are changing and our belief system is in a constant state of fine-tuning. Energetically, you will notice a difference in the way you feel and your energy will be more vibrant, lighter, bouncier and freer. Others will also notice the difference; your aura will be different and you will shift the energy in a room before you even say anything.

Expansion does not come without its challenges, and the extent to which you experience them is directly related to your willingness to let go of the past and the outdated beliefs and behaviors that no longer serve you. Challenges also come in the form of other people who want the "old you" back. While a comprehensive presentation of such challenges and symptoms is beyond the scope of this book, I can tell you from firsthand experience that the smoothest way through this is to take the path of least resistance. Step into your truth and embrace your expansion with boundless energy and conviction and the trust-filled knowingness that you've got this. Don't look back. You're not going that way. You're going forward. Lead the way and others will follow.

The key to ascension is self-love. It all starts with you and the investments you make in yourself. Your life is like a tree. You are the trunk and all other aspects of your life are the branches, including your family, your relationships, your job, career, your personal development and everything else that encompasses you. The roots are your support system and are made up of the investments you've made in yourself, like self-care, self-love and your resources. Without a strong support system that extends deeply into nutrient-rich soil, your tree won't have the nourishment it needs to grow strong and tall. The weather conditions are your life experiences. Some days will be filled with sunshine and include birds chirping and flying against a blue sky scattered with white puffy clouds. Other days will bring dark skies with thunder, lightning and a heavy downpour. Don't despair. The rain plays an important role in pulling the nutrients out of the soil that will strengthen your tree.

It is in your ascension that you will begin to harness your true power. You will no longer worry about being inadequate or not enough. You will not doubt whether you have the necessary skills or potential. If you have any worries or concerns, they will be more along the lines of wondering if you are really ready for what you are manifesting. You'll be so immensely powerful that you'll feel Source Energy coursing through your veins every moment of every day. You'll feel unlimited, energized and untethered as you live a life with unlimited power.

Discovering Your Authenticity

- What growth have you witnessed in yourself in the last year? The last five years?
- What adjustments in your life and lifestyle need to be made to support your ascension?
- What additional resources do you need?
- Are you willing to disengage and disconnect from the things that no longer serve you in exchange for your personal growth and expansion?
- How might you handle pushback from others?
- As you ascend through the levels of consciousness, how do you feel differently than you used to?

28

DEAR UNIVERSE

I am grateful for all of my divinely-curated life experiences, as they each have played a significant role in ushering me into my authentic reality.

Dear Universe,

I am once again truly awe-struck at the pure amazingness you deliver to my life when I surrender and trust you. Every once in a while I stop and observe my life as it is today, and never in my wildest dreams did I ever think I would be standing squarely at the intersection of joy, peace and truth. Truth be told, most days I have to pinch myself to make sure I'm not dreaming. You have always known what I hold in my heart, and have always flawlessly orchestrated the events in my life and never fail to deliver precisely what I need in each moment. Some things we have co-created together, and other things have come in the form of surprises that you have sprinkled in to make this journey even sweeter.

When you delivered the message you promised on March 8, 2017, I knew two things. First, I knew that I wanted to go from being tethered to being free, so taking a huge leap of faith was the only way I could step into my authentic reality. Secondly, I knew that this large-scale, transformative endeavor could only be carried out if I surrendered, trusted your process and played an active part in co-creating my new reality with you. The only way out was through. So, each day I got up and walked this path with you. Some days putting one foot in front of the other felt like pure drudgery and other days I had a little more spring in my step. Regardless of my pace, you were always right there walking next to me. Together, we walked step by step until we got to the other side of the bridge.

I knew that while at times it felt like I was being dragged down, you were meticulously curating plans to launch me to a higher place. I knew that I needed to trust you and your process. I knew that I needed to flow with the current rather than against it. I knew that I needed to trust my gut. I knew that I needed to shut the door on fear and only let love in. I knew that I needed to keep telling myself that everything is always supporting my highest good. I knew that I needed to keep reminding myself that the best is yet to come.

As you know, I am a big believer of bookending every unit of my life, from the most minute to the most grandiose, with gratitude. Each day begins and ends that way. In the morning, I'm grateful for the opportunity to drive my kids to school. I'm grateful for the mound of dishes I have to do after I get home because it means that they still live here and I can have breakfast with them. I'm grateful to have a lifestyle that allows me to share these special moments with them. In the evening, I'm grateful for yet another day in my physical form shared with those who are an important part of my life.

Each momentous chapter begins and ends that way....

I am grateful for all of my life experiences. They are all gifts, even the challenging ones. Every single one of them has played a major role in shaping who I am.

I am grateful for the courage to embrace change, and as a result I no longer fear the unknown.

I am grateful that you have sequenced my life events in such a way that I have discovered my purpose.

I am grateful for the most significant influences in my life, including but not limited to, my parents and my tribe.

I am grateful for the four amazing children with whom I get to share my Earthly journey.

I am grateful to have the opportunity to co-parent with one of the most amazing dads in the world. His dedication and commitment to his kids are unparalleled and it is truly and honor and a privilege to carry out this mission together.

I am grateful for my audience, whether it turns out to be one person or many.

I am grateful that you have introduced me to Abraham-Hicks, whose teachings have been a powerful and a grounding force in helping me navigate my Earthly journey.

I am grateful for everyone who played a part in turning the dream of writing this book into a reality.

Sometimes I stress that 100 years won't be enough time to soak up all the amazingness that this world has to offer. Sometimes I stress that I won't have enough time to accomplish everything I want to accomplish in my time here. But, then I anchor back on the phrase that grounds and centers me every single time… "Trust the process." Everything is as it should be, in every moment. The best is yet to come, and together, as co-creators, we will ensure that always holds true.

Love is always the answer,
Pam

29

THIS WORLD

This world doesn't need another happiness hack. What it needs most is for people to roll up their sleeves and commit to a life of self-mastery.

This world needs healing and it needs you. There is so much despair, suffering, disconnection and separatism. It needs you to become the best version of yourself by rising up to not only meet your obstacles but to overcome them by healing yourself first and by choosing love every single day. By virtue of simply being our authentic selves, our spark will naturally ignite the flame in others.

The healing that needs to take place first is whatever you have right in front of you. We are all dealing with something. If we weren't, we would have already transitioned from this Earthly classroom. None of us are exempt from that. We all have experienced pain in the past, may currently be experiencing it to some degree and can expect to feel pain in the future. Our efforts must be directed not toward avoiding pain, but toward transmuting our pain, which will give rise to growth and transformation and will give us the strength and confidence to claim our own personal power.

We can all be healers for one another; no special training or license is required. If you know how to smile at someone, you are healer. If you know how to listen actively as someone invites you into their world by sharing their life experiences, you are a healer. If you know how to reach out and hold someone's hand, you are a healer. If you try to step into someone else's human experience and try to understand their actions rather than reacting first, you are a healer. If you are kind, you are a healer. If you believe that there is no "right" or "wrong" and that we are all students and teachers for each other, you are a healer. If you believe there is no hierarchy, you are a healer. If you know how to live in the moment, you are a healer. If you know how to look not only at someone, but into them and see their soul, you are a healer. If you have ever helped someone without being asked, you are a healer. If you have met someone in the depths of his or her pain and played a part in ushering the person through it, you are a healer. If you share your knowledge, you are a healer. If you are committed to growth, you are a healer.

You have come to this Earth with preselected lessons your soul needs to master and a purpose to fulfill. Everything you have experienced up to this point in your life has been specifically bestowed upon you with a very specific objective in mind, which is to give you the opportunity to grow and transform. Remember we are here to love and to grow. That's it. Everything else in our physical world just complicates our experience with things that get in the way. Connecting with others and sharing your gifts and your healing touch is unequivocally the most powerful thing you can do every day.

We make life so complicated but, in actuality, it's pretty simple. We are here to love and to grow.

You are not in this alone. While your journey is individual, your resources are many. Your spirit guides, ancestors, angels, Source Energy, infinite wisdom and people in your life, are all here for you. All you have to do is ask for help, and keep asking yourself "What would love do?" every single day.

Now it's time for you to take flight. You're an eagle, and the Universe is the wind. Simply spread your wings and glide wherever the Universe takes you. When the winds are fierce, you will fly above the storm. When the winds are gentle, you will admire the beauty of this world from above. Allow the winds of the Universe to lift you up to new heights. It is your time to soar.

For a special bonus on how your can change the world, visit https://liveauthentically.today/soar-resources to download the guide.

I would love to hear your personal story of growth and transformation. How has this book inspired you to step into your authentic reality? What changes are you feeling moved to make in your life?

Go to https://liveauthentically.today/soar-resources and share your story!

AFTERWORD: WHAT DO I BELIEVE?

The lenses through which I see the world, the way in which I navigate my reality, and my belief system are all wildly different than they were at prior points in my evolution. Every iteration has played an essential role and served as a stepping stone as I progressed through my evolution, and I have crafted my own personal belief system based on my personal experiences. Rather than reciting doctrines and creeds that were developed by others, I created my own.

My Creed
I believe we are all one
I believe we are all gods and goddesses
I believe we each have a purpose
I believe we are all infinitely powerful
I believe we are all creatively limitless
I believe everything is perfect in every moment
I believe finding and maintaining happiness is my responsibility
I believe that everything is a choice
I believe our truth already exists within us
I believe our heart always has our answers
I believe we are here to grow
I believe that every experience is a gift
I believe that love is always the answer

I believe that we are all spiritual beings living in a physical world reality. This belief system has helped me navigate my way around this Earthly Classroom with love, as I simultaneously greet all of my experiences with gratitude. This includes every triumph and every challenge, for each is a generous gift. It is the accumulation of all of our experiences that play a part in establishing our uniqueness and define our individual essence and make us who we are.

Wherever you are on your journey, may you be infused with the trust-filled knowingness that everything is unfolding according to a divine plan. As you continue on your journey, I invite you to anchor to this backdrop during your human experience, as you play the role of co-creator and marvel at the magic and wonderment of the Universe.

Spirituality

Spirituality is a lifestyle, not a religion
Spirituality is a marathon, not a sprint
Spirituality is a process, not a competition
Spirituality is about being real, not about being polished
Spirituality is about being present, not about being ready
Spirituality is about being authentic, not about being disguised
Spirituality is about expressing gratitude, not about expressing wants
Spirituality is about introspection, not about publicity
Spirituality is about progress, not about perfection.
Spirituality is about the journey, not about the destination
Spirituality is about looking in the mirror, not about looking out the window
Spirituality is about experiences, not about possessions
Spirituality is about love, not about fear
Spirituality is about you, not about them

REFERENCES

"Abraham-Hicks Publications - Law of Attraction Official Site." Home of Abraham-Hicks Law of Attraction, 9 July 2019, www.abraham-hicks.com/.

Bullard, Shelly, and Mft. "The 4 Qualities Of A Conscious Relationship." Mindbodygreen, Mindbodygreen, 9 Oct. 2017, www.mindbodygreen.com/0-21277/the-4-qualities-of-a-conscious-relationship.html.

Clarey, Christopher. "Olympians Use Imagery as Mental Training." The New York Times, The New York Times, 22 Feb. 2014, www.nytimes.com/2014/02/23/sports/olympics/olympians-use-imagery-as-mental-training.html.

Golfer, / The Grateful. "Putting: Arnold Palmer Style." The Grateful Golfer, 12 May 2019, thegratefulgolfer.com/2019/05/14/putting-arnold-palmer-style/.

"The Shadow." Society of Analytical Psychology, www.thesap.org.uk/resources/articles-on-jungian-psychology-2/about-analysis-and-therapy/the-shadow/.

UNUniversity. "New Research Says Plant-Based Diet Best for Planet and People." Our World, ourworld.unu.edu/en/new-research-says-plant-based-diet-best-for-planet-and-people.

Made in the USA
Columbia, SC
25 November 2020